Internati   ;

Summer 200(

Analysis

Contributors

Talat Ahmed teaches history at Goldsmiths, University of London, and is the author of *Literature and Politics in the Age of Nationalism: the Progressive Episode in South Asia, 1932-56.*

Roland Boer is a research professor at the University of Newcastle, Australia. Apart from writing and Marx, he loves to travel by ship and cycle as far as he can. His most recent works are *Political Myth* and *Criticism of Heaven*.

Jonathon Collerson is a retail worker in Sydney.

Denis Godard is a member of the National Political Council of France's New Anticapitalist Party and a member of the team at the journal *Que Faire?*

Mike Haynes has written widely on modern capitalism and co-authored *A Century of State Murder? Death and Public Policy in Russia.*

Henry Heller is a professor of history at the University of Manitoba and author of *The Bourgeois Revolution in France (1789-1815).*

Charlie Hore has written extensively on China for *International Socialism* and *Socialist Review.*

Sartaj Khan is a member of the International Socialists of Pakistan.

Charlie Kimber is a leading member of the Socialist Workers Party.

Ken Olende is co-author of the pamphlet *Sri Lanka: the Struggle for Tamil Freedom.*

Farah Reza is a socialist and campaigner for abortion rights.

John Rose is the author of *Myths of Zionism.*

David Seddon was until 2006 a professor in the school of development studies at the University of East Anglia. He is now a professorial fellow, freelance writer, consultant and political activist.

Jeong Seong-jin is a professor of economics at Gyeongsang National University, South Korea. His books include *Marx and the Korean Economy* and *Marx and Trotsky.*

Martin Smith is coordinator of Love Music Hate Racism, a leading member of the Socialist Workers Party and author of the pamphlet *Why "British Jobs for British Workers" is not the Answer.*

Luke Stobart is an executive officer for Birkbeck College students' union and has coordinated books in Spain on the anti-war and anti-globalisation movements.

GM Tamás is a professor of philosophy in Budapest, a prominent Hungarian dissident and former member of parliament, and a prolific author.

Megan Trudell is currently researching Italy in the wake of the First World War.

Toxic shocks

The results of elections to the European Parliament have delivered a devastating shock to New Labour. Its share of the vote was the lowest since something approaching universal suffrage was conceded in 1918, and it trailed behind the right populists of the UK Independence Party (UKIP). David Cameron's Tories now seem the inevitable victors in the general election set to take place in the next ten months. And the success of the Nazi British National Party (BNP) in gaining two seats adds to the toxicity of the shock.

Behind the figures lies a simple reality. Big chunks of Labour's supporters have abandoned it because they feel it has abandoned them. This applies both to manual workers who have voted Labour for three generations and to white collar workers, the majority of who first swung behind the party in 1997.

The reasons are easy to see. Unemployment is expected to rise to three million over the coming year and millions more do not know whether their jobs are safe. Real wages of manual workers (still 45 percent of the workforce) have been declining for four or five years—and over the past year so have those of white collar workers. On top of that came the scandal over MPs' expenses, with half respondents in an opinion poll believing all MPs are corrupt. Traditional Labour voters have woken up each morning to hear that their MPs have been claiming more in expenses than many workers are paid. The issue hurts Labour more than the Tories because Labour's core vote has come from those with some class sense, however vague, who assume that the Tories are only concerned with enriching themselves.

For commentators in the liberal media the UKIP and BNP votes are to be expected from "the white working class". Their simplistic arguments are not supported by research into voting patterns (see Martin Smith's article on the BNP in this issue). They also pay little account to the realities of working class consciousness in Britain. This has always contained contradictory elements, with a sense of class solidarity intermingling with acceptance of what Karl Marx called "the ideas of the ruling class". This contradictory combination always characterised old Labour and the core of the trade union bureaucracy, with their diluted class message on the one hand and their acceptance of nationalism, "Britishness", the monarchy and the "civilising role" of the empire on the other.

The mixture was never homogenous across the working class. A minority always accepted ruling class ideas wholesale—the third of manual workers who, as "deference voters", opted for the Tories in election after election, accounting for half of Tory votes from the 1940s to the 1970s. At the other end of the spectrum was another minority with left Labour or Communist-influenced ideas who held strongly class-based attitudes and were determinedly anti-racist, even if there remained a tinge of nationalism emanating from leaders integrated into the political establishment. In between were the majority of workers who would shift in one direction and then the other under the influence of events—particularly the success or failure of class struggles—and of the ideas coming from either side.

Under the impact of the crisis UKIP and the BNP are providing a focus for the right wing minority and enabling it to set the tone for many in the middle, while the left are paralysed and atomised, despite playing a central role in holding together unions that remain the biggest "civil society" organisations.

The paralysis of the left wing minority goes back to something we have stressed again and again in this journal—the stultifying refusal of the main union leaderships and most of the former Labour left to provide any clear lead in opposition to the effects of the crisis and to the policies pursued by New Labour. It is worth remembering that only last September many union leaders, including those running the biggest union, Unite, as well as figures on the left such as Ken Livingstone, were praising Gordon Brown's response to the crisis. Since then we have had the spectacle of one of Unite's leaders, Derek Simpson, encouraging workers to raise the slogan "British jobs for British workers". Some on the left have gone so far as to praise as a "victory" the outcome of a construction dispute in Wales that led to Polish workers being sacked, with use of the phrase "social dumping" to describe unemployed workers seeking jobs outside their country or region of birth.

Such an approach can only encourage workers to accept the argument of the right that people of all classes in Britain should unite together against immigrants. It plays into the hands of the BNP, who have been able to adopt the "British Jobs for British Workers" slogan as their own, and of UKIP with its slogan "No to unlimited immigration".

What could have been a step forward for the left, the decision of Bob Crow of the RMT rail workers' union to back a national list in the European elections, went off track because of the same willingness to substitute the politics of nation for those of class. The list's name, "No to EU, Yes to Democracy", gives the game away. It implies that the European Union is not just one source of exploitation and oppression but the major one, ignoring the role of British capital—and this at a time when the New Labour government has been handing billions to British bankers. A slogan such as "No to the bankers" might have been able to tap the basic, even if diffuse, class anger that exploded on the City of London demonstration on 1 April. No2EU failed miserably to do so—confusing the left, getting only about 1 percent of the vote and failing to provide any focus for working class bitterness.

Yet the potential for class feeling to come to the fore still exists. This was shown by the sequence of events that led from the occupation over redundancies at the Waterford Crystal factory in Ireland to that of the Visteon factories in Belfast and then in Enfield, north London. The Enfield plant was not one with any great record of militancy in recent decades. But the other examples were enough to spur the workers to take action—and then to discover that they had enough power to force Ford (which sold off Visteon some years back but which still depended on it for components to such a degree that it had lent the firm millions to keep it operating) to agree to significant redundancy payments. Huge votes for strike action by tube workers and postal workers suggest we are going to see more real expressions of class feeling.

The Euro election results only express one element in popular consciousness. Moods can change rapidly, as we have seen at least twice in the past four decades at the fag end of Labour governments. In 1968 London's dockers struck for the day and marched in support of the racist Enoch Powell, yet from early 1969 onwards there was an upsurge of militancy led by networks of left influenced shop stewards which shifted the whole political spectrum. In 1977 the Nazis of the National Front picked up more than 100,000 votes in the Greater London Council elections. Yet they lost their influence as networks of left activists led resistance to the Thatcher government, starting with the huge 100,000-strong demonstrations against unemployment in 1981 and culminating in the miners' strike of 1984-5. The resistance on that occasion may not have been successful but it did provide an extra-parliamentary focus for the left.

Anti-fascist agitation was immensely important on both occasions—particularly the role of the Anti Nazi League in the late 1970s. Likewise, mobilisations by Unite Against Fascism will be crucial in beating back the Nazis today. But such activity can only be of limited effectiveness without a wider sense of an alternative to what is happening to people's lives.

This is especially true today, as the economic crisis puts pressure on capitalism to launch assaults on wide sections of the working class, with about half of all workers saying they face wage freezes or even cuts, major employers scrapping final salary pension schemes and the leaders of all three mainstream parties agreeing on massive public sector cuts after the next general election.

It has been in the interests of all parties' leaders to keep quiet about the coming attacks. New Labour went into attack mode when the Tories' shadow health minister, Andrew Lansley, let slip that they expect to implement 10 percent cuts, yet the *Financial Times* reports that this is what Treasury officials, working for Labour, "boasted behind the scenes" that they were preparing back in April. David Cameron let it be known that he will move to take such measures quickly if he wins the election. He apparently believes that "Margaret Thatcher made a mistake by waiting two years after her 1979 election victory before delivering her tough economic medicine". But he also recognises how difficult and unpopular this might be.

The worries for those in high places are not only electoral. There is also concern that a Tory government will enter office merely in reaction to the disenchantment with New Labour and will not have the aura of legitimacy required to push through the measures our rulers believe are necessary. Business organisations have been expressing anxieties about the furore over MPs' expenses. They complain it is a distraction from the real tasks of government and opposition alike. Their fears are justified. Coming so soon after the anger over bankers' bonuses, it throws into a clear light the gap between the "suits" of all sorts—in the City, the political establishment and industry—and those expected to pay for the mess they have led the economy into.

They will be doing their best over the next few months to try to rectify things. For the tabloids this will, no doubt, mean more attacks on asylum seekers, more stories about the luxurious lives supposedly led by those on benefits, more gratuitous Islamophobia and the message that we all have to make sacrifices.

This pushes to the fore once again the urgent necessity for the left to try to pull its forces together to fill the political vacuum. There are hundreds of thousands of activists in Britain who think of themselves as being to the left of Labour. Most will have wished, as they heard the European election results, that there had been a viable left alternative on the ballot paper. This was clear, for instance, in the reception to an open letter issued by the Socialist Workers Party. And there are millions of people who would vote for a pole of attraction to the left of Labour in the general elections—and so provide a counter-focus to the racist and semi-racist right—if they thought a viable one existed.

The British "first past the post" electoral system, with minority votes often seeming like wasted votes, has always created difficulties in providing such a focus. It is even harder than in countries such as France where 4 percent of votes makes you a recognised part of the political scene, or Germany where 5 percent wins dozens of parliamentary seats. But that does not do away with the urgency of campaigning to pull the left's forces together. The central obstacle to past attempts to do so is that key national figures of the left—most left union leaders, the handful of left MPs—have insisted that there cannot be a break with Labour, despite half the membership of the party leaving over the past dozen years. This was, in the final analysis, what doomed the Socialist Labour Party, the Socialist Alliance, Respect and now No2EU.

Sometimes a threatening shock spurs people to sudden action. There was a sign of this with the magnificent and militant protests against the BNP after the election results emerged. Now is the time to see if the feeling can take on a new political form. The alternative is to cling to the hull of the Labour Party as it sinks into a sea infested with UKIP and BNP sharks.

We do not know whether campaigning for a political alternative will gain enough critical mass to bring it about before the general election. But in any case, the networks drawn together in the process would help in the wider extra-parliamentary resistance to what capitalism has in store for us. There will be an urgent need in the months ahead for coordination in support of whatever struggles occur, in standing by those subject to abuse by the gutter press and in preparing for the fightback against the inevitable onslaught on the public services.

Green shoots or wilting blossoms?

We do not know whether the green shoots of recovery some observers claim to have seen in the late spring will wither in the summer heat. But they are unlikely to blossom this year or, for that matter, next. Stock exchanges may have risen by about 20 percent between February and June but the underlying reality is that the world economy is continuing to contract, with any limited revival in China or slowing of the decline in the US outbalanced by continued deterioration in continental Europe. Talk of "recovery" is still talk of a reduction in the speed of contraction in the worst crisis the system has known since the Second World War.[1]

This is recognised by those capitalist commentators not bemused by the small shifts in market indices that can create quick speculative profits. They see that the huge debts run up by the banking system during the bubble can still return to plague it, despite the unprecedented sums thrown into the system. The IMF has raised its estimate of aggregate financial write-downs to $4.1 trillion, about twice the figure of a year ago, while the estimated total excess of government expenditure over taxation across the OECD area for next year is 8.7 percent of gross domestic product.[2]

The scale of the debts opened up a debate in the upper echelons of the US ruling class in the early spring, which we mentioned in our previous issue, over whether it was necessary to nationalise the whole banking system. The Obama administration managed to bury that idea with "stress tests" supposedly showing most of the banks were relatively healthy (see Megan Trudell's piece in this issue). But that has not stilled the voices of those who suspect the tests were designed to get the right result and those who worry that the steps taken by the American, Chinese and to a lesser extent British governments have not been replicated in continental Europe. And now another debate is coming to the fore, on what to do with the burden of debt now weighing on governments as well as banks.

On one side of this debate stand those who believe that the US government should continue with its "Keynesian" stimulus policies. To worry

1: For the decline in the US up to April, see the graph from Paul Krugman in "The Great Recession Versus the Great Depression", available from http://krugman.blogs.nytimes.com/2009/03/20/ For a more pessimistic picture of the world as whole see the graphs of Barry Eichengreen and Kevin O'Rourke at www.voxeu.org/?q=node/3421

2: *Financial Times*, 21 April 2009.

about the cost now, they warn, could cut any revival dead, just as tax rises did in the middle of the New Deal in the US in 1937. What is more, any inflationary impact of government deficits can make the debt burden lighter. "What I hear more and more, both from bankers and from economists," writes Wolfgang Münchau, "is that the only way to end our financial crisis is through inflation. Their argument is that high inflation would reduce the real level of debt, allowing indebted households and banks to deleverage faster and with less pain".[3]

That has produced a backlash from those financial interests who would lose out—and from commentators who claim any danger of deflation has passed and the fear now must be of an inflationary spiral, a new bubble and then a new crash. These figures argue that the only solution is to squeeze the mass of the population to pay for the debts. As Gideon Rachman writes, "Panic has passed; something less frightening and rather bleaker is beckoning. Welcome to the politics of austerity".[4]

The US government may be in a position to avoid a clampdown on spending for the time being. It remains the most powerful player in the world system, even if humbled by the crisis and by its setbacks in Iraq, Afghanistan and elsewhere. It biggest creditors, the Chinese and other governments, dare not crack the whip over the scale of its debts for fear of causing a collapse in value of the hundreds of billions in dollar assets they hold. The British state, with a deficit unprecedented except in time of all-out war, is not in the same position. It is this, rather than simply their ideological fixation on neoliberalism, that lies behind the rush towards cuts by the mainstream parties. Martin Wolf of the *Financial Times* spells out the pressure on them:

> The UK has lost control over public spending. It has to get it back again. Whether they like it or not, UK voters will have to elect a government willing to achieve this end... The next government will...find itself in a war of attrition with its own servants.... Government spending must be cut down to size... This must mean: a sustained freeze on the pay bill; decentralised pay bargaining; employee contributions to public pensions; and a pruning of benefits. It is obvious, too, that this will mean massive and painful conflict between governments and public workers... The next prime minister is likely to end up quite as hated as Margaret Thatcher was.[5]

3: *Financial Times*, 25 May 2009.

4: *Financial Times*, 25 May 2009.

5: *Financial Times*, 7 May 2009.

Willem Buiter, a former member of the Bank of England's monetary policy committee, shares Wolf's belief in the necessity of a savage attack on living standards and the public service: "Under the best possible scenario, taxes will have to be raised and/or public spending cut on a permanent basis by between 5 and 6 percent of GDP." He warns: "The pain will be widely felt. This pain will not be the result of a war fought by a united nation against a hated enemy... It is therefore not clear that the necessary social and political cohesion to accept joint fiscal burden-sharing will be present." But he continues, "If the necessary fiscal tightening is not forthcoming, markets could panic and Britain could face an emerging market style 'sudden stop', with the rest of the world withholding financing from its public and private sectors".[6]

In other words, forget the hype about green shoots. Whether they eventually take root or not, we are in for a period of bitter struggles and the likelihood of social and political turmoil. That is all the more reason for the forces to the left of Labour to get their act together and stop leaving a vacuum to be filled by the Nazis of the BNP and the only slightly less nasty types who run the UK Independence Party UKIP.

6: *Financial Times*, 22 April 2009.

Obama's 100 days

Megan Trudell

The first 100 days of the Obama administration have made clear that the tremendous expectations driving last year's dramatic election are already coming into conflict with the realities of US capitalism in crisis. The desire for change on the part of ordinary Americans could not but be reflected in early policy decisions. However, there is deep counter-pressure from US business and the military to which Barack Obama is already bending.

The reversals of George Bush's policies on "moral" issues have been both symbolic and important; the lifting of bans on stem cell research and on US funding for international organisations that offer advice on or carry out abortions are both unquestionably progressive. Obama has also passed executive orders requiring employers to notify workers of their right to join a union and giving preference in awarding federal construction contracts to union labour. Such reforms—even if they do return to pre-Bush policy rather than institute anything really new—mark a significant ideological break from the right wing moralism of the Bush era, and they make a difference to people's lives. The sense of the wind being in progressive sails has no doubt also contributed to the votes for gay marriage in three US states (although Obama himself does not favour same-sex marriage).

Most importantly, Obama has ordered a $787 billion stimulus package for the economy and his $3.2 trillion budget for the coming year includes significant government spending.

For liberals desperate for a presidential saviour, these changes prove that Obama is in the same class as Franklin D Roosevelt, president at the high point of reform in the US. Marking the first 100 days—itself a challenge for US presidents thrown down by FDR's legislative response to the economic depression in 1933—the *Guardian* exulted: "The changes racked up already suggest a potential to become one of the most liberal presidents in US history".[1] Jonathan Alter, author of Obama's preparatory reading before becoming president,[2] makes a quantitative comparison: "FDR had 15 major bills and Obama has ten to his credit. He might not have as many bills as FDR but in terms of dollars spent he is right up there with FDR. The times are not as serious as the 1930s but the response of Obama is as aggressive. I am surprised by how he has kept his foot on the gas".[3]

Others have been more critical. A much borrowed phrase, used by commentators as varied as Martin Wolf in the *Financial Times* and France's New Anti-capitalist Party to describe the first 100 days, has been the Italian aristocrat Tancredi's assertion in Lampedusa's *The Leopard* that "for things to remain the same, everything must change".[4] This assessment is sadly the more accurate one, as a brief outline of Obama's first few months illustrates.

The economy

Wolf makes the point that it is precisely Obama's conservatism that supports the comparison with FDR: "What we have seen unfolding, from the president's choice of Lawrence Summers and Tim Geithner as his principal policy advisers, to last week's 'stress tests', is classic conservative policy making. The aim is simply to get the show back on the road".[5] Roosevelt's project in his first months was to stabilise US capitalism, not to overturn it. According to one historian, FDR "enacted an impeccably conservative programme, underwriting the existing banking structure and slashing government spending".[6]

Obama is certainly doing the former. His government had spent, at time of writing, $700 billion on its troubled asset relief programme (Tarp) bank bail-out, and there will be more to come. Following the recent bank "stress tests", Treasury secretary Geithner conceded that more public money would be handed over to the likes of the Bank of America and Wells Fargo if the $76 billion capital it is estimated the banks need cannot be raised

1: The *Guardian*, 29 April 2009.

2: Alter's book on Roosevelt, *The Defining Moment: FDR's First Hundred Days and the Triumph of Hope*, was cited by Obama before his inauguration.

3: Quoted in the *Guardian*, 29 April 2009.

4: Martin Wolf, "Obama's Conservatism May Not Prove Good Enough", *Financial Times*, 12 May 2009; http://tinyurl.com/NPA-obama

5: Martin Wolf, *Financial Times*, 12 May 2009.

6: Badger, 2008, pp26-27.

privately. The tests have been widely criticised for not being stressful enough, underestimating both the likely unemployment rate over the next two years and the extent of the fall in house prices. Dean Baker of the Centre for Economic and Policy Research argues, "It is hard not to conclude that these stress tests, and certainly the PR campaign around them, were intended to paint as positive a picture as possible of the banks' financial condition".[7] His own estimate is that an extra $120 billion could be needed unless there is another stimulus package to prevent further unemployment.

The existing $787 billion stimulus package (the American Recovery and Reinvestment Act), which aims to "create or save" 150,000 jobs, includes money for public works, assistance for states, and tax relief for individuals and business. However, nearly three months after approval, less than 6 percent of the money has been spent and, while some states are holding back from sacking teachers or construction workers in the anticipation of government money, it is unlikely to be enough preserve the status quo when it does arrive.[8]

A Centre for Economic Policy Research report argues that since the recession has pushed state governments into the red, increased central funding will be cancelled out or at least have its impact reduced:

> The vast majority of [local] governments are facing budget deficits in 2009 and 2010 due to the economic downturn. Virtually all of these governments are required by their constitutions or charters to balance their budgets. Therefore, the projected deficits will force them to either cut spending and/or raise taxes. These spending cuts and tax increases will partially offset the impact of the stimulus.

The shortfall between 2009 and 2011 "is projected to be more than $100 billion a year".[9] What will happen when the federal money trickles through remains to be seen, but it is likely to fall well short of the challenge. The creation or salvation (and the two are not the same thing) of 150,000 jobs would be welcome but puny. Unemployment rose by 563,000 to 13.7 million in April, with the unemployment rate rising to 8.9 percent. Over the past year that is a rise of 6 million in the numbers of unemployed Americans, and the average conceals higher rates of unemployment for black Americans (15 percent) and Hispanics (11 percent); 21 percent of

7: Dean Baker, *The American Prospect*, 8 May 2009.

8: *Washington Post*, 12 May 2009.

9: Baker and Deutsch, 2009.

young people are out of work.[10] Those job losses have been widely spread across private sector industries and 1.2 million are manufacturing jobs, reflecting the fact that manufacturing production has fallen by 16 percent since December 2007. US industry as a whole is operating at 69.1 percent of its capacity, the lowest rate since 1967.[11]

Obama's government spending is raising howls from Republicans, who regard the $3.4 trillion budget plan in much the same terms, minus the celebratory tone, as the *Guardian* does. It is, we are told, "the biggest redistribution of wealth from the rich to the poor in US history".[12] Given that the bank bail-out probably represented a hefty redistribution in the opposite direction, this would be fair enough. But it's not likely.

The Treasury has already made $17 billion in cuts from the budget including an early years childhood literacy programme. One of Obama's key campaign pledges reflected in the budget is healthcare reform; in May the announcement that groups representing hospitals, pharmaceutical companies and insurance providers have agreed to cut spending by $2 trillion (£1.3 trillion) over ten years was heralded as "historic".[13] There has been some scepticism regarding these players' commitment to facilitating reform to extend coverage and lower costs to some of the 46 million Americans without healthcare. As one surgeon in Ohio put it, the collection of interests offering to "reform" healthcare was reminiscent of foxes guarding the henhouse: "They are adamantly against any kind of government sponsored public health plan that would be available to middle class [read working class] Americans. Health insurers are fearful that such a plan would cut into their profits and just might drive them out of business".[14]

Those profiting from selling healthcare may have no choice but to engage with reform, and Obama would no doubt prefer they were—in Lyndon Johnson's words—inside the tent pissing out, but they surely intend to water it down or render it unworkable, if not to resist it altogether. Obama also faces opposition to healthcare reform from Republicans and, crucially, Democrats in Congress: "Already apparently dead is a plan to raise $267 billion over the next decade to pay for his healthcare initiative by curbing the ability of wealthier people to reduce their tax bills through deductions for mortgage interest, charitable contributions and state and local taxes".[15]

10: Bureau of Labour Statistics.
11: Federal Reserve figures.
12: The *Guardian*, 26 February 2009.
13: *BBC News*, 11 May 2009.
14: Dr S Amjad Hussain, *Toledo Blade*, 18 May 2009.
15: The *Guardian*, 11 May 2009.

Other aspects of the budget have also been removed, including a plan to limit tax deductions for the wealthy, or they have been limited, like the Make Work Pay tax credits which are only funded until 2010.

Critically, the budget requires that any reform in education, healthcare and energy provision must not increase the overall budget deficit—calculated at just over $7 trillion between 2010 and 2019. Again the Obama figures are optimistic. The budget deficit for 2009 has reached $1.84 trillion as a result of the bail-outs and stimulus measures, and the $7 trillion figure is based on projected growth in the US economy of 3.2 percent in 2010, almost twice that predicted by a survey of private economists, who also see unemployment as continuing to rise through 2010.[16]

The Obama government's intervention in the car industry illustrates starkly the gap between rhetoric and action from the administration. The collapse of General Motors, until last year the world's largest car maker, is the biggest failure of an industrial corporation in US history and has serious implications for the company's 235,000 workers. Following the initial bailout of $17.4 billion for GM and Chrysler, the forced resignation of GM head Rick Wagoner and the Fiat takeover of Chrysler, the Obama administration made its assistance dependent on further cuts and concessions from car workers. A recent United Autoworkers (UAW) deal with Ford negotiating "givebacks" and cuts in bonuses, unemployment benefit and healthcare set the tone (indeed Ford may well follow GM and Chrysler into bankruptcy proceedings). UAW members are owed over $20 billion by GM, although the bankruptcy proceedings protect the company from claims from creditors.

In a speech outlining the condition of the car industry, Obama placed the blame squarely on the executives in Detroit and politicians in Washington under Bush, but it will be car workers who continue to pay the price. Seven weeks after his sacking Wagoner was still being paid by GM, while the Treasury decided whether he should receive a $20 million severance package! The Obama government underwrote GM's move to bankruptcy on 1 June to the tune of a further $30 billion and a 60 percent government stake in the company. Despite criticism of GM's executives, the restructuring plan involves the closure of nine additional plants with a further three being mothballed, and a loss of 21,000 US jobs in an industry that has seen 400,000 workers thrown out of work in the past year. The priority for GM, under new chief executive Fritz Henderson, is to restore profitability, and Obama made it clear that car workers are being expected to pay for the company's losses.

16: The Blue Chip Economic Indicators survey, reported on *Reuters*, 10 April, 2009.

The war

The reversal of the Bush government's torture policies has also shown the vacillation of the government under pressure. In January Obama ordered the closure of the prison camp at Guantánamo Bay "within a year", the end of its military commissions, an end to the use of torture, the closure of the CIA's secret prisons and the lifting of the ban on media publication of pictures of US casualties returning from Iraq and Afghanistan.

However, new CIA chief Leon Panetta has been permitted to retain the use of extraordinary rendition; on his 114th day Obama reneged on a deal with the American Civil Liberties Union to release photographs of the abuse of prisoners in Iraq and Afghanistan by US soldiers; and on day 116 Obama reversed his decision on military trials at Guantánamo. Obama's alleged willingness to talk with leaders of Iran and Syria was refreshing after Bush, yet his government has extended sanctions against both countries.

During his presidential campaign Obama pledged to withdraw the 142,000 troops from Iraq within 16 months of taking office. That date has now been put back to August 2010 and between 35,000 and 50,000 troops will be kept in the country to execute a "drawdown plan". Meanwhile, US emphasis in the "war on terror"—or "contingency operations" as US imperialism is now called in another linguistic change that preserves the essence of the previous policy—has shifted to Afghanistan and Pakistan.[17]

The "exit strategy" from Afghanistan involves sending more troops in. Obama ordered an extra 17,000 US troops which will take the total over 60,000 by autumn as well as increasing the size of the Afghan army and police force and extending the war further into Pakistan, including the use of Predator drones in the Baluchistan region.[18] Despite having been elected on a surge of anti-war feeling, Obama is committing more troops to a conflict that could well become his Iraq—plus he still has Iraq itself to deal with.

Anthony Cordesman of the Centre for Strategic and International Studies, has summed up Obama's dilemma:

> The centre of gravity in the war of terrorism is now in Pakistan, and the threat of instability in a nuclear Pakistan has more strategic importance than the future government and stability of Afghanistan. More broadly, the US is now losing the war in Afghanistan that has been popular in US politics, but it is far from clear it has won the unpopular war in Iraq in ways that allow it to rapidly deploy large reinforcements to US forces in Afghanistan. The US

17: The *Guardian*, 25 March 2009.

18: See Simon Assaf, "Afghanistan's Disasters Of War", *Socialist Worker*, 5 May 2009.

> also now faces the most serious financial crisis since the Great Depression, an uncertain Afghanistan government, and growing uncertainty as to how long those of its allies that are now in the fight will sustain their commitment.[19]

The war in Afghanistan may have been "popular" in comparison with Iraq among US voters, but a recent poll has demonstrated a sharp change—42 percent of Americans now say that sending troops to Afghanistan was a mistake, a significant rise from 30 percent in January.[20] Another ominous development is the change of personnel organising the war. Defence secretary Robert Gates has appointed General Stanley McChrystal as military commander in Afghanistan. McChrystal was in charge of Joint Special Operations Command as part of Cheney's "dark side" forces employed in Iraq and was responsible for the taskforce accused of the abuse of detainees at Camp Nama in Baghdad in 2006.

However, the priorities of the war in Afghanistan have also led to some tensions between the US and Israel—visible in Obama's Cairo speech in which he pointed to Palestinian suffering and called for an end to Israeli settlements. It remains to be seen how these will be played out.

Hope misplaced?

The contradictions in Obama's first 100 days are the result of the class fault-lines that characterised his election and that are further widening as the impact of the recession is felt. Not all Americans are in the crisis together. Obama worked hard, and diluted policy, in order to win Republican support but not a single Republican voted for the budget. From Dick Cheney's robust defence of the Bush government's torture policies to the cries of "Socialism!" from Republicans opposed to the expansion of government intervention in the budget, Obama's initiatives are coming under fire. Although polls show that he remains popular, his ratings are split on partisan lines: overall his approval rating is 63 percent, but it falls to 30 percent among Republicans. These results may sound unimportant but it is the most polarised result for any president in the past four decades.[21]

Obama's handling of the economy, the budget deficit and healthcare gain significantly more approval from workers on lower incomes than from better off Americans. According to the Pew Research Centre, people with incomes of less than $30,000 approve of Obama's overall job performance

---

19: Cordesman, 2009.
20: Poll conducted by Gallup.
21: Poll by the Pew Research Centre.

by 71 percent with 16 percent disapproving; of those on between $30,000 and $75,000, 61 percent approve and 30 percent disapprove, while among those with incomes of $75,000 or more 58 percent approve against 31 percent disapproval. This suggests that, while the lower income Americans who voted for Obama in such numbers have kept the faith, higher income voters (especially in the highest bracket) are peeling away.

However, the generally high figures suggest that working Americans are prepared to give Obama time. The measures the administration have taken so far have benefited the rich over the poor but after eight years of Bush the sense of change and the chance of improvement created by the Obama presidency persist.

One historian's description of the atmosphere following FDR's election as president in 1932 could have described the excitement generated by Obama's election: "Where once there had been apathy and despondency, there was now an immense sense of movement. If the country did not know in what direction it was moving, it had great expectations; the spell of lassitude had been snapped".[22]

Close to two million people turned out on inauguration day stirred by similar hopes for change and expectation of transformation that was shared by millions more worldwide. Those expectations may well be misplaced in the figure of Obama and his capacity or inclination to challenge business interests. But just as it would be a mistake to sow illusions in Obama's ability to bring real change in isolation from a movement pushing him to do so, it would also be an error to decouple the hopes raised in the campaign from the necessity of fighting for and developing collective class action to protect workers and their families from the effects of the crisis.

Of course it is true that change, or the appearance of change, can act to preserve class power by appearing to answer more radical hopes while not altering the status quo. But even minor concessions to the deep sense of frustration and bitterness in society can also fuel expectations and encourage the development of collective impulses to deliver more profound and lasting transformation.

The impact of the current crisis on workers and poor in the US is immense. Thirteen million are unemployed, including one in ten in Michigan; three million Americans lost their homes last year with a further three million forecast for 2009; images of police tearing down tent cities in California and Florida are reminiscent of scenes from Steinbeck's *Grapes of Wrath*; the retirement savings of millions of middle aged Americans have

22: Leuchtenburg, 1963, p47.

been wiped out in stock market falls; in 2008 the amount that US households were collectively worth fell by 18 percent, the biggest loss since the Second World War.[23] Such economic pain can challenge the ideological conceptions that many have of US society and the drawing of class lines in the crisis can expose the priorities of bankers and business leaders, coming as it does after three decades in which the gap between the rich and the poor in the United States tripled. While the US economy was growing between 2000 and 2005, productivity went up by 16.6 percent but family incomes fell 2 percent; during the Bush years workers were made to work harder in order to further enrich the wealthy.[24] Politically, the experience of the Bush governments has been to broaden resistance (from the 1999 Seattle protest through the anti-war protests to immigrant rights marches), and to expose US imperialism and racism, through two wars and Hurricane Katrina, in the eyes of far wider numbers of people.

Under these circumstances the Obama administration, heavy with Clinton (and Bush) era politicians, though appearing radical in comparison with the recent past, may be exposed as being in no way radical enough to help those who are suffering. If Obama continues the direction of the first 100 days, his rhetoric may be seen to be merely sugaring the pill. However, it is also possible that the erosion of patience with government and with economic conditions can combine with those aspirations for change expressed in the election to force Obama's government leftwards to deliver real reform.

Perhaps in the comparisons with FDR it is worth considering that the bulk of the progressive legislation of the Roosevelt presidency came well after the 100-day mark and came in response to class anger as the inability of early measures to alleviate the suffering of urban workers and farmers provoked protests and a series of strikes. Roosevelt's popularity did not collapse with the big strikes in 1933 and especially in 1934[25]—the Democrats won majorities in the congressional elections that year and FDR won a landslide victory in 1936—but they did propel the reforms of the "Second New Deal" as FDR reluctantly responded to pressure from below: "It was only later on in the depression decade...that the emphasis shifted decisively from salvage operations to work relief programmes, and other measures that directly benefited the working class".[26]

23: The *Wall Street Journal*, 13 March 2009.

24: BBC News, 4 September 2006.

25: See Newsinger, 2009.

26: Foster and McChesney, 2009.

Socialist argument—and this is true in Europe where Obama is a more popular politician by far than Gordon Brown, Nicolas Sarkozy, Silvio Berlusconi or Angela Merkel, as well as in the US—can relate to people's desires for better lives, expose and explain the class realities expressed in Obama's legislation thus far and attempt to lay the basis for a new ideological framework through which people can express their experiences as they alter under the impact of the crisis.

References

Badger, Anthony J, 2008, *FDR: The First Hundred Days* (Hill & Wang).

Baker, Dean, and Rivka Deutsch, 2009, "The State and Local Drag on the Stimulus", Centre for Economic Policy Research, www.cepr.net/documents/publications/stimulus-2009-05.pdf

Cordesman, Anthony, 2009, "The Afghan-Pakistan Conflict: US Strategic Options", Centre for Strategic and International Studies, www.csis.org/media/csis/pubs/090317_afghpakconfl.pdf

Foster, John Bellamy, and Robert W McChesney, 2009, "A New New Deal under Obama?", *Monthly Review*, February 2009.

Leuchtenburg, William E, 1963, *Franklin D Roosevelt and the New Deal* (Harper Perennial).

Newsinger, John, 2009, "1934: Year of the Fightback", *International Socialism 122* (spring 2009), www.isj.org.uk/?id=530

Imperialism, religion and class in Swat

Sartaj Khan

The Pakistan military claimed at the beginning of June that it had achieved success in its all-out assault on Taliban insurgents after driving more than two million people from the Swat Valley and other areas of the north west of the country. The assault followed the breakdown of an agreement reached in February between the government and Sufi Mohammad, leader of one of the Islamist groups, for Swat's legal code to be based on Nizam-e-Adl*—an attempt to mix constitutional rules with the local interpretation of sharia law. The agreement was meant to bring an end to fighting between the Pakistan army and the Swat Taliban, led by Sufi Muhammad's son in law, Maulana Fazullah.*

The military onslaught happened after pressure from the US, which worried about the implications an agreement between the Pakistan government and the Taliban would have for its operations in Afghanistan and elsewhere in Pakistan. But the assault found favour with most liberal and "civil society" opinion, and much of the left, even if this was sometimes mixed with horror at the effects on civilians. Articles in the Pakistani press habitually refer to the "barbarity" of "terrorist" rule in Swat. This feeling was given a sharp edge by a mobile phone video supposedly showing a 17 year old woman receiving 30 whippings for "illicit" relations with a man—although other reports claim that the video was fraudulent and that the woman has denied she was whipped.[1] *Whatever the truth of the matter, the video played a role in leading much of the left internationally to take a similar approach to the Pakistani liberals, treating the Pakistan Taliban as if it were as much a foreign force in Swat as the Pakistan army*

1: "Swat Girl Denies Flogging by Taliban", *The News*, Karachi, 6 April 2009.

or the US army in Afghanistan. Yet there is strong evidence of a class element to the conflict. The New York Times *could report in April, "The Taliban have advanced deeper into Pakistan by engineering a class revolt that exploits profound fissures between a small group of wealthy landlords and their landless tenants...the Taliban seized control by pushing out about four dozen landlords who held the most power. To do so, the militants organised peasants into armed gangs that became their shock troops."*

The Karachi newspaper The News *has carried a debate which, according to one far left contributor, "has pitted those who claim that the situation in Swat is a reflection of longstanding class inequities against those who refute this notion of 'class war'; while the former suggest that the 'Taliban' has generated support amongst the subordinate classes, the latter argue that the 'Taliban' has imposed itself in the area on the basis of brute force".[2] One of the articles prompting the debate, reprinted in edited form here, came from Sartaj Khan of the International Socialists of Pakistan.*

Society in Swat is divided bitterly on ethnic and class bases. Those known as *Khans* are feudals, while those known as *Pushtun*, *Sayed* and *Miagan* are owners of considerable cultivated land. These groups were dominant for centuries before they were challenged from two sides—by the emerging commercial bourgeoisies and new middle classes on one side and the landless on the other. There are two sets of non-landowning groups. First there are the old inhabitants of the valley—the *Gujars, Ajar, Khostanis* and *Kami Kamins*—marginalised by the conquest by the elite groups in the 16th century. These are the "wretched of the earth" who have been denied their right to the land. Then there are the "commoners", the traditional petty bourgeoisie, such as blacksmiths, cobblers and barbers.

The anthropologist Fredrik Barth, who studied the area 40 years ago, described the divisions as analogous to that of the caste system in India, with separate mosques and graveyards for elite groups and the commons. He found the non-landowning groups to be "directly or indirectly dependent on the landowners both politically and economically".

However, a commercial bourgeoisie and a so-called "new middle class" emerged to challenge the old Khanite landed classes across the North West Frontier Province (NWFP). This is connected with the migration of large numbers of Swat's inhabitants to industrial zones such as in Karachi since the 1960s. Most worked in the textile industry but a small minority did emerge as middle class. From the 1980s onwards people from Swat have

2: Asim Sjjadd Akhtar, "Some Observations On The War In Swat", *The News*, Karachi, 29 January, 2009, www.thenews.com.pk/editorial_detail.asp?id=159609

also travelled to the United Arab Emirates and Saudi Arabia. The impact of the remittances from these migrants is uneven. Abid Qaiym Suleri and Kevin Savage claim that "remittance households are generally better off than non-remittance, own better houses and more valuable assets"; a Sustainable Development Policy Institute discussion paper notes "the poverty alleviation often associated with labour migration has yet to reach rural NWFP".

Further contributing to the growth of the middle class has been the money made by selling off forest, and smuggling goods, weapons and drugs. Real estate agents, transporters, contractors, traders, personnel in the state bureaucracy and the armed forces, and, above all, government agents from the periods of the Zia and Musharraf military regimes have wealth and power from sources other than land. So too do some from the old exploiting classes. These changes have considerable implications for the social order.

NWFP is the poorest province of Pakistan with 43 percent poverty. Some 85 percent of the population live in the rural areas. Swat is 17th out of 24 districts in NWFP ranked in terms of average income. The situation is deteriorating with every passing day.

The rise of Islamism

Three movements, all in the guise of Islamism, arose to give expression to the desires of the petty bourgeoisies and new middle classes. They have each challenged the dominance of the Khanite landed autocracy. *Tehrik Nifaz-i-Shariat Muhammad* (TNSM) was founded by Sufi Muhammad in 1992. It enjoyed the support of former servicemen and the commercial bourgeoisie, capitalising on two vital issues: the judicial system imposed on Provincially Tribal Administered Areas (PATA) and the corrupt national political system. Both systems alienated the masses of Swat.

Swat was a "princely state" until it was fully absorbed into Pakistan in 1969 and subjected to the PATA regulations.[3] The old *Jirga of Kheels* (council of tribes) that had endorsed previous rulers was replaced by the corrupt *Dala* (or *Para-Jamba*) system, where leaders supported adherents by hook or crook, concentrated on petty issues and ignored the common cause. The year Swat merged with Pakistan was also a year of the mass peasant upheaval in the country. The landless occupied the land they cultivated. Thanks to this movement, *Gujars*, mostly peasants, acquired up to 42 percent of land in some villages. But settlements of these cases are still pending in the courts.

The judicial system in Pakistan is corrupt to the core and land cases take decades to process. The more remote the rural area is, the greater the

---

3: Kalim Bahadur, *Democracy in Pakistan* (Har-Anand Publications, 1998), p310.

likelihood that the case will be prolonged. A common view is that a single generation never sees a settlement in its own lifetime.

The arrival of neoliberalism in the 1990s saw a speculative boom in real estate. But the real estate agents who hoped to benefit from this also saw their land deals and commissions held up by the judicial system. Sufi Muhammad's TNSM gained support because of these judicial delays. It presented sharia law as the answer to the public grievances, most significantly the rapid settlement of land disputes. But in 2001 TNSM's leaders were arrested after it mobilised publicly for *jihad* in Afghanistan against the US invasion. This allowed the reformist Islamists' political coalition, the MMA,[4] to gain in the elections of 2002. Their petty bourgeois leadership mobilised the rural poor to defeat the politics of *Dala-Para-Jamba* but they too were soon found to be corrupt, alienating the masses. The secular Pushtun nationalists of the Awami National Party[5] won the elections in 2008 but lost the support of the people even more quickly. The Pakistan Taliban were waiting in the wings.

The social base of the Taliban in Swat

Islamism builds at the expense of the liberal-left, secular nationalist movement. The Pushtun nationalism of the Awami National Party and Islamic reformism of the MMA failed to challenge the ruling elite or imperialism, mainly due to their class character. The anti-imperialist rhetoric of the Taliban largely displaced the secular nationalists, portraying corrupt rulers as puppets responsible for the poverty and misery in the country.

Poverty had increased in the 1990s, after declining in the 1970s and 1980s. The globalisation of war and the integration of Pakistan into the world market paved the way for the emergence of new movements and brought changes to old ones. Islam and Islamic leaders could transcend the boundaries of a society dominated by ethnic, cultural and tribal lineages, uniting people in a common cause. Class interests could be disseminated in the name of Islam and sharia. That is how Mullah Fazlullah, the leader of the Swat Taliban, appeared on the scene. A dropout from a school in Mingora and a wire-lift operator who worked for Rs 1500 (around £15) per month, he emerged at the age of 28 as the leader of his organisation.

He initially enjoyed support from all sections of society. Prince Asfandiar Amir Zeb, the descendant of the family that ruled Swat for years and the grandson of a former president of Pakistan, said, "Quick justice and

4: The coalition of Islamist parties that contests elections and ran the NWFP government until last year's elections.

5: The Awami National Party supports the Pakistani People's Party government.

efficient government" was what "people wanted" and this was "what the people saw" in Fazlullah. Fazlullah's *madrassa* (religious school) in Swat was built with the support of the petty bourgeoisie and the middle class, with people across the valley donating $2.5 million for the cause. Every village was given a specific target and a turn at working for the building.

But the big landlords kept their distance and as the movement gained momentum it changed rapidly. As it became more radicalised, resentment developed among sections of the middle classes. Today the militant sections of the movement come from the rural poor—a significant difference with the petty bourgeois and middle class domination of the TNSM in its prime.

According to Khadim Hussain (an academic who supports military action in Swat), Fazlullah "communicates with...groups that do not have a share in the land distribution of the area...in their language". His "supporters in the marginalised groups get a sense of empowerment... Both the state and the traditional elites along with the political elites of the valley...have all along failed to respond to the aspirations of those who remained marginalised."

Militants are targeting Khans regardless of their political affiliations. According to journalist Rahimullah Yusufzai, "The militants justify the attacks by alleging that the Khans committed excesses on the common and landless people in the past." The police and administration always sided with feudals so they too are being targeted.

The first political leader who came under attack from militants was Malik Bakhat Baidar. He was a businessman, vice-president of the Swat Awami National Party, belonged to a wealthy family and was in close contact with the armed forces. Even Prince Asfandiar Amir Zeb was not spared. He bitterly opposed Fazlullah and frequently requested that dictator General Musharraf undertake military operations against the TNSM. The Pakistan Peoples Party (PPP)[6] leader Mohammad Sher Khan and his family were targeted many times. He escaped narrowly but his brother, Kabir Khan, was killed along with his wife and son. The two brothers of another PPP leader, Mohammad Zimmer, were also assassinated.

After the collapse of the first peace talks and army operation in Swat last year, the feudals from the Awami National Party came under attack from the militants. The biggest Khan, former federal minister Afzal Khan Lala, was attacked several times but survived. Ministers from Swat and all

6: The party of the Bhutto family and of the current president, Asif Ali Zadari (Benazir Bhutto's widower); originally formed in the late 1960s with a social democratic colouring, it is dominated by rich landowners and supportive of US imperialism.

seven members of the provincial assembly were forced to take refuge in Peshawar or Islamabad.

The present conflict in Swat grew out of a broader struggle that has been waged by the exploited classes for centuries. The agreement in February was a victory for the militants, but they were led by the madrassa-owning and small landholding layer of petty bourgeoisie. Instead of liberation from the Khans and state rule, the leaders of the uprising agreed to share control with them, while continuing to use the rhetoric of liberation. The agreement allowed exceptional repressive power through the open-ended sharia, which was essential for the petty bourgeoisie to suppress the expectations of the lower classes. It recognised the failure of the neoliberal order but in a way that expressed the desire for liberation of the petty bourgeoisie alone. Everybody knew that the agreement would break down. The Pakistani military regarded it as only a temporary expedient. Their spokesman said on the eve of the agreement that it was only a pause.

Much of the left has taken the same position as over the occupation of Afghanistan: it is against the occupiers and occupied as well; against the imperialist invasion and "terrorism" at the same time. Generally the left is bankrupt and fails to understand the dynamics of capitalism or the implications of war, and consequently the resistance to it. It is still living in the era of the 1960s: if there is class struggle it must be waged under the leadership of an enlightened and educated Maoist intelligentsia under a red banner. No class war in the name of religion is seen as possible.

Meanwhile two and a half million people have been forced from their homes. The society of Swat, once considered a paradise, has turned into hell.

Hungary: "Where we went wrong"

GM Tamás, a prominent Hungarian dissident and now professor of philosophy in Budapest, spoke to Chris Harman about developments in Eastern Europe since the fall of Stalinism.

This is the 20th anniversary of the collapse of the Stalinist regime in Hungary and the fall of the Berlin Wall. It is also a year in which the world economic crisis has hit Eastern Europe with devastating effect. You were one of the dissidents before 1989.

The dissident movement here in Hungary was not very large. I was one of the leading figures in it and played a part in the resistance from the end of the 1970s. When I decided to take on the regime fully I was still a left wing person, a libertarian socialist. I and my friends in the dissident movement practically all came from the left and as a body became liberals. Some went quite far in that direction, including myself, others less so. The intellectual and sociological origins of these groups almost everywhere in Eastern Europe had been on the left. Our first quarrel had not been with socialism as such but with the Stalinist regimes.

Two ideological figures here were quite characteristic, János Kis and myself. János Kis was a second generation pupil of György Lukács and produced Marxist works of a high quality (which unfortunately are not generally translated).[1] I was less of a Marxist but a libertarian socialist and very much on the left. We all went in a liberal direction, together with our

1: János Kis was author together with György Bence of the book that appeared under the pseudonym Marc Rakovski—Rakovski, 1978. Bence, Kis and their former teacher, György Márkus, attempted in the 1970s a sytematic critique of Marx's *Capital* in an important book, as yet untranslated, which appeared in Hungarian only after 1989.

Polish and other brothers and sisters in arms. And by the time we reached the watershed—it was 1988 in Hungary—we were quite committed to a liberal human rights programme. This happened to practically everyone.

Miklós Haraszti, who wrote the book A Worker in a Workers' State,[2] *which had a big impact on the left in Britain, went the same way.*
Absolutely. He was originally a Guevarist and saw himself as a consistent communist. He is now press freedom commissioner of the Organisation for Security and Cooperation in Europe, and I saw him in a picture of a meeting of "coalition of the willing" types in Slovakia with George W Bush when he visited that country. Haraszti is a fighting liberal as far as press freedom is concerned and a fighting neoconservative as far as social and economic issues are concerned. Eventually I went a different way, but until the mid-1990s I was not different from the rest of my generation.

During more than 15 years of dissidence I was unemployed and lived by doing translations under other people's names and black-market language teaching work to support myself. I was a dissident intellectual, writing theory, political essays and political journalism in *samizdat*.[3] We did illegal seminars on historical, political, economic and sociological topics. Then from 1986 on I was allowed to teach abroad, in the US, Britain and France, and did some research at Oxford. Beginning in 1988, I participated in the increasingly organised and formalised resistance movement against the regime. I spoke at demonstrations and took an active part in protest actions. There was a flowering of civil society, thousands of new groups, discussion forums and clubs. It was a beautiful time. We didn't sleep very much—I didn't sleep much from 1988 to 1992. It was talk, talk, talk, talk among many, many people. It was a period of social imagination out of which nothing much came but it was a moment of perceived and hoped for freedom. I was at the centre of all that, later elected an MP for the Free Democratic Alliance, which was then the party of the dissidents and the second largest party in parliament. It was a liberal party and I was quite on the right wing of it.

"Liberal" in the European rather than the British or North American sense?
Both, actually. It was rather left wing as regards human rights, minority rights, cultural freedom, equal rights for gays and lesbians and so forth—in this respect very much like American liberalism. But economically it was neoconservative. And I, too, proposed a mixture of this kind.

2: Haraszti, 1977.

3: *Samizdat* was the Russian name given to uncensored dissident material.

We were immediately, unexpectedly, embroiled in a fight with the conservative right. Our first election campaign was designed to be directed against the main enemy, which was the post-Stalinist party. But that party apparently vanished and did not play any role for a while. A few of its members made it to parliament but they largely kept silent. And all of a sudden we were confronted with the conservative right with their talk of a "Jewish conspiracy", of "enemies to our breed" and so on. It was already the old conflict between "Westernisers" and "nationalists", "cosmopolitans" and "patriots"—and a very quaint expression on the Hungarian right, "the foreign-hearted" and the "well-rooted". This was in 1990, and it still goes on, boring and barren as it is. In 1988-9 we still had some threats from the old Stalinist guard—"You'll hang" and that sort of stuff. We expected more of that. Instead we got attacked by the nationalist right. All my posters were disfigured with the Star of David and the swastika. But at that time such attitudes were rejected by the majority of the electorate.

The right won the election but it was its moderate wing that was representative of majority opinion. And so this problem diminished for a while. By 1994 when I left professional politics—in utter confusion—the elections were won by a combination of social democrats and liberals, the mood was completely different and the right wing nationalist danger seemed to disappear.

What was important in hindsight was that in the first two years I spent in the highest chamber of my country as a lawmaker two million jobs were lost—and I don't think I noticed. That is one of the greatest shames of my life. I don't think it figured in political debates at that time. There were important debates concerning constitutional rights and republican versus monarchist symbols, fights over control of state radio and television. I won't say political conflicts were not important but compared to the economic disaster they were of less importance, and we did not see the interdependence between the two. Why did the ruling class need the centralisation of media power? Because it was losing majority support from the population that were getting impoverished. We were totally naive and our discourse at the time was that of classic liberalism and pretty ineffective. This liberal party will probably now, and quite deservedly, disappear from parliament.

I began to realise what was going on around me by the time that legislature came to an end and I decided not to stand again for parliament. It was not only a Hungarian problem. From Siberia to Prague and from Alma Ata to East Berlin there was the same problem. What happened was not the transformation of the economy but the destruction of the economy. We did not come up simply with a new capitalism but with a black hole. It was one of the great demonstrations of the destructive power of capitalism.

The methods were the same you can witness in other parts of the world—downsizing and outsourcing, privatisation and social dumping. Foreign capital arrived in search of consumer markets, closing down manufacturing industry it had bought for a song—but the difference was in the dimensions. Everywhere there has been a great loss in workforce, especially in manufacturing, but here a total way of life was lost. The quite successful cooperative agriculture practically disappeared; the new family farms did not prove commercially viable. Unemployment in the countryside is endemic. I remember well during the miners' strike in Britain, when people all of a sudden realised it was not only the mining industry that was going to go but the culture of hundreds of mining villages, so that Wales could never be the same afterwards. But here we have had a qualitative change, a situation in which a whole culture is gone. From the 1920s the Stalinist system—however monstrous, tyrannical and state capitalist it was—had through urbanisation and industrialisation created the livelihoods and life forms of hundreds of millions of people. They may have been disappointed and dissatisfied with the way of life but nevertheless it was theirs. And nobody had prepared them for what was to replace it. It was not something better, not something we might call "change", but instead the end to economy as such.

In large parts of Eastern Europe and the Eurasian landmass there was the loss of what we knew of as civilisation, which was very much dependent on the state. The state has barely started to function again in Putin's Russia—in a very unpleasant way—but it is starting to work regularly, making records, collecting revenue, paying civil servants, answering letters, receiving citizens with complaints. But in the early 1990s even that was not available: it was a total disaster. Meanwhile we, the froth at the top of it, were celebrating the triumph of freedom and openness and plurality and fantasy and pleasure and all that. That was frivolous, and I am deeply ashamed.

Somehow I knew there was trouble. This was reflected in my writings. But the analysis I offered was of a superficial political kind. There were signs—for instance, American policies towards the Balkans, the Gulf War, general dissatisfaction that things were not going well. But these were viewed as transitory phenomena: the transition was difficult but in the end everything would be all right—just the same approach as the "right believing" Communists had had to Stalinism. Terrible sacrifices for now—and then the radiant future, "*les lendemains qui chantent*".[4]

4: "The tomorrows that sing"—a French Communist slogan of the Second World War.

But everything was not and was not going to be all right. As someone as it were professionally engaged in theoretical research, I felt I had to understand it. So I started to read and re-read theory and economic science, and empirical sociology and history, and tried to understand what was going on, trying to find out what was wrong in the foundations of our thought and trying to find some way out. I even had a detour in conservative literature critical of liberalism and from there was a leap to Marxism. (Funnily enough, conservative criticism of liberal pieties such as that of Michael Oakeshott and of Leo Strauss eased my way towards Marxism.) So I spent long years in learning—rather than re-learning, for I had never been before a really knowledgeable Marx reader—and went back to school. I tried very slowly and thoroughly to understand the character of the former regime, why the transition to the market was the way it was and why market forms were not sufficient either in general or for the local endemic problems of East European state capitalism.

It took a long time, and an even longer time to formulate this publicly and articulate it politically and to change my discourse, my language, my vocabulary. It was like a long illness and a long recovery. But I think I may be finally at the beginning of a new life.

For me this is fantastically important, not just for you as an individual but because in the whole Eastern bloc tens of thousands of people were dedicated to liberal democratic change and believed it could come about through the market. We visited Poland during the strikes there in 1988 and talked to people who were generally on the left. I remember talking to people in Poznań and for them the transition was going to be towards Scandinavia. There was no understanding that it might be anywhere else in the world that was capitalist.[5] *Then early in 1989 I went to Leningrad, as it was known at the time, and talked to courageous people who were producing leaflets typed out individually by hand for the election. They had no understanding of what the Western form of capitalism meant. They assumed it meant liberty and prosperity and so forth.*

We were better informed. We came from the left. We were not ignorant of the crimes of modern capitalism. The leaders of the Hungarian opposition movement had all gone to the West in the 1980s and could see for themselves what it meant. We saw what Ronald Reagan meant. We knew what happened in 1973 in Chile and can't even flatter ourselves with the idea that we were ignorant. We were not. Many of us were enthusiastic readers of the *Spectator* (I even wrote for it), the *Weekly Standard* and *Commentary*.

5: The transcript of some of the discussion is contained in Zebrowski and others, 1988.

We accepted capitalism with all the blemishes, and our idea of it was not Scandinavia. It was the United States. By that time the welfare state had been unravelling for a long time. We went into that chapter with our eyes wide open. Of course, people in Poland and the Soviet Union were much more cut off from the West than we and the Yugoslavs were. We do not have that excuse.

There were secondary considerations. We could see that the last workers' movement that made people enthusiastic, the Solidarność workers' movement in Poland, was abandoned by German social democracy. Herbert Werner and Helmut Schmidt, the leaders of the German SPD, and Bruno Kreisky, the Austrian social democrat leader, were asking, "Why don't the Russians intervene?" They were afraid it might spread to East Germany and that there might be a working class unrest that would spread. Then there were people in the peace movement who were really engaged in the Cold War on the side of the Soviet Union (cf "unilateral disarmament"), and it seemed to us that the non-Communist left were not interested in the liberation of Eastern Europe from the Stalinist system. I always kept a respect for the anti-Stalinist left traditions and I think the others did as well. I still have a great respect for left communist and council communist traditions. I grew up on the works of Boris Souvarine and Victor Serge—one of the first books I read in French was *The Revolution Betrayed*. So we never said, "This is the same, every Marxist is a Gulagist, every communist a tankie." We were not that stupid. But it seemed to us that attempts to overcome the Soviet-style system from the left were doomed and that we had to pay the price of capitalism to put an end to the dictatorship. At first we were saying that it was a price that had to be paid, and then it was, alas, love for it.

But it did not last. My own case is a *cause célèbre* in Hungary because I was known as a leading dissident and then I was the chairman of the liberal party at one time. I had a high profile as someone who wrote and still writes for large circulation newspapers and who was on television. That does not mean that my case was important but it was visible.

I do not think it would have been possible for me to go back to the sort of confused libertarian leftism I subscribed to in the 1980s.[6] I still don't think either that the partly successful social democratic model of the welfare state can be relaunched. I also don't think the various models of it are that desirable. I am not inclined to forget that 1968, the most recent revolutionary moment in Western Europe, broke out in protest against the welfare state. We are apt to forget the problems of the welfare state and, even if it

6: See Tamás, 1985.

were possible to recreate it, they would still exist—the statism, conformism and authoritarian hierarchic models of doing politics. It is bad faith for the neoconservatives to criticise the welfare state in those terms but that does not mean the welfare state version of capitalism is that attractive—although in many ways it was superior to the present day version, was more egalitarian and allowed a modicum of counter-power and counter-hegemony. It was, after all, a system of compromise, while this is a system of complete domination by capital.

I do not think there are that many more versions of capitalism the system can come up with to hold out even fraudulently as a promise to people who do not own capital and who are not protected by the imperialist state. So if you break with capitalism now, you are likely to have fewer illusions than at any previous instance. We have seen all the compromises now. The old social democratic compromise in 1914, the Stalinist construction of a tyrannical state capitalism, *caudillismo* on the right and on the left, New Deal, National Socialism, militaristic systems, nationalistic systems, Catholic corporatism *à la* Seipel/Dollfuss, *à la* Salazar, neoconservatism. Most imaginable versions have been tried and the problems are resurfacing again and again.

By the time I came to break with the bourgeois mainstream there were no substitutes left, so I had to become a revolutionary Marxist. I did not see any other intelligent and credible solutions. You have to look the facts in the face. It is not a comfortable choice or a majority choice but that does not matter. I think that all the possibilities are exhausted.

It is now visible with the present day crisis. When the masters of the universe are experimenting with various mixes of old solutions and are even less intelligent and less radical than they were in the 1930s or 1950s, who can believe that they can save capitalism in a humanistic way from its worst aspects. It just does not seem possible. If I had broken with liberalism earlier, I might have become a social democrat. But where is social democracy? It is dead. It is a tradition but it is not a living political option. People are still voting Labour and social democrat, because it traditionally seemed to them to be the metaphorical home for working class and lower middle class people and to stand for greater equality. But that is a habit, not an idea, and there is a difference.

A few more questions about Hungary. Through the early 1980s Hungary was presented as the model market socialism, based upon massive foreign loans, and that came unstuck in 1988 and 1989, and you dissidents took over the government.
We never did. We stayed in opposition.

The non-Communist forces took over. But the central structures of the state remained the same—the police chiefs, those running the armed forces, the enterprises?
Yes. But the most important institution of the state was the party, and that was no longer there. So the changes were enormous, even in the state apparatus. The party was the backbone of the state structures both territorially and in all the economic branches (ie horizontally and vertically), so that it created a unity in the state steering of life in all respects. In classical capitalist countries the state bureaucracy remains outside the factory. But the party was the same in the government and in enterprise management, an instrument for keeping order and an instrument for modernising. It was a structure that offered discipline, and culture and leisure, which created the life of so many, offering the means of advancement, indoctrination, a sense of place, a sense of belonging and a seemingly solid project for the future. So you cannot say everything remained the same. We should not underestimate the changes, although the policies of the Communist Party leadership in the 1970s and 1980s were dogmatically pro-market.

At the same time the crucial elements of continuity should not be forgotten. Soviet-type state capitalism was a commodity-producing, wage labour based, unequal, hierarchic, repressive money economy and a class society to outclass all class societies which was extremely efficient in suppressing proletarian resistance. Revolts against that regime have always been socialist revolutions, in 1956 the workers' councils in Hungary, in 1968 the humanistic socialism in Czechoslovakia. Solidarność was in fact no trade union but a network of territorially organised workers' councils which initially wanted a self-management proletarian republic of a self-governing people, before repression made it into a bitterly conservative, pessimistic and Catholic movement to disintegrate at the moment of political "victory". The Central European style of "enlightened absolutism", of top-down reforms devised by scientifically and philosophically trained elite planners has not changed since the 18th century. "Communist" economic planners were painlessly transmogrified into neoconservative monetarist planners. For them, in a characteristically positivist manner, "socialism" was but an error in economic calculus. Marginal utility seemed more "modern" than the labour theory of value—and bureaucrats go more willingly with the prevailing fashion than couturiers.[7]

And the people from the Communist Party kept their power?
Yes, especially in the provinces—in the local councils, the police, economic

7: See Tamás, 2007, pp66-75, and Tamás, 2008, pp61-67.

life, the chambers of commerce and the bourgeois parties. One of the difficulties of my former liberal party was that coming from dissidents it did not attract former Communist Party members. So it remained without those roots in local administrations, among local bosses and local cliques.

As regards the economy in the 1980s Hungary had not only depended on foreign loans but had also participated in the well protected trade mechanism of the Comecon.[8] So even quite backward technologies and low cost production could be exported to the Soviet Union with its huge internal market. That kept old-fashioned manufacturing industry in place at the same time as attracting investment through Western loans. So the sellers' market in the Soviet Union and the foreign investment together provided advantages. The market was there for the other "Stalinist" countries, but without the loans.

One reason the regime collapsed everywhere was that the Communist Party could not survive without its ideology and its sense of identity. However much it was an instrument of power and control, it was very much dependent on the voluntary commitment of party members, and the party tried to castrate the members ideologically. Marxism was uncomfortable for them, because if you kept Marxism flourishing, it produced rebels. So they neutered Marxist research and thinking in various ways—in Hungary through Weberian "modernising" theories and rampant aestheticism, in Poland and Romania through nationalism. Certainly by the 1980s Marxism was a minority worldview confined to old comrades who did not play any role in the socialisation of new party cadres. Those in the socialist parties in Eastern Europe who are in their forties and fifties and come from the old state parties never read a Marxist book in their lives. Everywhere in Eastern Europe, including of course the Soviet Union, the party had lost its ideological core. It functioned without it for a time, totally empty, power being its own justification, but it fell with the first real challenge, a fairly banal one, from human rights liberals and democratic nationalists. They could not say anything. Their attitude was, "We want the same thing (that is, liberal capitalism) but a little more slowly."

They broke up extremely violently the 16 June 1988 demonstration on the anniversary of the death of Imre Nagy (and beat you up in the front of TV cameras), yet just twelve months later they collapsed when large numbers of East Germans came through Hungary to cross the Austrian border to the West.

To have stopped the East Germans crossing would have required a massive

8: The Comecon was the Russian-led Council for Mutual Economic Assistance.

show of force, which they could not do. On the whole, the changes in Eastern Europe were bloodless—with a few exceptions, for instance in Romania. No one would shoot and there was no one in the old "Communist" parties who would give their lives. No one has lifted a little finger in the defence of the system created after all by the October Revolution. There was no real motivation to resist the change. What would have been the *raison d'être* for the ruling "Communist" parties? The difference between a monetarised and marketised state capitalism and capitalism proper is infinitesimal. They could have chosen the Chinese way (savage capitalism plus one-party rule) but for that they lacked economic autarky and the genuine revolutionary roots of the Chinese Communist Party. The main driving force in East Central Europe was, quite simply, the West. The "Communist" party leaders have not had anything to say and transmogrified themselves insouciantly into "social-liberal" parliamentary *panjandrums*. These are different from the other parties only because of the past of their members, not because of their present. The political programmes and manifestoes of these former "Communist" parties are no different from those of the rest.

I remember I was elected in a by-election in 1989 to the old parliament as the first opposition member—the only one—and I made a speech calling the "Communist" prime minister a liar to his face, and this was broadcast live on television. This was the first time anyone had said any such thing in public for 40 years and it caused an enormous stir. But then the secretary general of the party walked up to me in the lobby, introduced himself (we had, of course, never met before) and told me to my great surprise that I was absolutely right. The cracks had become visible. Even the façade was crumbling. The number 1 denounced the number 2 to the Enemy of the People...

Tell me some things about Hungary today.

While industry and agriculture were collapsing, the dominant political forces said they were about to transform Hungary into a financial services centre of the world. It was nonsense. After the total collapse of the early 1990s some foreign investment arrived and, cheap labour being copiously available, there was some construction here and there. But the buy-outs were mostly for liquidating competitors and clearing consumer markets for the multinationals. However, as workers lost their jobs, these consumer markets naturally went up into thin air. By now the multinationals are packing up and leaving. On the whole it was still the state that somehow tried to provide for the increasing number of people left without any resources. We have many more pensioners than gainfully employed people in the private sector. Living standards have plummeted, working hours have got longer for those still employed, and unemployment is everywhere, with the dole for only six months. Many people are going hungry and they are not used to it. In the 1970s and 1980s Hungary was prosperous compared to the rest of the region, especially in the 1970s when there were rising living standards. All this is collapsing.

What determines the political conflicts here is a desperate fight for diminishing state resources. It is a fight between the middle class and the rest. This is the basis of the extreme right. There is not enough for everybody. There is a desperate scramble for social assistance, income support, social housing benefits, European grants, etc, and the "socialist" government's policy of cuts, more cuts and then some cuts opposes the middle class to the "modernisers" representing multinational capital, and thus "foreigners".

The opposition to neoliberal globalisation takes in the main nationalistic forms. It is necessary within a more or less democratic country to explain to the nation how and why they dare to deny such resources to the needy. The answer is criminalising and racialising the conflict—to say that all the people who need social assistance are racially different from us, racially inferior in the case of the Roma, or ne'er do wells and lazy, benefit-dependent spongers in the case of the "white trash". The answer then is to build more prisons, get more police and keep the proletariat, the precariat and the underclass in their place as inferiors. It is quite extraordinary how much the general response to the crisis, to galloping anomie and to spreading poverty is anti-plebeian. The open hatred against old age pensioners, the unemployed and social welfare claimants as "parasites" is counterbalanced by a hatred of the ruling order of capital as "foreign". Western liberal criticism of East European racism, xenophobia and neo-fascism is perceived as a feint to subdue "national" resistance to rootless cosmopolitan finance capital and life-destroying "political correctness". The strengthening of the right is not only disgusting quasi-fascist traditions coming back to life but also a response to social collapse and disintegration. The right is promising order, social cohesion and survival for the middle class, especially for young white, gentile, Christian middle class families.

And this is happening at a time when the working class is without any political representation, even of a minority or vanguard type representation that may make a difference in a situation of conflict. There is not even a symbolic representation such as the Labour Party or radical minority representation like yourselves in the Socialist Workers Party. The working class here is silent. It is the slumbering giant. It is the only class in Eastern Europe that is waiting, that is not doing anything, that is politically inexistent. They are neither joining the extreme right in its gallant fight against the underclass nor are they joining any socialist or social democratic opposition because it does not exist. The trade unions are scared out of their wits in case they lose their privileges and their usual bargaining positions.

I do not know how long things will stay like this. For the moment the only visible fight is that of the middle class against the underclass and against the crisis, which is conceived as a conspiracy from abroad, as something imposed on us by the West, by the plutocratic, cosmopolitan, anti-Hungarian, anti-Polish global order. On the one hand, we have the neoconservative parties in power at the moment—representing the global capitalist wing of the dominant forces—and on the other a "national conservative" right that is symbolically representing middle class interests but not declaring itself as such. The tension is enormous but the real political terms are not presented to public opinion. This is what a few of us are combating, but it is an uphill struggle, at the moment just a question of propaganda and enlightenment. We might get there in the end but it may be too late.

You have a small group of people around you and you are involved in an electoral project.

There is an informal group of intellectuals on the left that is trying to help the unions in their work—doing free public relations for them and making them more acceptable for mainstream society, where they are stigmatised. They are the people who are organising May Day festivals with balloons and sausages and beer. They are treated with contempt. People in this society do not keep secret their sheer contempt for those who do physical work, and even so-called centre-left publications will openly make fun of people who have dirty hands. It is like the 1920s: anti-democratic and anti working class, and furiously anti-communist, in the absence of any organised socialist left.

So we do not only say we dislike inequality in principle. We go to railway workers and metal workers and try to help and to talk to them and to learn. I did not form this new electoral group. I was asked by leaders of one of the small orthodox successor groups to the Communist Party plus Greens and feminists to be head of their candidates' list in the European elections. I hesitated for a long time. It is difficult for me, as an unrepentant fighter against the former system, to align myself with however modest, non-paid, totally innocent heirs to it. Not that they ever had any power—the leader of this party is a young engineer who was 20 when the system ended. I said yes in the end. Meanwhile other groups have joined us—Attac Hungary, leftish "civil society" groups, and we have some small, subdued union support. We are making a shoestring campaign without any expectations; nevertheless, we are attracting some attention. We might make people sit up and listen, and then perhaps take our literature and start something.[9]

So we are the very beginning of any left wing, socialist, Marxist organising but at least we have begun. It is a slow and uphill struggle but I am more convinced than ever that it is absolutely necessary. There is a sharp upside-down class struggle. There are the bourgeoisie and the middle class, multinational capital and the domestic middle class, with different but partially coinciding interests, attacking the proletariat and the underclass, and there is no answer—but there should be an answer.

It will also be in the interests of some of the middle classes to have an alliance with new proletarian forces, as in the olden times, if they do not want some kind of authoritarian nationalist semi-dictatorship. People will realise this but I fear it might be too late. Because what is threatening us now is an alliance between the conservatives and the extreme right, in which the diktat of global capital will be accepted while veiled by nationalist sloganeering and the racialising and criminalising of proletarian resistance.

You see how this bourgeois establishment is trying to push out everybody who seems to be on the outside. Gay and lesbian clubs, women's groups attacked—burnt, torched—as well as the Roma. There are tightly knit neo-Nazi terrorist organisations which have already murdered a few Gypsies and tried to assassinate socialist and liberal politicians. "National conservative" politicians on the whole are reluctant to condemn such goings-on. Hungary has the only National Socialist daily newspaper and National Socialist TV station in Europe, perhaps the world. Hundreds of openly anti-Semitic comments are posted daily on the websites of mainstream centre-left newspapers, not to speak of other outlets. Authoritarian education reform is advocated using corporal punishment for children—something forbidden since 1945. There are calls for the re-establishment of the ill-famed gendarmerie whose zeal and cruelty in deporting Hungarian Jews in 1944 surprised even Eichmann. Timorous anti-segregation measures in schools are vociferously opposed and rejected by local authorities. Dark-skinned children have their own miserable "educational" institutions. Modern art is ridiculed in a way that has not happened since the 1930s. The Enlightenment and modernist heritage are again presented as

9: Since this interview, the Hungarian Green Left managed to gather the necessary 20,000 signatures to stand but were prevented by bureaucratic shenanigans from taking part. The result was a huge international scandal with the German Die Linke protesting everywhere. The organisation called on sympathisers to invalidate their vote by writing "Green Left" across the ballot papers as a silent protest. There was some solidarity even in the mainstream media.

degenerate and diabolical. All these things are seen as having a rebellious potential. All the reactionary clichés are coming out.[10] Reaction is teaching East Europeans how these struggles hang together. We are learning our lessons the hard way. We don't need to be told socialists and feminists, gay and lesbian activists, minority rights campaigners and trade unionists belong together because we all are being clobbered by the same enemy.

References

Haraszti, Miklós, 1977, *A Worker in a Workers' State* (Penguin).

Rakovski, Marc, 1978, *Towards an East European Marxism* (Macmillan).

Tamás, GM, 1985, *L'Oeil et la Main* (Editions Noir).

Tamás, GM, 1989, *Les Idoles de la Tribu* (Editions de l'Arcantère).

Tamás, GM, 1996, "Ethnarchy and Ethno-Anarchism", Social Research, volume 63, number 1 (Spring 1996).

Tamás, GM, 2000, "On Post-Fascism", *Boston Review* (Summer 2000), www.bostonreview.net/BR25.3/tamas.html

Tamás, GM, 2007, "A Capitalism Pure and Simple", *Left Curve 32*.

Tamás, GM, 2008, "Counter-Revolution Against A Counter-Revolution", *Left Curve 33*.

Zebrowski, Andy, and others, 1988, "Solidarity at the Crossroads", *International Socialism 41* (winter 1988).

10: See Tamás, 1989; Tamás, 1996, pp147-190, Tamás, 2000.

How do we stop the BNP?

Martin Smith

The fascist British National Party (BNP) made a major electoral breakthrough when it won two seats in the European elections in June. BNP leader Nick Griffin won a seat in the North West region and Andrew Brons won a second seat in Yorkshire & Humberside. Across the country the BNP polled 943,598 votes (see table 1).

Going into this election Nick Griffin had a lot to be confident about. He described the political situation as the "Perfect Storm" for the BNP. The British economy is in the middle of the worst economic crisis since the 1930s, unemployment is rising and millions are anxious about what the future will bring. It was against this background that the expenses scandal broke. The Tories were exposed with shocking claims of servants' quarters and "duck islands", but it was the corruption of Labour MPs that provoked deep bitterness among Labour voters—despite everything working class voters still expected more from Labour. There was another critical ingredient: the popularising of the slogan "British Jobs for British Workers" first used by Gordon Brown but then taken up by groups of striking construction workers.

We have BNP members on local and county councils, one in the London Assembly and now two sitting in the European Parliament. The BNP hopes this will make it a legitimate party and part of the political establishment.

Worryingly, during the election campaign sections of the Labour Party tried to downplay the threat of BNP election victories. They were backed by some sections of the media. The *Independent* published an editorial with the headline "Stop Exaggerating The Threat Of The BNP". Even the anti-fascist magazine *Searchlight* claimed the BNP election campaign had come off the rails.[1] This clearly was a mistake and one that should not be made again.

Table 1: European election results 2004 and 2009 for the UK (excluding Northern Ireland)

	Number of MEPs (2004 figure)	2004 BNP vote	2004 UKIP vote	2004 BNP plus UKIP	2009 BNP vote	2009 UKIP vote	2009 BNP plus UKIP
East Midlands	5 (6)	91,860 (6.5%)	366,498 (26.1%)	458,358 (32.6%)	106,319 (8.7%)	201,984 (16.4%)	308,303 (25.1%)
East of England	7 (7)	65,557 (4.3%)	296,160 (19.6%)	361,717 (23.9%)	97,013 (6.1%)	313,921 (19.6%)	410,934 (25.7%)
London	8 (9)	76,152 (4%)	232,633 (12.3%)	308,785 (16.3%)	86,420 (4.9%)	188,440 (10.8%)	274,860 (15.7%)
North East	3 (3)	50,249 (6.4%)	94,887 (12.2%)	145,136 (18.6%)	52,700 (8.9%)	90,700 (15.4%)	143,400 (24.3%)
North West	8 (9)	134,959 (6.4%)	257,158 (11.7%)	392,117 (18.1%)	132,094 (8%)	261,740 (15.8%)	393,834 (23.8%)
South East	10 (10)	64,877 (2.9%)	431,111 (19.5%)	495,988 (22.4%)	101,769 (4.4%)	440,002 (18.8%)	541,771 (23.2%)
South West	6 (7)	43,653 (3%)	326,784 (22.6%)	370,437 (25.6%)	60,889 (3.9%)	341,845 (22.1%)	402,734 (26%)
West Midlands	6 (7)	107,794 (7.5%)	251,366 (17.5%)	359,160 (25%)	121,967 (8.6%)	300,471 (21.3%)	422,438 (29.9%)
Yorkshire & Humberside	6 (6)	126,538 (8%)	228,666 (14.5%)	355,204 (22.5%)	120,139 (9.8%)	213,750 (17.4%)	333,889 (27.2%)
Wales	4 (4)	27,135 (3%)	96,677 (10.5%)	123,812 (13.5%)	37,114 (5.4%)	87,585 (12.8%)	124,699 (18.2%)
Scotland	6 (7)	19,427 (1.7%)	78,828 (6.7%)	98,255 (8.4%)	27,174 (2.5%)	57,788 (5.2%)	84,962 (7.7%)
Total	72 (78)	808,201 (4.9%)	2,650,768 (16.1%)	3,458,969 (21%)	943,598 (6.2%)	2,498,226 (16.5%)	3,441,824 (22.7%)

1: The *Independent*, 25 May 2009; *Searchlight*, June 2009, www.searchlightmagazine.com

However, it is important to put the BNP's electoral gains in perspective. It did not witness a massive surge in support. Overall its national vote went up by 135,397 from the 2004 Euro election figure, increasing its share of votes by 1.3 percent. Griffin's share of the vote only increased by 1.6 percent. The number of votes for the BNP in the two seats it won was lower than in 2004.

There are two reasons why the BNP was able to win its two Euro seats. The first was the collapse of Labour's vote. Labour came third behind UKIP with just 15.7 percent of the vote, an all time low. The result in Wales was like a punch in the solar plexus for Labour. They were beaten into second place by the Tories—this is unprecedented. In the South West and South East regions Labour came in fifth with just 7.7 percent and 8.2 percent of the vote respectively. The second reason was the low turnout. Only 33 percent of the electorate voted. We have to continue to call on people to vote to keep the BNP out. If 5,000 more people had voted Green in the North West, Griffin would not have won a seat.

The purpose of this article is to demonstrate that despite its clever attempt to politically reposition itself as a respectable party of the right the BNP remains a fascist party at its core. I also want to look at the rise of the BNP and the factors that have propelled it to the centre of the political arena. I write these lines just two days after the results of the elections were announced. Across the north of England we have witnessed a number of protests against the BNP, and when Griffin decided to call a press conference outside parliament hundreds of Unite Against Fascism activists gathered at a few hours notice and chased him away. Across the country the election results and such protests have provoked debate and raised the question "How do we stop the BNP?"

What is fascism?

Ever since Benito Mussolini and his fascists took over the Italian state in 1922 and Adolf Hitler's Nazi Party was handed control of the German state in 1933 socialists have attempted to understand the political phenomenon of fascism and Nazism.[2] Trotsky's writings remain key texts in any analysis of the nature of fascism. He argues that what distinguishes fascism from other forms of dictatorship is the methods it deploys, its ultimate political goal and the social base of the movement.

Many people believe that virulent racism is the key component of a

2: There is a debate among historians about the differences between fascism and Nazism. For the purposes of this article I use both terms interchangeably.

fascist party. Of course racism and anti-Semitism are profoundly important to fascists. They use racism to hold their supporters together and create a scapegoat for discontent. But the main aim of fascism is not restricted to the annihilation of one racial group within society. For example, Mussolini's Blackshirts did not use anti-Semitism to build their organisation. Since then fascist parties have increasingly used racism as a way of gaining support. The victims vary from country to country. In Hitler's Germany the main target was the Jews; in Hungary today it is Roma Gypsies.

However, there is much more to fascism than racist ideology. Its primary aim is to destroy working class organisations and democracy, and to install a dictatorship. Trotsky argues:

> Fascism is not merely a system of reprisals, of brutal force and of police terror. Fascism is a particular governmental system based on the uprooting of all elements of proletarian democracy within bourgeois society... To this end the physical annihilation of the most revolutionary section of the workers does not suffice. It is also necessary to smash all independent and voluntary organisations, to demolish all the defensive bulwarks of the proletariat, and to uproot whatever has been achieved during three quarters of a century by the Social Democracy and the trade unions.[3]

For most of the time ruling classes have no need for fascism. They control society and make profits through democratic institutions, relying on the fact that the majority of people accept the way the system works most of the time. On occasions they use parts of the state to quell disorder. However, during times of major social crisis the state can find itself unable to defend the status quo. It can find that its armies are prone to mutiny and mass uprisings can make the police ineffective. In such a situation the very existence of capitalism is threatened. It is at such junctures that the ruling class can turn towards fascism. Fascist organisations can only take power under certain conditions. The first is that sections of the ruling class have to be so desperate that they feel compelled to abandon bourgeois democracy and throw in their lot in with the fascists. The other is that the fascists must have proved that they are powerful enough to smash the working class. To achieve this they have to be a mass party.

Fascism is different from other counter-revolutionary movements in another important way. It is a mass movement of the petty bourgeoisie—shopkeepers, doctors, low-level officials, foreman and the

3: Trotsky, 1971, p144.

self-employed. This class occupies a contradictory position in society. When capitalism is relatively stable the petty bourgeoisie tends to tail either the main capitalist parties or the parties of the working class. But during extreme economic crises the petty bourgeoisie can look to create its own movement—a movement of despair.

Members of this class are individualised and isolated, and during political and social crisis these tendencies are often heightened. The capitalist class is usually able to ride out the storm by living off the wealth it has accumulated; the working class has its trade unions that give it some protection against the ravages of the crisis. The petty bourgeoisie believe that they suffer most. Their small businesses often go to the wall first and their savings can be eaten away by inflation as the stocks and shares they own are rendered worthless. Their status in society is also threatened. They fear the long drop into the working class or, worse, unemployment. The shame of bankruptcy eats away at their soul and it is at this point that their prejudices and jealousies come pouring out. They are drawn to organisations with a radical rhetoric against the system, whose focus of activity is on the street. Fascism articulates their fears and it also articulates their political aspirations. It talks about protecting the "little man" from the "twin evils" of capitalism and communism. This does not mean that fascist parties do not win support among people outside the middle class. The bigger a fascist movement becomes the more it is able to recruit from the unemployed and from sections of the working class.

In the 1920s and 1930s fascist parties built mass movements based on the middle class, but they could not take power without the political and financial support of the ruling class. Hitler's Nazis were bankrolled by business leader Fritz Thyssen and other sections of German capitalism. Mussolini's fascists were backed by the Pirelli brothers and other industrialists.[4] The fascist parties offered the ruling class a solution in the form of a mass movement of counter-revolution.

Fascist movements use a dual strategy of building brute force on the ground and creating a "respectable" political facade. Hitler developed a similar strategy in Germany in the 1920s. At first he tried to seize power by force with the "Beer Hall Putsch" of 1923 but this ended in humiliation and defeat for his fledgling Nazi Party.

Fascism has never taken power in a country simply through elections—fascist parties have always been handed power by ruling classes in crisis. So Adolf Hitler was appointed chancellor in 1933 as Germany's

---

4: Guerin, 1972, pp33-40, 27-33.

rulers faced an extreme economic crisis that they feared could spark a workers' revolution. Mussolini's fascist party arose out of former veterans of the First World War who organised themselves into right wing gangs to attack socialists and trade unionists. Mussolini combined these gangs with a "respectable" nationalist political organisation. At first Italy's rulers were suspicious but by 1922 their fear of the rising workers' movement overcame their distrust and Mussolini was granted power.

The cost of Hitler's Nazi Party taking power was a catastrophe. It led to the destruction of the most powerful working class in the world and culminated in the Holocaust, the systematic murder of six million Jews and millions of "Slavs", Gypsies, gays and lesbians, the mentally ill and the disabled.

The legacy of the Nazi regime poses a real problem for today's fascists. If they ape their political messiahs—Hitler and Mussolini—they find themselves at the fringes of political life. They have been forced to deny their political heritage and rebrand their political ideas. Today the BNP spends a great deal of time and energy denying that it is a fascist party. I hope in the coming sections of this article to demonstrate that the BNP remains committed in deed and thought to the goals of fascism.

The resistible rise of the BNP

In electoral terms the BNP has been by far the most successful fascist organisation in Britain but its rise has not been inexorable and over the past 28 years its support has ebbed and flowed. The party was founded in 1982 after a split from the National Front (NF), then the biggest fascist organisation in Britain. During most of the 1980s the BNP, led by John Tyndall who ran the party as his own personal fiefdom, stood in the shadow of the NF. But its fortunes began to improve from the late 1980s. A key factor was the first electoral breakthrough in Tower Hamlets, east London, in 1993.

East London has been a traditional stomping ground for right wing and fascist parties. The British Brothers' League had led a vicious campaign against Jewish migrants at the beginning of the 20th century; east London was a stronghold for Oswald Mosley's British Union of Fascists, which polled 23 percent of the vote in North Bethnal Green in 1937 and continued to organise there even after the Second World War; the area was fertile ground for the NF in the 1970s. Yet it would be wrong to characterise east London as a racist enclave. It has a rich tradition of fighting racism and fascism stretching back to the socialists who campaigned against the British Brothers' League, through the actions of the Communists, Independent Labour Party members, and Jewish and Irish workers who stopped Mosley at the battle of

Cable Street in 1936, to the Anti Nazi League campaign against the National Front in the 1970s.

In 1990 the BNP gained votes of 9.71, 8.4 and 12.1 percent respectively in council elections in the Globe Town, Park and St Peters wards of Tower Hamlets. These results were the highest votes gained by any fascist party for a dozen years. Two years later it focused its general election efforts in east London, with John Tyndall getting 3 percent of the vote in Bethnal Green & Stepney and his right hand man Richard Edmonds getting 3.6 percent in neighbouring Bow & Poplar. Polling data suggested it got a number of votes from the Isle of Dogs area despite a lack of campaigning,[5] and this was where the BNP won 20 percent of the vote (657 votes) in a council by-election in October 1992. The BNP flooded the area and began systematically working on the estates. Then, in a council by-election in the same ward on 23 September 1993, its candidate Derek Beackon gained 34 percent of the vote (1,480 votes) and it won its first ever election.

How did the BNP make this electoral breakthrough? First and foremost the Liberal Democrats, who controlled the council at the time, made the BNP's racism respectable. Housing was and still remains a key issue for working class people and a source of racial tension. The Liberal Democrats introduced a "sons and daughters" housing scheme that prioritised housing through a points scheme based on the length of residency of people's parents. This scheme favoured white residents and pushed migrant workers further down the housing priority list. The Liberal Democrats were also more than happy to play the race card. One local paper reported that a Liberal Democrat councillor was travelling to Bangladesh to argue that Tower Hamlets had "no room for immigrants".[6] In the run-up to the 23 September 1993 council elections they produced leaflets suggesting that they favoured white residents.

Instead of taking a firm stand against all this the local Labour Party caved in and implied that they supported the "sons and daughters" policy. Worse, in order to weaken the Liberal Democrat challenge Labour published false canvassing returns suggesting that the BNP could win. The idea behind this crazy plan was to win back Labour voters, but all it did was legitimise the BNP.

The local BNP branch also found new ways to tap into the frustration and discontent in the borough. It organised a "Rights for Whites" campaign and demonstration in 1990 after a local white boy was injured in

---

5: *Patriot*, spring 1997.

6: *East London Advertiser*, 8 November 1991.

a fight with a gang of Asian youths. I was there that day on a counter-BNP picket. Theirs was not your usual Nazi protest. The Nazi regalia and flags were absent and the skinheads were told to stay away. This was a demonstration coordinated by Nazis in their Sunday best joined by 300 to 400 local people waving St George's flags and singing "chirpy" cockney songs.

The BNP boasted that it was able to speak to "literally thousands of local people, selling them papers and creating the image they wanted to create of the BNP, as opposed to the negative media stereotype".[7] The BNP tried to project its members as local activists and pillars of the community but the brutal reality was never far from the surface. In 1992 BNP thugs organised several attacks on Anti Nazi League (ANL) stalls in Tower Hamlets and just a week before the election a gang of 30 to 40 BNP members went on the rampage on Brick Lane attacking shops and breaking windows.

The reaction by the left to the BNP victory was instant. A Socialist Workers Party member and Unison union steward led a section of Tower Hamlets council workers out on strike. The ANL organised a picket of the BNP newspaper sale at the top of Brick Lane. The BNP, and before it the NF, had sold there for years. It was a provocation to the local Bengali community. The picket drove the BNP sellers away and they have never returned. Across the country the ANL organised a mass campaign involving leafleting of estates and workplaces to get the anti-Nazi message across. Finally the TUC organised a 40,000-strong demonstration against the BNP through Tower Hamlets.

The BNP predicted that Beackon would hold on to his seat in May 1994 council elections. It was wrong. He lost the seat to the Labour Party although he still came second with 2,041 votes (28 percent). The BNP stood 29 candidates across the country getting an average of 13.7 percent.[8] Many party activists were demoralised by the result and for the rest of the decade the BNP remained at the margins of British political life with only 0.1 percent of the vote in the 1997 general election and 0.19 percent in 2001.

Nick Griffin

In September 1999 Nick Griffin won the party's first ever leadership election, taking 1,082 votes to incumbent John Tyndall's 411. This signalled a change in direction for the BNP. Griffin was no stranger to fascism. He went to his first meeting of the NF aged 15. As a student at Cambridge University he established the "Young National Front Students" society.

7: *Patriot*, winter 1997.
8: Copsey, 2004, p66.

He also took up boxing after he was driven off the streets by anti-fascists in Lewisham, south London, in 1977.[9] In 1980 he became a member of the NF governing body, the National Directorate, set up the NF Student Organisation and launched the magazine *Nationalism Today*.

He left the NF in 1989 and with Derek Holland formed the International Third Position (ITP). The organisation was named after an old fascist slogan—Nazism was the "third way" between "Jewish" capitalism and "Jewish" Bolshevism. The ITP was a secretive organisation. Included in its ranks was the Italian fascist Roberto Fiore, wanted at the time by the Italian state in connection with the bombing of Bologna which left 85 dead and 200 injured.[10] Tyndall asked Griffin to join the BNP in 1995. He immediately began to edit the BNP publication *Spearhead*. He was also the editor of *The Rune*, an anti-Semitic newspaper. In issue 12 Griffin called the Holocaust "the Holohoax" and criticised Holocaust denier David Irving for admitting in an interview that up to four million Jews might have died. Griffin wrote, "True revisionists will not be fooled by this new twist to the sorry tale of the hoax of the 20th century".[11]

During his 1998 prosecution for incitement to racial hatred Griffin said, "I am well aware that the orthodox opinion is that six million Jews were gassed and cremated and turned into lampshades. Orthodox opinion also once held that the world is flat... I have reached the conclusion that the 'extermination' tale is a mixture of Allied wartime propaganda, extremely profitable lie, and witch-hysteria".[12]

The BNP was divided into two camps when Griffin took over the leadership in 1999. Those around Tyndall and John Edmonds wanted to continue with an out and out fascist party modelled on the NF and Hitler's Nazi Party; others such as Tony Lecomber, Michael Newland, Steve Edwards and Sharon Edwards wanted to see a new repackaged BNP that presented itself as more voter-friendly. Griffin united with the second group. He outlined the direction he wanted to take the BNP in the magazine *Patriot*, run by Nazi thug and convicted bomber Tony Lecomber:

> Politics is always the art of the possible, so we must judge every policy by one simple criterion: is it realistically possible that a decisive proportion of the British people will support it? If not, then to scale down our short-term

9: The *Guardian*, 19 November 2008.
10: *Searchlight*, July 1998.
11: BBC, 2001.
12: BBC, 2001.

ambitions to a point at which the answer becomes "yes" is not a sell out, but the only possible step closer to our eventual goal.[13]

Griffin's objectives were clear. The party would have to water down its policies in order to win an electoral base. He decreed that the BNP had to do away with the "three Hs—'hard talk', 'hobbyism' and 'Hitler'".[14] He was urging his members to stay away from violence, football hooliganism, skinhead culture and Hitler worship. But the party's ultimate "goal" remained a fascist state. He spelt this out absolutely clearly in the same issue of *Patriot*:

> Instead of presenting the party as a revolutionary alternative to the system, we must present them [the electorate] with an image of moderate reasonableness... Of course we must teach the truth to the hardcore. But when it comes to influencing the public, forget about racial differences, genetics, Zionism, historical revisionism and so on.

Griffin has used a great deal of political capital fighting those in his party who are frustrated by electoral politics and want to go back to "street fighting", fascist style rallies and parades—the "traditionalists". He expelled John Tyndall and John Edmonds for being disruptive in 2002. Griffin's drive to ditch the BNP's fascist image and repackage its ideology to make it more politically acceptable to a section of the electorate is not new. Historically fascist organisations have always been divided between an electoral wing and those who want to see a movement based on the streets.

Griffin is copying the strategy put forward by French National Front (FN) leader Jean-Marie Le Pen. Le Pen argued that in order to build up the FN's strength its members could no longer openly proclaim their dedication to Hitler and genocidal racism. Instead they would present themselves as nationalists who were concerned about immigration and multiculturalism. Le Pen famously described his politics as "neither left nor right, but French". Just as with Griffin this did not mean dropping fascism but hiding it. Le Pen continues to leave open the possibility of a more revolutionary strategy should the circumstances prove favourable. Just how far Griffin has gone in imitating his French allies could be seen when Griffin launched a bi-monthly magazine called *Identity*. Le Pen's bi-monthly magazine was also called *Identité*. The name, an editorial said, was chosen to reflect the "new modernist nationalism

13: *Patriot*, spring 1999.
14: Searchlight, August 2002.

to which the British National Party is now firmly committed" aimed at "the preservation of the identity of the traditional inhabitants and cultures of Britain". The more contentious term "race" would disappear.[15]

The electoral rise of the BNP

In the 1999 European elections the BNP only gained 1 percent of the national vote. But from the polling returns it was able to glean the areas it had polled well in. Two towns stood out—Oldham and Burnley. In both it gained over 10 percent of the vote and these became key target areas. The BNP reaped the harvest in the 2002 council elections, taking an average of 27 percent of the vote across the five wards it contested in Oldham. In Burnley it did even better, winning three council seats. It was the electoral breakthrough Griffin was looking for.

The BNP did not even have an active branch in Oldham in 1997. But again it was the establishment that helped it on its way. In January 2001 the head of Oldham police division, chief superintendent Eric Hewitt, voiced concerns about a rising number of attacks by Asian youth on white men in the town. Hewitt was just pandering to racists since ethnic minorities were six and a half times more likely to be victims of racist attacks than their white counterparts. The local press ran a series of scare stories that had the effect of whipping up racist tensions in the area. The BNP seized the political opportunity, campaigning against plans to build a mosque and organising an "Equal Rights for Oldham Whites" protest outside the police station. It was Tower Hamlets all over again. Tensions were further stoked up when the NF proposed a march through the city. According to one former member the BNP was deliberately issuing fake NF press releases in an attempt to raise the political temperature.[16]

Tensions grew in April 2001 as more than 450 Stoke City football hooligans ran amok in a predominantly Asian area of the town, and in the following weeks various fascist groups and gangs of white youth roamed around the town intimidating Asian people. The town exploded on the night of 26 May 2001 into a full-scale riot between the police and Asian youth that continued for three nights.

Obviously fascist groups were able to stir up the situation but the independent *Ritchie Report* stated that the riot revealed wider problems: "Poverty and social exclusion aggravated by a lack of government funding had caused the three nights of violence" and it suggested that the council

15: *Identity*, January-February 2000.
16: Copsey, 2004, p127.

was doing little to challenge the racial segregation in housing and education that had gone on in the town for 30 years. It also noted that only 2.6 percent of the council's staff came from ethnic minorities, "a form of institutional racism" and evidence of an "unwillingness" of the council to face realities.[17]

After the riots the BNP was able to distance itself from the NF with the help of the local paper which allowed Griffin to claim, "We're not here to put others down or cause trouble; all we want is a fair deal for our own people: equal rights for whites!"[18]

There is a common liberal argument that if you do not give fascist parties publicity by attacking them, no one would notice their existence and vote for them. But as figures 1 and 2, and table 2, show, the BNP has been able to build on its council election victories since its initial breakthrough in 2002. There are now 20 constituencies across the country where it polls above 7 percent. BNP council seats are not only found "in a few troubled towns and cities in the north west".[19] It currently has 55 councillors in places such as Stoke, London, Yorkshire, the Midlands and Sevenoaks, and a member on the London Assembly (these figures do not include the 2009 June elections).[20] As table 2 and figure 2 show, there is an ever growing list of wards at risk to the BNP as all the mainstream parties find it more and more difficult to turn out their vote.

Electorally the BNP is Britain's most successful fascist party. Mosley's British Union of Fascists won only two council seats in the 1930s, while the NF, Britain's largest fascist group, failed to win any seats in the 1970s.

Table 2: The BNPs results in the 2005 general election

Number of seats where BNP got more than 5 percent	33
Number of seats where BNP got more than 6 percent	21
Number of seats where BNP got more than 7 percent	10
Number of seats where BNP got more than 9 percent	7
Number of seats where BNP got more than 10 percent	3

17: www.oldhamir.org.uk
18: *Oldham Chronicle*, 29 May 2001.
19: The *Independent*, 25 May 2009.
20: www.uaf.org.uk/news.asp?choice=70503

Figure 1: Number of BNP councillors

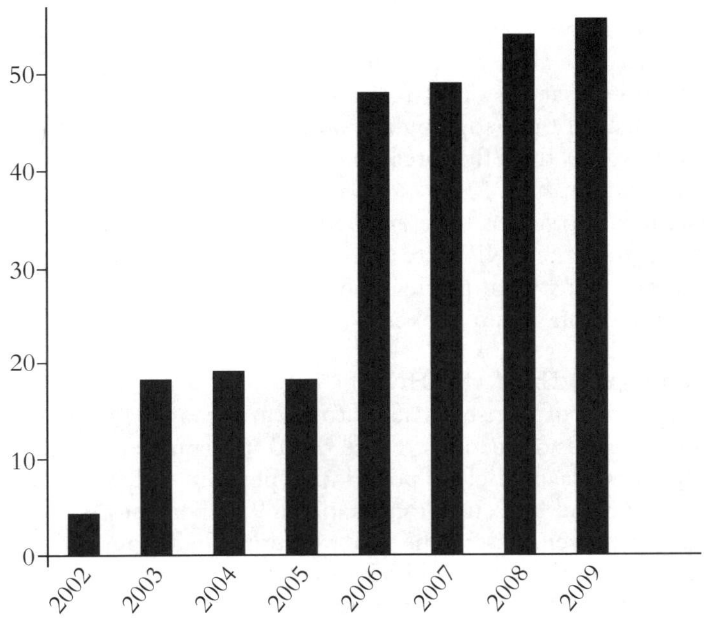

Figure 2: General election votes for the BNP

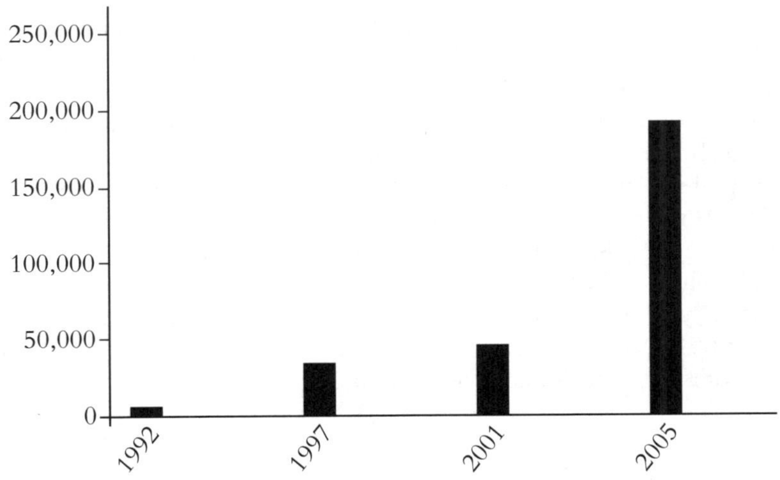

There was also a rise in the BNP's votes in the London Assembly elections from 2000 to 2004. In 2008 another rise, this time of just 0.6 percent of the poll, allowed the BNP to cross the 5 percent threshold needed to win a seat. The BNP vote in the mayoral election was 69,710, just over half the vote that they got in the London Assembly elections. This indicates that half of the people who voted BNP tactically voted for the Tory Boris Johnson as their first preference—the BNP had called for a second preference vote for him.[21]

Of course, local variations have enabled the BNP to win particular seats. In all of these areas the BNP were aided by three interrelated factors: the collapse of local mainstream parties, the politicisation of race by the three major parties and anti asylum seeker hysteria.

Racism and the growth of the BNP

We have seen a growth of fascist parties across Europe over the past 30 years. In the 2004 European elections, while the BNP gained 4.9 percent of the vote, Belgium's Vlaams Belang polled 23.2 percent, Italy's Alleanza Nazionale 11.5 percent and Le Pen's Front National 9.81 percent. At a local council level the gap is even wider. The Front National had close to 2,000 councillors by the end of the 1990s and Vlaams Belang had 809 municipal and 88 provincial councillors elected in 2006 compared to the BNP's 55. The so-called "new fascist" parties have all seen their fortunes grow when the mainstream political parties of the centre have collapsed or have been politically damaged by scandal or political crisis. They have also grown while the mainstream parties legitimise racism or attack ethnic minority communities.

Is Britain becoming a more racist society? There is not a yes or no answer; the issue is more complex than that. The proportion of people surveyed who said they were either very or a little prejudiced dropped between 1983 and 2001 from 35 percent to 25 percent, and 25 percent remained the figure in a poll in August 2005 (a month after the London bombings of 7 July 2005).[22] But although the general levels of racism have fallen over the past 30 years the levels of racism have increased in three areas—over the question of asylum seekers, Islamophobia and migration. The political class and the media have driven these forward as perceived problems playing into the hands of the BNP.[23] Wherever the BNP has gained ground it has been on the basis of a rise in racism and concessions made to the racist agenda.

21: *Unite to Stop the British National Party*, Unite Against Fascism pamphlet, pp8-9.

22: BBC "Multicultural Poll", conducted by Mori.

23: Finney and Simpson, 2009, p52.

The wave of racism against asylum seekers

There was a racist onslaught on asylum seekers by both the media and many mainstream politicians at the fag end of John Major's Tory government and in the first years under Tony Blair. National newspapers such as the *Daily Mail* and *Daily Express* ran stories on a daily basis scapegoating asylum seekers and accusing them of being "bogus", "scroungers" and "rapists". Some local newspapers went further, with an editorial in the *Dover Express* describing asylum seekers as "human sewage".[24] The Tories introduced the inhumane anti-asylum laws, which gave the authorities the right to lock asylum seekers up in prisons and camps. Labour promised to repeal the Tory laws. However, in office it not only kept them but also introduced dehumanising vouchers and dispersal schemes.

Police figures in April 2000 showed that the number of racist incidents had doubled in the previous 12 months. There were 1,500 racist incidents in the first three months of 2000, compared with 1,000 for the whole of the previous year.[25] Bill Morris, Britain's first ever black trade union leader, delivered a powerful warning to Britain's politicians:

> The United Nations has charged the Tories with whipping up racial intolerance. But the [Labour] home secretary and the Home Office must accept responsibility for creating the environment where it is acceptable. The mood music is playing a hostile tune for black Britons. By heralding measure after measure to stop people entering Britain, the Home Office has given life to racists.[26]

The constant attacks on asylum seekers helped the BNP gain support and legitimacy. Griffin told a *Guardian* reporter, "The asylum seeker issue has been great for us... It's been quite fun to watch government ministers and the Tories play the race card in far cruder terms than we would ever use. The issue legitimises us".[27]

Figure 3 shows that the majority of people do not have fixed racist positions on the question of immigration and asylum. People's fears and concerns rise and fall depending on a number of factors, of which the most important are the role of the media and the condition of the economy. There is no evidence to show that the BNP prospers in areas where there are large numbers of asylum seekers. The Democratic Audit (a think tank based

---

24: The *Dover Express* ran a number of stories during October 1998 attacking Kosovan asylum seekers. The most infamous was published on 1 October 1998.

25: Hassan Mahamdallie, *Refugees are not to Blame*, *Socialist Worker* pamphlet, p4.

26: The *Independent*, 14 April 2000.

27: *Guardian* magazine, 20 May 2000.

at Essex University) found that the higher the numbers of asylum seekers allocated to a locality the lower the level of BNP support. But its explanation, that the government avoids sending asylum seekers to areas with high or potentially high levels of such support, is wrong. The real explanation is that racist attitudes arise from perceived ideas, not reality. So the BNP performs better electorally in so-called "whiter" areas on the periphery of higher "ethnic minority/asylum seeker" populations. This corresponds to a pattern of voting detected in France, referred to by the Front National as a "halo effect". It is the fear of immigrants rather than the direct contact with migrant communities that favours the fascists.[28] Integration of asylum seekers into an area actually undermines the BNP and its racist ideas.

Figure 3: Percent ranking "race relations/immigrants/ immigration" as the most important issue
Source: Mori

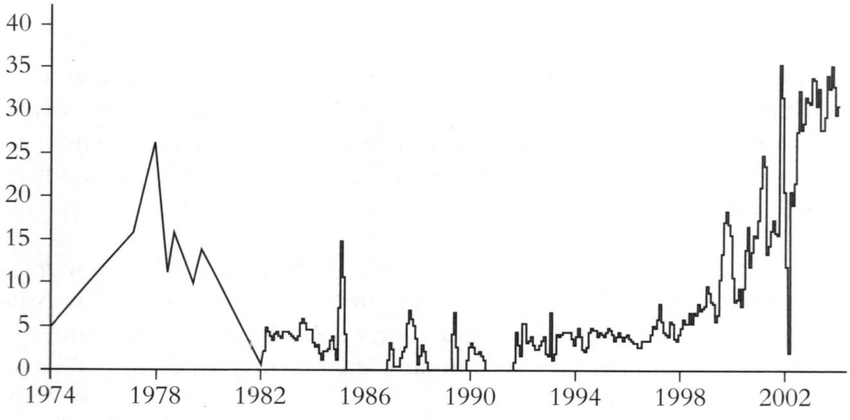

Islamophobia

The next wave of racism came in the wake of 9/11 in 2001, the US/UK invasion of Iraq in 2003 and the London bombings of July 2005. Each event brought with it an increase in anti-Muslim violence, verbal abuse and attacks on property. As far as the British political, media and literary establishment were concerned the normal rules of engagement were suspended.

28: Magretts, John, Rowlance and Weir, 2006, pp17,28.

Peter Oborne and James Jones have highlighted a number of high profile media stories depicting Muslims in a racist manner. They also show that many of these stories were either entirely made up or distorted.[29] This was not just true of the right wing gutter press. Take journalist Polly Toynbee, normally regarded as a model liberal and champion of the oppressed. As long ago as 1997 she wrote in the *Independent*, "I am an Islamophobe, and proud of it".[30] Can you imagine her declaring, "I am an anti-Semite and proud of it"? A Conservative columnist wrote in the *Independent*, "There are widespread fears that Muslim immigrants...will succeed where Islamic armies failed and change irrevocably the character of European civilisation".[31]

Such disgraceful assaults on Muslims allow Griffin to push the argument even further. He told one journalist for the *Financial Times*, just days before the Euro elections, that he had "nothing against Sikhs and Hindus"—even though they cannot join the party and he will offer large sums to encourage them to voluntarily repatriate—but he is avowedly "anti-Islam".[32] The BNP has tapped into the hysteria against Muslims through what some critics call the "new racism" or "neo-racism"—a type of racism that denies it is racist and stresses cultural differences.

In Stoke on Trent the BNP has nine councillors. Its leaflets contrast pictures of the local area 70 years ago with silhouettes of mosques and of three women wearing *niqabs*. The headline asks "Is this what you want for your city centre?" It has campaigned against the building of a mosque and has distributed leaflets claiming Muslims were getting priority for council housing.[33] In Dudley its leaflets claimed that the council gave funds to build mosques when in fact Muslims raised the money themselves. In Bradford leaflets claimed that Asian men were grooming under-age white teenagers for sex. The campaign was made easier for the BNP when the local Labour MP Anne Cryer told journalists, "I think there is a problem with the view Asian men generally have about white women. Their view about white women is generally fairly low".[34]

Migration

The fascists have always tried to gain support by campaigning against migration into Britain and they have always been boosted by government

29: Oborne and Jones, 2008.
30: Cited in the *Independent*, 4 July 2008.
31: Oborne and Jones, 2008.
32: *Financial Times*, 1 June 2009.
33: G2, the *Guardian*, 28 May 2008.
34: The *Times*, 11 August 2007.

action to limit it. This is what happened in 1968. Racist Tory MPs such as Enoch Powell and Duncan Sandys claimed, wrongly as it turned out, that 20,000 Asians holding UK passports in Kenya would "pour" into Britain. The Labour government panicked and passed the 1968 Commonwealth Immigrants Bill, which removed the right to entry and settlement in Britain from UK passport holders lacking a "close connection" through birth in the country or a British parent or grandparent. According to the Runnymeade Trust, "The close connection device was designed to ensure that white settlers in East Africa retained the right of entry while black settlers, despite holding the same passport, did not".[35]

Far from weakening the racists the passing of the act gave Powell the confidence to raise the stakes and make his notorious "rivers of blood" speech on 20 April 1968. He was sacked from the Tory shadow cabinet, but racism was made to look respectable and 1,500 dockers struck in support of Powell and marched to parliament. Tyndall has said that the hysteria and Powell's speech helped unite the recently formed NF and gave it a taste for propaganda work. The NF's membership doubled—according to some historians to 17,500. A second wave of hysteria in the media about Asian immigration, this time from Uganda, in 1972-4 saw Tyndall's right hand man Martin Webster poll over 16 percent in West Bromwich. There was a third wave of media hysteria in 1976, when just 130 Malawian Asians were allowed into Britain. Once again the NF's fortunes were boosted. It believed its time was coming when it polled 120,000 votes in the Greater London Council elections. Once again the Labour government rolled over in the face of this racist backlash. Home secretary Merlyn Rees was asked by a TV reporter, "What you really mean is that immigration control is a device to keep out coloured people?" He replied, "That is what it is".[36]

A massive campaign organised by the Anti Nazi League and Rock Against Racism put a stop to the NF's rise. But the lessons of the late 1960s and 1970s were that concessions to the racists did not hold them back. As Paul Foot wrote, "One of the most constant rules in the history of immigration controls is that those demanding controls are encouraged, and not silenced, by concessions. The Commonwealth Immigrants Act of 1968, far from stemming the tide, encouraged it still further".[37]

We have seen this again over the past dozen years. So long as the economy remained relatively healthy, the Blair and Brown governments

---

35: Quoted in Alexander, 1987, p37.
36: *Weekend World*, 4 February 1978.
37: Foot, 1969, p111.

encouraged migrant workers from Eastern Europe to come and work in Britain. Government figures for 2004/2005 record that 264,000 came from Poland, 50,535 from Lithuania and 44,300 from Slovakia. We have an accurate breakdown of their occupations—the biggest groups were warehouse workers, care assistants, shop workers and caterers.[38] Far from being a drain on society they contributed massively to the wealth of this country. But as soon as the economy went into a tailspin, Brown and his ministers made a U-turn. The saviours of the British economy suddenly become the problem. Immigration minister Phil Woolas summed up how low Labour would stoop in an interview with the *Times*:

> It was, he says, fighting racism that got him into politics... Mr Woolas describes dealing with immigration as "my lifelong purpose" but he is not going to be pandering to what he calls Hampstead liberals... The government must, he insists, face up to the voters' concerns about the level of immigration—particularly as recession looms. The economic downturn changes everything, he says. "Clearly if people are being made unemployed, then the question of immigration becomes extremely thorny." Employers should, he believes, put British people first, or they risk fuelling racism. "In times of economic difficulties, racial stereotyping becomes stronger but also if you've got skills shortages you should as a government attempt to fill those skill shortages with your indigenous population... I'm going to help the British back to work".[39]

Just as in the past, Labour's shift to accommodate the racists' arguments did not protect them at the ballot box. It only strengthened the likes of UKIP and the BNP.

The BNP and the economic crisis

Within weeks of the collapse of Lehman Brothers, Nick Griffin was outlining his party's views on the economic crisis and the possibilities it opens up for them:

> The "credit crunch" and the resultant banking collapse have utterly discredited the twin doctrines of globalisation and unrestrained international capitalism. There is now likely to be a period of fierce competition between different ideas about what should take their place. Indeed, there is even a risk

38: Smith, 2007, pp63-64.
39: The *Times*, 18 October 2008.

> that we may now witness a resurgence of sterile Marxist-Leninist economics, as old-fashioned state socialists try to portray their bankrupt theories as the only possible alternative to "red in tooth and claw" capitalism. There is a coherent and intellectually rigorous alternative to the false dichotomy between Marx and capital in the form of Economic Nationalism, the economic system favoured by the British National Party.[40]

This is fascist "third way" economics in its purest form. Just like Hitler in the 1930s, Griffin is addressing the concerns of the "little man"—the small business man, the self-employed van driver or the former soldier who has fallen on hard times. Griffin has a long-term strategy for the BNP to take power. He believes—hopes—that the entire economic system will experience systemic collapse. He predicts that this will lead to Third World instability, Islamic radicalisation and mass migration that will swamp the West.[41] The BNP, by establishing a permanent foothold in British political life, will then become a beacon for the "indigenous", "white" Britons. He even told a Radio 4 reporter in 2007 that he believed the BNP would be in power by 2040![42] By January 2009 Griffin was becoming even more confident, telling supporters at a by-election meeting in Haywards Heath, "Our time is coming."

"British jobs for British workers"

In February 2009 workers at the Lindsey Oil Refinery walked out on strike. They were joined by up to 10,000 refinery, power and construction workers from across Britain. These wildcat strikes were a reaction to growing unemployment in the industry and the fear that foreign workers were undermining pay and conditions. The slogan adopted by many of the workers was "British jobs for British workers". Sadly, many union leaders were also happy to use the slogan. Yet it leads workers up a blind alley. It pits worker against worker instead of worker against boss

The slogan originated in a speech by Gordon Brown to delegates at the Labour Party conference 2007. Why did Brown use such an inflammatory statement? After all it was used by Mosley's fascists in the 1930s and the NF in the 1970s. Some inside Labour claim that Brown's aim was to undermine the BNP. But far from weakening them, it has, in the words of Griffin, "made our message more respectable". The slogan was perfect for

40: *Identity*, October 2008.
41: *Identity*, July 2006.
42: "Turning Right", BBC Radio 4, broadcast 8 May 2007.

the BNP. It had political legitimacy; it was used by Brown and sections of the trade union leadership. But most of all it promoted the idea of British identity and values—the terrain the new fascists want to fight on.

It gave fascists a route in to organise around a strike, something we have not seen in Britain for over 30 years. Tony Woodley, the joint secretary of the Unite union, told reporters, "The British National Party are seriously and sizably involved, infiltrating meetings and posing as organisers".[43] A BNP ad van toured some picket lines and youth BNP members gave out leaflets on many picket lines. The "Wildcat" website referred to by many strikers was run by BNP members. The BNP did not lead the dispute, they just worked around the edges of it, and union stewards to their credit chased the BNP off the Lindsey picket lines after four days. The real prize for the BNP was that it was able to popularise the slogan on the streets. It immediately put out a leaflet supporting the strikes with the headline "British Jobs for British Workers", and on ballot papers for the Euro elections it described itself as "British National Party—Protecting British Jobs".

The crisis of Labour

The BNP's initial Isle of Dogs breakthrough in the early 1990s was against a backdrop of the prolonged demise of the Tories under John Major. The BNP was unable to build on its election victory for two reasons. First, the Anti Nazi League organised a hard-hitting national campaign to confront the BNP and label it as a Nazi Party. This made it hard for the BNP to pose as "respectable" and cut it off politically from much of its electoral base. Second, Labour was in opposition in the early 1990s and could position itself as an alternative to the Tories.

Today the BNP is growing under a Labour government, a government that has left many of its supporters angry and demoralised. Backing for Labour among its traditional working class base is shrinking. The war on Iraq, the economic crisis and the MPs' expenses scandal have weakened the party and reduced the legitimacy of parliament. Patrick Seyd, a politics professor at Sheffield University who has written extensively on Labour, noticed that members were leaving the organisation and refusing to vote for it within 18 months of Blair's election. He put this down to the government's attacks on the poor and single mothers.[44]

How far Labour has its lost support among working class people is demonstrated by Alexander Lee and Timothy Stanley. In 1997 50 percent

43: *Financial Times*, 5 February 2009.

44: Interview in *Socialist Review*, July 1998.

of C2 voters (a sociological category for skilled manual workers) and 59 percent of DE voters (semi-skilled and unskilled workers) supported Labour. By 2005 this had dropped to 40 percent and 48 percent respectively. In areas like Burnley, Yorkshire & Humberside, Barking and the north west Labour's share of the vote had seriously diminished.[45] These are areas where the BNP has made electoral breakthroughs.

It is not just Labour's voting base that is haemorrhaging. Party membership is also falling. At the end of 2007 it was 176,891. That was scarcely 40 percent of the 405,000 peak reached in 1997 and is thought to be the lowest total since individual membership of the party began. But it is also widely believed that Labour's real membership now stands at 120,000. From its membership subscription income one can infer that there are just 100,000 standard rate-paying members.[46]

Labour's "triangulation" strategy[47] involved shifting party policy to the centre ground in order to increase electability and outmanoeuvre the opposition. It assumes that neglecting the party's traditional base does not matter since it has had nowhere else to go. It has left activists demoralised and an electorate who rightly believe Labour no longer cares about them. Labour's vote in the Euro election shows how far the decline has gone.

The collapse of Labour has left a political space that Griffin and the BNP have been quick to exploit. Soon after winning the BNP's leadership contest Griffin proclaimed that the party would become "the focus of the neglected and oppressed white working class".[48] Again Richard Barnbrook, then the BNP's candidate in Barking & Dagenham and its London organiser, told the authors of one report that the BNP was "more Labour than Labour".[49]

Who votes BNP?

The media regularly claims that the BNP gets most support from dissatisfied sections of the white working class and that the average BNP member comes from this social background. Many on the left accept this view. The reality is more complicated. Historically, as we have seen, fascism has been a primarily middle class movement. There is evidence that this is just as true of present day fascist organisations. The Nazi thugs who went on the rampage in Luton in May 2009 or the fascist gangs that attacked students at Rome University in 2008 may have been working class males. Nevertheless, the popular appeal

45: Lee and Stanley, 2006, pp4-6.
46: Lee and Stanley, 2006, p38.
47: Copied from Bill Clinton's strategy in the US in the 1990s.
48: Interview on BBC London South East News.
49: Magretts, John, Rowlance and Weir, 2006, p7.

of the so-called new Nazis is still largely located among the middle class. An article published by the French newspaper *Le Monde* in April 1998 studied the voting base of the Front National. It found 31 percent of Le Pen's supporters to be small business owners, 21 percent professional people (doctors, lawyers and so on), 21 percent shop workers, 19 percent unemployed, 8 percent farmers and 16 percent factory workers. Its electoral support came mainly from the classic right and middle class but there was a minority of voters who came from the left.[50] Just as with Hitler's party, the bigger the Nazi vote the greater penetration it has inside the working class.

Is the BNP different? The Democratic Audit report points out that while the BNP has done well in places where Labour had once been strong this does not mean that former Labour voters are simply switching over to the BNP. "The BNP gains its electoral support from all three of the largest parties; and in fact it gains the most from the Conservatives and the least from Labour".[51] Almost a third of the council seats the BNP has won are in previously Tory or independent wards.

We now have a much more accurate picture of the kind of people who join the BNP thanks to a disgruntled member leaking the party's membership list last year. Table 3 shows the breakdown of occupations of the 584 members who provided this information. Even the most conservative reading of the statistics suggests that at least two thirds of those BNP members who recorded their occupation work in "traditional" middle class professions or are petty bourgeois. It is worth pointing out that only 584 out of 12,000 people on the list stated their occupation. But it gives at least a partial snapshot of the BNP.

A more detailed look at the list reveals that there are over 110 "ex-servicemen" and 16 serving soldiers. Over 20 are described as former members of the police and Territorial Army. There are another 25 working in "security", from doormen to personal protection. The list includes five current civil servants, 15 teachers, several ministers of religion (not counting the two witches) and a columnist with the Tory-supporing *Spectator* magazine. There are four former Labour councillors, 11 former Tory councillors and two former Green candidates. The BNP's influence inside the union movement is thankfully pitiful. There are four shop stewards and four "former shop stewards".

The BNP still attracts more than its fair share of Colonel Blimp types. Descriptions written next to some of the members give a glimpse of the kind

50: See Bambery, 1993, p61

51: Magretts, John, Rowlance and Weir, 2006, p23.

of people who back the party. In Surrey, for instance, someone is described as a "retired accountant. Fellow of the Institute of Chartered Accountants/ Management Accountants. MA (Oxon). Hobbies: military history, ethnology/anthropology, carpentry/cabinet-making. Ex-serviceman & TA Captain." He claims he is a former district councillor and letter writer. In Gloucestershire there is a business owner (antiquities), who has two suits of 14th- and 15th-century armour and can joust for rallies.

Table 3: Occupations of BNP members[52]

Armed forces	19%
Company and shop owners	13%
Unspecified workers	12%
Construction	10%
Professionals	9%
Managers	7%
HGV and taxi drivers or driving instructors	7%
Artists	7%
Teachers	4%
Police and prison workers	4%
Security	4%
Health workers (not doctors)	2%

Looking at where the people on the list live and the kinds of jobs they do tells us a lot about the nature of its support. In some areas where the BNP has done well electorally there are relatively high numbers of supporters. So Lancashire has 861 names on the list. West Yorkshire has 858. Yorkshire as a whole has more than 1,600 BNP supporters, including 164 in Kirklees, 190 in Bradford and more than 100 each in Barnsley, Sheffield

52: Thanks to *Socialist Worker* journalist Simon Basketter, who spent hours trawling through the BNP membership list to work out the occupations of many of the members. When the list was first released it was put up on dozens of websites. Sadly under the data protection act, these lists have had to be removed. However, if you have not seen the list, every so often it is posted up.

and Wakefield. Essex is up there too with just over 670 members, including 73 in Barking & Dagenham. However, despite the fact that 22 percent of those on the list live in areas with above average deprivation some 16 percent live in well off areas. So there are more supporters on the list who live in the Tory heartland of Surrey than in Britain's second biggest city, Birmingham—192 compared to 187. The BNP list contradicts the idea that supporters live in areas with high levels of immigration. Only 5 percent live in areas classified as having higher than average Asian populations and just 2 percent in areas with higher than average African Caribbean populations.

Further evidence of the class composition of the BNP was supplied by an ex-member of the Tower Hamlets branch of the BNP. He approached me and another member of Unite Against Fascism and went through the active branch membership list. Again it makes interesting reading.

Table 4: Occupations of members of Tower Hamlets BNP

Work in the City	4
Retired	4
Newspaper sellers	3
Unemployed	2
Self-employed	2
Shop owners	2
Market stall-holders	2
Housewives	2
Painters and decorators	1

Two things are worth noting. Tower Hamlets is one of the poorest boroughs in London and therefore one would expect it to be more working class in composition than, say, a BNP branch in Surrey or North Wales. But even in the Tower Hamlets branch the vast majority of its members are petty bourgeois and none of them work in the council or NHS, the borough's two biggest employers. In addition, the Tower Hamlets branch is known to have been the home of some of the BNP's streetfighters. In fact Combat 18 was able to take over the branch after Beackon lost his council seat in

1994.[53] Far from being working class hooligans the six notorious streetfighters in the branch worked in the City or sold newspapers outside tube stations. The ex-member described the streetfighters as "rich kids getting their rocks off on their weekend dose of ultra-violence".

When Griffin rejects both organised labour and capital he is appealing to the middle class. He blames big foreign multinational corporations for economic problems—making a big play of blaming Jewish owned businesses for the crisis—and blacks, Asians and Jews for social problems. The BNP does draw support from some angry and frustrated working class people. But the vast majority of these people are not fascists and at times of high levels of class struggle many can be mobilised to fight the bosses and break with the BNP. The BNP was nowhere during the miners' strike in Britain in 1984-5 and was completely marginal during the public sector disputes in France in 1995 and earlier this year.

The strengths and weaknesses of the BNP

In order to achieve a relatively low level of political legitimacy Griffin and the BNP have had to disguise their core fascist beliefs. There are real strengths to this strategy. It has gained the BNP a level of electoral success and political legitimacy unmatched by its predecessors. By hiding its real agenda it has also made it harder for the anti-fascist movement to expose it. In fact, some sections of the left have taken what the BNP says at face value and argued that we should no longer call it a fascist organisation. However, the BNP's strategy has also opened up real weaknesses. Griffin and his hardcore supporters are well aware of them and they are working hard to resolve them.

When the NF marched in the 1970s it could claim 17,000 members and could mobilise a few thousand to its marches. Despite the BNP's success at the polls it still only has 3,000 members (the leaked BNP membership list of 12,000 went back several years and contained a large number of people who had left the organisation or people who regarded themselves only as sympathisers). For a fascist party to be successful it has to demonstrate to the ruling class that it can control the streets and can break the back of working class resistance. At the moment the BNP has not been able to put large numbers onto the streets. A few years ago it called a protest in one of its "strongholds"—Dagenham in East London. Despite making it a national

53: Combat 18 was a group of hardcore Nazis who rejected electoralism in favour of violence, terrorism and intimidation. Its name was a homage to its political guru—the one and eight correspond to the first and eighth letters of the alphabet, "A" and "H", and stand for Adolf Hitler.

mobilisation fewer than 100 BNP supporters turned up. And the BNP is fearful of calling a national demonstration for the fear of being driven off the streets as the NF was at Lewisham in 1977, or humiliated as Mosley was at Cable Street in 1936.

Many of the new members who have joined the BNP have not been won to its full fascist programme. Colin Auty is one such example. In 2006 he became the BNP councillor for Dewsbury in West Yorkshire. In May 2008 he announced that he was going to stand against Nick Griffin for the leadership of the BNP. On his blog Auty blames Griffin for the BNP's poor public image. He even complained about Griffin's racism and anti-Semitism. He said persuading people to vote BNP is like "trying to sell a new car with a scratched bonnet". He also launched a vehement attack on the BNP's constitution, describing it as "a dictator's dream".[54] Shed no tears for Auty but his comments are revealing.

There was also the case of Burnley BNP councillor Maureen Stowe, who resigned from the organisation when she discovered it was a racist party. She told *Socialist Worker*, "The BNP really hid the racism, certainly in my presence. There was a lot of talk about money going into the Asian area of Daneshouse and Stoneyholme. I admit it seemed that way to me. But I've seen the figures and it's just not true." Maureen was never invited to the "inner core" meetings of the BNP. "I wasn't formally a member of the BNP".[55] Of course, the majority of people who join the BNP know what they are joining but these two examples show that while the BNP is able to recruit people on the basis of its "softer" policies it still has a problem when it tries to turn them into fascist cadre.

The so called "liquidation" of the BNP creates other problems for the leadership. The BNP contains in its ranks both a section of streetfighters and those who want to use electoral methods to take power. This makes the BNP prone to splits and faction fights. Griffin is happy to use the electoral strategy so long as it helps build the party. For him it is only a tactic that will enable the BNP to carry out its real aims.

Italy shows how these new fascist parties are happy to move from electoral work to a movement on the streets at a blink of an eye. Last year the National Alliance stood Gianni Alemanno as Mayor of Rome. Despite his connections with a number of small neo-fascist groups in Rome he presented himself as a pillar of the community and a friend of working people. He said he would stop financing cultural events such as film

54: *Searchlight*, June 2008.
55: *Socialist Worker*, 6 March 2004.

festivals that just benefited the middle class and instead spend the money on the poor. But he said he would deal with the issues of public "security" in a way that focused on immigrants living in the city. Alemanno won. This was a green light for the fascist organisations in Rome to take to the streets. New Force, a small fascist organisation, attacked left wing students at Sapienza University in Rome and there were also fascist attacks on the shops of immigrants. The media and the right wing parties defended the attacks, claiming that the immigrants in these shops were dealing drugs.

So far Griffin has been able to hold back the street fighters mainly because of the party's electoral successes. However, if the BNP was to do badly in an election, there is a real possibility that it could descend into another period of internal strife. Likewise, electoral gains can increase tensions inside the party, giving confidence to those who want to march and control the streets while drawing into the party large numbers who do not fully share its Nazi ideas.

Griffin, while still out to make the party "respectable", is trying to protect the core values—fascism—from being watered down. In 2007 he proposed a new membership structure designed to safeguard the party and ensure that it remains in the control of a minority of politically educated and ideological activists. There is a two-tier membership. "Standard members" can vote in leadership elections and stand as candidates. But only "voting members" can bring forward policy motions and vote at the BNP's annual conference. The criteria to be a voting member are two years unbroken membership, undertaking one three-hour session of party work a week, a financial commitment of £10 a month and attendance at education and training schools.[56]

Griffin is expending a lot of effort attempting to radicalise his party. He set up the Red, White and Blue Festival—once again an idea stolen from Le Pen who organises an annual *Bleu, Blanc, Rouge* fete.[57] Griffin's event tries to both create a family friendly image of the party and provide a platform for British and European fascists and an outlet for Nazi propaganda.

How do we stop the BNP?

The growth of the BNP has posed a big question for the left and the anti-fascist movement. Nick Lowles, editor of the anti-fascist magazine *Searchlight*, wrote an article last year discussing the way forward for the

56: Copsey, 2004, pp170-171.

57: If you want to get an idea of how Le Pen runs the *Bleu Blanc Rouge* festival, there is a fascinating account in Marcus, 1995, pp1-5.

movement. Much of what he argues I would agree with but he does draw a number of conclusions that would weaken the struggle against the BNP. First, Lowles rejects the slogan "Don't vote Nazi". He writes:

> A simple "Don't vote Nazi" is an irrelevant slogan that needs to be discarded immediately. That is not to say that we should not highlight the real politics of the BNP and its leadership but we must address people where they currently are. And in terms of that, very few people see the BNP as a Nazi party.[58]

But if we are not to call them Nazis what political tag does he suggest we use—far right, neo-fascist or post-fascist? These are all terms *Searchlight* has used to describe the BNP. Are they terms your average 16 year old would understand? And what does "far right" mean? It could be used to describe Margaret Thatcher or Nicolas Sarkozy. It is meaningless as a political term. It does not explain the strategy and tactics the BNP deploy. Of course, there are many young people who do not know about Hitler and his Nazi regime. But surely part of the anti-fascist movement's task is to educate young people about the dangers of fascism. Millions of people in Britain do understand who the Nazis were and do make a connection to the BNP today. That is why a recent poll found that 76 percent of those asked said they could never vote for the BNP.[59]

There is another reason why it is vital that we continue to call the BNP Nazi or fascist: that is exactly what it is. The point of Le Pen's modernisation strategy is to build the FN as a fascist party by distancing it from its Nazi and collaborationist past. The BNP leadership are also anxious to cover up their fascist politics and their history.

As well as rejecting the slogan "Don't vote Nazi" *Searchlight* has argued in many campaigns for the slogan "Vote Labour to keep out the BNP". This slogan actually weakens our movement. Many people from many different political traditions want to stop the BNP—revolutionary socialists, greens, anarchists and activists who do not support any political organisation. If you force the anti-fascist movement to call for a vote for Labour you end up excluding these forces from the campaign to beat back the BNP. The slogan "Don't vote Nazi" unites everyone. The slogan does have its problems. During the Anti Nazi League campaigns of the early 1990s when you went around the estates handing out leaflets saying "Don't vote Nazi" the question, "Well, who do you vote for?" was rarely if ever

58: Lowles, 2008, p7.

59: Magretts, John, Rowlance and Weir, 2006, p22.

asked on the doorsteps. Labour in the 1990s was in opposition and, if nothing else, at least offered the illusion that it was going to be better than the Tories. Today Labour is in office and support for it is at an all time low. The question, "Who do I vote for?" is therefore a common response.

In part the BNP has been able to grow because of the failure of Labour to address working people's problems. This is another reason why the slogan "Vote Labour to keep out the BNP" does not work. For many people the reason they are going to vote BNP is precisely as a protest against the mainstream parties. Sadly there is no short cut for the left; the only answer to that question is the creation of a genuine party to the left of Labour.

Lowes puts forward an additional, particularly dangerous, argument: that we need to ally with all the mainstream parties against the Nazis. He writes, "There will be some who argue for a solely class based approach to anti-fascism but a refusal to work with the mainstream parties will only hand dozens of seats to the BNP and quicken its electoral advance".[60] In relation to Barking & Dagenham Lowles goes even further: "There is also a job for the other main parties [besides Labour]. Even though they are hardly represented on the council (there are no Liberal Democrats and only one Conservative) both parties need to be encouraged to rebuild their local organisations".[61]

The musician Billy Bragg has an equally misguided argument which he calls "progressive patriotism". Put simply, he believes the left have allowed the fascists to capture the flag of St George and so claim to be the inheritors of English nationalism. The way to fight them, he argues, is to reclaim the flag and use English nationalism to create a positive agenda. He uses an anecdote in his book *The Progressive Patriot* about being on an anti-BNP demo in Shaftesbury in the south west of England. A lone Nazi waved his England flag at the protest. On his way home Billy stopped at a petrol station and saw a tub full of plastic St George's flags.

> A thought crossed my mind: what if I'd brought these flags, all of them, and distributed them to my fellow marchers? What would the lonely counter-demonstrator have done if he had seen 200 people coming towards him, half of them holding anti-BNP placards, the other half carrying their English flags? Would he still have been able to express his opposition by waving his own English flag or would we have forced him to find some other method to display his racist beliefs? A Nazi salute perhaps?[62]

60: Lowles, 2008, p8.
61: Lowles, 2008, p11.
62: Bragg, 2006, pp168-169.

Unfortunately we know exactly how the BNP would react if the left was to attempt to reclaim the St George's flag. Over the past few years Sandwell council in the Midlands has adopted Bragg's idea and held a St George's Day parade. Each year growing numbers of BNP members have joined the march and last year the BNP held a rally at the end of the parade. The Labour group pulled their support for the parade this year and the organisers banned political parties from the march. What did Griffin do—stand on the sidelines giving a Nazi salute? No, he just marched on his own, telling the press, "I'm here as an Englishman, not to be party political".[63]

Reclaiming the flag and trying to put a left wing gloss on English nationalism has not weakened the BNP by pushing it to the margins. It has legitimised it and placed it at the centre of political discourse. Funnily enough the method used by the Anti Nazi League and Rock Against Racism to undercut the NF can also be found in the pages of Bragg's book:

> While the National Front marched beneath their ranks of Union Jacks, we gathered amid our union banners, yellow Anti Nazi League roundels and punk pink RAR stars. We walked the six miles to Victoria Park in high spirits. Ten thousand whistles had been handed out and we all took turns on the megaphone to lead chants of "The National Front is a fascist front! Smash the National Front".[64]

Lowles's and Bragg's arguments both have parallels in history—in particular in the strategy of the popular front developed by Stalinist parties across Europe in the 1930s.

United front versus popular front

The Communist International first developed the theory of the united front in the years following the Russian Revolution. The "Thesis on Comintern Tactics" of 1922 stated:

> The united front tactic is simply an initiative whereby Communists propose to join with all workers belonging to other political parties and groups, and unaligned workers, in a common struggle to defend the immediate, basic interests of the working class against the bourgeoisie. Every action, for even the most trivial everyday demand, can lead to revolutionary awareness and revolutionary education; it is the experience of struggle that will convince

63: http://lancasteruaf.blogspot.com/2009/04/bnp-leader-infiltrates-west-bromwich-st.html
64: Bragg, 2006, p195.

workers of the inevitability of revolution and the historic importance of communism.

Leon Trotsky saw this tactic as central to the fight against fascism in the 1930s. To see why, we have to look at what happened in the cases of Germany and France in this period.

Hitler and his Nazi Party polled just 2.6 percent of the vote in 1928. The two main parties of the left were far stronger. The social democratic SPD (the equivalent of the Britain's Labour Party) had a million members and polled almost seven million votes, and the Communist KPD got three million votes. Two years later the German economy was in ruins as the worldwide slump hit. Industrial production fell by half and the official unemployment figure reached 3,252,000, with some historians estimating the true total closer to six million, 40 percent of the workforce.[65]

From nowhere Hitler's Nazis gained 18.3 percent of the vote in 1930 and 37.4 percent in the July 1932 elections.[66] This was the highest vote they achieved and by the November 1932 elections it had fallen to 33.1 percent. The Nazis were not primarily an electoral machine. They had over one million members and a private army of 400,000 SA and SS stormtroopers. They also had the support of some major sections of German capitalism.[67] The combined vote of the SPD and KPD was greater than that of the Nazis in every free election except July 1932. But, as Trotsky wrote in 1931, you cannot judge the balance of forces by votes alone:

> The main strength of the fascists is their strength in numbers. Yes, they have received many votes. But in the social struggle, votes are not decisive. The main army of fascism still consists of the petty bourgeoisie and the new middle classes… On the scale of electoral statistics, 1,000 fascist votes weigh as much as 1,000 Communist votes. But on the scales of revolutionary struggle 1,000 workers in one big car factory represent a force 100 times greater than 1,000 petty officials, clerks, their wives and their mothers in law. The great bulk of fascists consist of human dust.[68]

The roots of Hitler's success lay in the failure on the part of the two left parties to unite against the Nazis on the streets and in workplaces.

65: James, 1986, pp110–161. Also Roger Eatwell, 2003, makes a compelling case about the real levels of unemployment in Germany in 1930-3.

66: Gluckstein, 1999, p79.

67: Gluckstein, 1999, p68.

68: Trotsky, 1971, pp92-93.

The SPD refused to face up to the Nazis since it was totally committed to working through parliament and the state institutions. When the reactionary Field Marshal Hindenburg was nominated for president the leadership of the SPD backed him on the basis that he was the "lesser of two evils". At the start of 1933 the SPD leaders even accepted Hitler's appointment as chancellor on the grounds that it was carried out in a constitutional manner. The problem with the KPD was not its failure to confront the Nazis. Its members regularly fought them. The problem was that it adopted an approach that made it impossible to unite in struggle with the SPD. In line with the "third period" policy imposed on Communists everywhere by Joseph Stalin the KPD branded the SPD and not the Nazis as the main enemy. It even called the SPD "social fascists". This disastrous policy cut the KPD off from the larger numbers of workers who identified with the SPD.

In a series of articles about the events in Germany, Trotsky argued, "Worker communists, if fascism comes to power it will ride like a terrific tank over your skulls and spines. Your salvation lies in merciless struggle. Only a fighting unity with Social Democratic workers can bring victory".[69] Unity, Trotsky urged, should include all those prepared to back a struggle: "The policy of the united front has as its task to separate those who want to fight from those who do not." That did not mean burying the differences between those who wanted to reform the system and those who wanted to topple it. It meant agreeing to fight around one issue while continuing to argue their positions. Trotsky summed it up: "March separately but strike together! Agree only on how to strike, who to strike and when to strike".[70]

Tragically that never happened. A united resistance to Hitler was never achieved and the Nazis were able to march through the middle. The result was, as Trotsky described it, "undoubtedly the greatest defeat of the working class in history".[71]

The way to fight the fascists was shown in France a year later. The circumstances were desperate for the French working class in February 1934. The French fascists were exploiting despair caused by economic depression. The largest far right group, the Croix de Feu, claimed 50,000 members. The fascists attempted to smash their way into power by calling an armed demonstration for 6 February and storming parliament. Fifteen people were killed and 1,435 injured as the police beat back the assault. The fascists did not seize power but they did force a change of government to the type of right wing

69: Trotsky, 1971, p141.
70: Trotsky, 1971, pp138–139.
71: Trotsky, 1971, p416.

authoritarian regime that paved the way for Hitler in Germany. Panic spread throughout factories and working class areas as news of the fascists' action circulated. The largest union confederation, the CGT, called a general strike on 12 February. It was an outstanding success. Almost five million workers downed tools. One million took to the streets across France as the leaders of the Socialist and Communist Parties were forced to march together. Here was the unity against the fascists that had not happened in Germany.

But the lessons were not learnt. Fearful of an invasion of Russia by Nazi Germany, Stalin's regime looked in 1935 to a new form of unity—a pact against Hitler with the right wing governments of France and Britain. There was a complete U-turn. No longer were reformist parties denounced as "social fascists". Communist Parties now argued that unity had to be achieved with everyone—even politicians representing the middle and ruling classes. This was known as the popular front.

In France the Communist Party spent 18 months organising a pact with a party called the Radicals—they were not radical; they were the equivalent of the modern day "one nation" Tories. In January 1936 the Communists, Socialists and Radicals agreed the Popular Front programme to fight a general election. To keep the Radicals on board the programme was far tamer than even the mealy-mouthed policies of the Socialists. But it was a left wing tide that swept the Popular Front alliance into office in June 1936, with the Socialists and Communists gaining seats while the Radicals suffered losses. The electoral defeat of the main bosses' parties sparked a new confidence among workers. Strikes erupted and their size and demands went way beyond what the new government and trade union leaders wanted. There were 12,142 strikes and 1.8 million strikers in June 1936 alone. That was higher than the previous annual record for strikes. Over three quarters of the strikes involved factory occupations.

The ruling class thought France was on the brink of revolution. Socialist Leon Blum headed the new government. His first act was to stop the strike wave by organising talks between the bosses and the unions. The near revolutionary strikes compelled the employers to give significant concessions. But the upsurge continued. The Socialist Party and trade union leaders could not halt it. But the Communist Party could. It did not join the government but supported it. To keep its alliance with the Radicals the Communist Party used its influence in the factories to end the strike movement.

Within less than a year the Popular Front government, elected with such left wing hopes, began behaving like the right wing government it had replaced. It attacked workers' conditions and openly supported French capitalists. The fascists gained a new lease of life as workers' confidence fell back and disillusionment with the government spread. The Popular Front government finally fell apart in April 1938 and power shifted back to the right. In 1940 the majority of the parliament elected by the Popular Front in 1936 voted to hand power over to Marshal Pétain's collaborationist regime.

The popular front strategy was also deployed against Franco and his fascist supporters in Spain in 1936. Just as in France, it was a disaster, subordinating working class struggle to efforts to maintain unity with the liberal politicians. Although the situation in Britain today is nowhere near as serious as in France and Spain in the 1930s it is worth looking concretely at what it would mean if the popular front strategy were implemented in Britain. The Tories would certainly veto any hard-hitting anti-racist campaign. Boris Johnson won't even support London's anti-racist Rise festival. And can you imagine members of the Tory Party, let alone the leadership, supporting a physical confrontation with the BNP?

Stopping the BNP today

The BNP can be defeated and driven back. A successful campaign against it requires mass mobilisations and detailed local work. There are no quick fixes. Unlike in the 1990s when the BNP only had one councillor, today it has seats in many towns and cities. Griffin's strategy has so far largely moved away from calling demonstrations and street rallies. So anti-fascists cannot rely on countering the BNP on the streets (although this could change since the BNP did organise a number of "flash" protests and stalls in the run-up to the election).[72] We need to develop a strategy to undercut its electoral support.

This requires a shield and a sword.

Our shield has to be the anti-fascist movement. Unite Against Fascism (UAF) is not the classical united front described in Trotsky's writings on the 1930s. The Socialist Workers Party (SWP) is not a mass revolutionary party able to call on the Labour Party to work with it on a single issue. But UAF, just like the ANL before it and the Stop the War Coalition today, does deploy the spirit of Trotsky's united front method. The leadership of UAF contains supporters of the Labour Party, a number of trade union leaders and activists, anti-racist campaigners and the SWP. It attempts to bring together all those threatened by the fascists—trade unionists, Asians, black people, ethnic minorities, LGBT organisations, students, the disabled, anti-racists and the parties of the left.

72: "Flash" protests and street stalls are where the BNP turns up in a town centre, leaflets and then clears off. So far, with one or two exceptions, the BNP is not holding regular sales.

UAF is also trying to create a broad based organisation that can carry the anti-fascist message to the widest number of people. It does not shy away from calling the BNP Nazi and fascist. Whenever fascists try to encourage attacks on black, Asian or migrant communities, UAF will be there to offer to support resistance. That requires a national organisation. But a grassroots organisation is also needed. For example, when the BNP put out leaflets attacking the building of a mosque in Oldham the local UAF group put out a leaflet exposing the BNP and defending the right of Muslims to build a place of worship. Local knowledge and roots make campaigning stronger.

The leadership of the BNP are fascist to the core. However, many of those who vote BNP are not. Clearly they hold racist ideas but they are not yet won over to fascism. That is why many of the people who vote BNP are ashamed of their actions. Good propaganda campaigns that offer an alternative way of fighting back can pull these people away from the BNP. Part of UAF's job must be to try to drive a wedge between the fascists in the BNP and the racists who vote for them.

We also need to take the anti-fascist message to the young. In the 1970s members of the SWP along with other anti-fascist activists and musicians set up Rock Against Racism. It organised a number of massive carnivals and hundreds of local concerts against the NF. It played a big role in radicalising young people and pulling young people away from the NF who at the time were trying to build a base among punks, skinheads and mods. Love Music Hate Racism (LMHR) is the child of Rock Against Racism. Like its predecessor it uses music to carry an anti-racist and anti-fascist message to young people. It has organised a number of festivals: two in Trafalgar Square in London that pulled crowds of over 40,000 people, a 100,000-strong festival at Victoria Park in east London in the run up to the London elections last year, a 6,000-strong event in Rotherham, South Yorkshire, and this May a 24,000-strong festival in Stoke on Trent. It has also organised hundreds of small LHMR concerts and has put on anti-racist events in schools and colleges.

Some people, including *Searchlight*, challenge the effectiveness of such events.[73] Of course, as one of the organisers of LMHR I would dispute this. But on occasions it is best to let others speak up on your organisation's behalf. Stoke on Trent has nine BNP councillors and that is why LMHR decided to organise a carnival in the city. The local newspaper *The Stoke Sentinel*, which has a reputation for being "soft" on the BNP, ran the following editorial under the headline "Equality Was The Winner":

73: Lowles, 2008, p8.

> It was billed as an event to celebrate Britain's multi-cultural society and to unite people through music. For the 20,000 sun-drenched revellers at the Britannia Stadium, it comfortably achieved both. But to the wider community Saturday's Love Music Hate Racism festival said so much more. In a city where the BNP has established a foothold, there was a resounding show of unity and a determination to oppose racism in all its forms... In the audience, the crowd responded with a defiant message: "This city is moving forwards, not backwards." Whether it's election time or not, the area constantly needs to be reminded of its multi-cultural make up and diversity. Love Music Hate Racism was the perfect way to do it... There is no place in our society for the bigotry expounded by racist groups. There is no place on our streets for the hatred they preach. Getting that over to 20,000 people on Saturday was an admirable start. But it mustn't end there. The onus is on us all to ensure the racists don't succeed. We need to learn from a young age. Saturday was an opportunity to bring together people from different backgrounds and different walks of life. But, moreover, it was a chance for the city to show a united front against prejudice and extremism. It did just that.[74]

Much of what LMHR and UAF do is, by its nature, a reaction to the BNP's activities. But propaganda and campaigning are never enough. The BNP is not a democratic party. Its aim is to create a fascist state which would not only see the destruction of the left and ethnic minorities but also dismantle every vestige of democracy. That means any talk of dealing with it simply through "constitutional means" is a flawed strategy that means fighting them with one hand tied behind your back. Just as our forebears stopped Mosley at Cable Street and dozens of other places in the 1930s, and just as many of us halted the NF's marches and parades in the 1970s, we also have to be prepared to physically confront the BNP if it attempts to march. This does not mean small squads of streetfighters but thousands and, if possible, tens of thousands of activists.

One weapon we must deploy in our armoury is the tactic of "No Platform for Fascists". Liberal common sense tells us that democracy is a matter of exchanging views and of critical reasoning. Liberals tend to frame the argument in terms of free speech, saying that however reprehensible the fascists are they should be defeated through debate just like any other political current. Socialists, by contrast, argue that fascism is not a political current like any other and should not be treated as such. The BNP is not like any other political party—when Tories march to defend their "Nimby"

74: *The Stoke Sentinel*, 1 June 2008.

way of life they do not create violence or physically attack people. When the BNP comes to town it brings with it fear and murder. Its freedom of speech denies everybody else's rights and freedoms. For the BNP the ballot box is only a tactic. The rationale of fascism is to become a mass movement on the streets that can smash all democratic institutions.

There is a clear link between BNP activity in an area and a rise in racist violence. When the BNP took its first council seat in Tower Hamlets racist incidents in the borough increased by 300 percent compared to the previous year. Barking & Dagenham Race Equality Council recorded a 30 percent increase in the numbers of racist attacks in the two years after the BNP won its first council seats in that borough, during a period when racist attacks across London as a whole fell.

One cannot rationally "debate" with those who systematically lie about their real aims and views nor can one "debate" with those who use terror tactics and thuggery against ethnic minorities, trade unionists and anyone else who disagrees with them. That means we have to campaign to deprive the BNP of the oxygen of publicity. We have to organise in the union movement, student bodies, our communities and the media to deny it a platform. We say no platform for fascists because of what they are and what they do, not because of their "opinions", objectionable though these undoubtedly are.

We also need a sword to beat back the BNP.

One of the main reasons the BNP is growing is the despair created by the economic crisis and the hatred directed towards a Labour government that fails to build council housing and lets our public services go to ruin while it finds billions to wage war and bail out the bankers. The BNP feeds off this despair.

That's why the occupations by workers at Waterford Glass, Visteon and Prisme, and the strikes by the post and tube workers are so important. They point to a different tradition, a different way of fighting, one that does not blame migrant workers, black or Asian people for our problems.

We also have to be honest. The left faces another serious problem in the fight against the BNP. At the moment the BNP is using the ballot box to build a base and is feeding off the despair created by a failed Labour government. As the European elections demonstrated, we cannot point to a left electoral alternative. That does not mean we cannot stop them. After all we beat back the NF in the 1970s and the BNP in the early 1990s and there was no serious left of Labour organisation to vote for then. But in the coming months the left as a whole is going to have to address this problem and try to create a left pole of attraction.

Finally, we need to address a wider problem. My grandfather fought

Mosley's fascists in the 1930s. As a young school student I campaigned against the NF (I still have my "Skateboarders Against the Nazis" badge). I helped coordinate the resistance to Derek Beackon and the BNP in east London in the early 1990s. Today I am the coordinator for LMHR and on the steering committee of UAF.

This time I think we face the most serious threat in my lifetime. I believe we can push the Nazis back again. But I am frustrated with having to counter the fascists every ten years or so when they raise their ugly heads above the parapet. Fascism is not an aberration of capitalism; it is a product of a system, a system that in times of crisis has been prepared to unleash the monster of fascism against working class people. It seems obvious to me that, as well as fighting to drive the fascists out from our communities, we need to fight to create a socialist society.

References

Alexander, Peter, 1987, *Racism, Resistance and Revolution* (Bookmarks).

Bambery, Chris, 1993, "Euro-fascism: The Lessons of the Past and Current Tasks", *International Socialism 60* (autumn 1993).

BBC, 2001, "BNP: Under the Skin", website for the special episode of Panarama, http://news.bbc.co.uk/hi/english/static/in_depth/programmes/2001/bnp_special/default.stm

Bragg, Billy, 2006, *The Progressive Patriot: A Search for Belonging* (Bantam).

Copsey, Nigel, 2004, *Contemporary British Fascism: The British National Party and the Quest for Legitimacy* (Palgrave Macmillan).

Eatwell, Roger, 2003, *Fascism: A History* (Pimlico).

Finney, Nissa, and Ludi Simpson, 2009, *Sleepwalking into Segregation?* (Policy Press).

Foot, Paul, 1969, *The Rise of Enoch Powell* (Cornmarket).

Gluckstein, Donny, 1999, *The Nazis, Capitalism and the Working Class* (Bookmarks).

Guerin, Daniel, 1972, *Fascism and Big Business* (Pathfinder).

James, Harold, 1987, *The German Slump* (Clarendon).

Lee, Alexander, and Timothy Stanley, 2006, *The End of Politics: Triangulation, Realignment and the Battle for the Centre Ground* (Politicos).

Lowles, Nick, 2008, "Where Now?", *Searchlight*, June 2008.

Magretts, Helen, Peter John, David Rowlance and Stuart Weir, 2006, "The BNP: The Roots of its Appeal", Democratic Audit, University of Essex, www.jrct.org.uk/core/documents/download.asp?id=300

Marcus, Jonathan, 1995, *The National Front and French Politics* (Palgrave Macmillan).

Oborne, Peter, and James Jones, 2008, "Muslims Under Siege: Alienating a Vulnerable Community", Democratic Audit, University of Essex, www.channel4.com/news/media/pdfs/Muslims_under_siege_LR.pdf

Smith, Martin, 2007, "The Shape of the Working Class", *International Socialism 113* (winter 2007), www.isj.org.uk/?id=293

Trotsky, Leon, 1971, *The Struggle Against Fascism in Germany* (Pathfinder).

Marxist accounts of the current crisis

Joseph Choonara

Just as medical science progresses through pathology, Marxist political economy develops through the analysis of the actual crises of capitalism. It is therefore no surprise that the current paroxysm has sparked both a revival of interest in Marxism[1] and a flurry of responses by prominent Marxists. My focus here should not be taken to indicate that non-Marxist accounts are unworthy of engagement. A number of mainstream economists have been forced, whether enthusiastically or reluctantly, to grapple with the realities of the system.[2] But the crisis has also revealed the paucity of what passes for academic economic theory, captured in an astonishing admission by Willem Buiter, a London School of Economics professor and a former member of the Bank of England monetary policy committee:

1: This has been the object of some fascination in the mainstream press, which has reported a seven-fold increase in sales of Marx's *Capital* in Germany, the success of a Manga comic version of the work in Japan and now a musical, currently in production in Shanghai, which, according to the director, "will bring Marx's economic theories to life in a trendy, interesting and educational play that will be fun to watch".

2: For instance, Graham Turner's recent book (2008) or, from a more right wing perspective, Martin Wolf's latest work—see Callinicos, 2009. On Turner's book, see also Murphy, 2009.

The typical graduate macroeconomics and monetary economics training received at Anglo-American universities during the past 30 years or so may have set back by decades serious investigations of aggregate economic behaviour and economic policy-relevant understanding. It was a privately and socially costly waste of time and other resources. Most mainstream macroeconomic theoretical innovations since the 1970s...have turned out to be self-referential, inward-looking distractions at best. Research tended to be motivated by the internal logic, intellectual sunk capital and aesthetic puzzles of established research programmes, rather than by a powerful desire to understand how the economy works—let alone how the economy works during times of stress and financial instability. So the economics profession was caught unprepared when the crisis struck.[3]

The record of Marxists has been better. Nonetheless, their approaches to the crisis are far from homogenous, have often been developed in isolation from each other and diverge on several points. Here I consider widely accessible accounts that have appeared in English over the past few months, appraising their strengths and weaknesses relative to each other and to the tradition associated with this journal.[4]

The "real" and the financial

All Marxist accounts of the current crisis have been forced to recognise its financial dimension. The crisis has been marked by the near collapse of the banking system in several countries and began with the bursting of the subprime mortgage bubble in the US. One of the first Marxist accounts to draw attention to subprime was produced by Robin Blackburn, who wrote on this subject as early as spring 2007, a few months before the real panic began:

In recent months "subprime" defaults have jumped. A Lehman Brothers analyst warns that some $225 billion worth of subprime loans will be in default by the end of 2007 but others say the figure will be nearer $300 billion. The "equity tranch" [the riskiest slice of the repackaged debt] is now dubbed "toxic waste" by the insiders and analysts are waiting to see which bodies float to the surface... The default crunch will not only cause

3: Willem Buiter, "The Unfortunate Uselessness Of Most 'State Of The Art' Academic Monetary Economics", *Maverecon*, 3 March 2009, http://blogs.ft.com/maverecon

4: For an illuminating discussion of the International Socialist tradition in political economy, listen to Alex Callinicos's recent seminar on the subject—available from www.isj.org.uk/?s=resources#alexseminar

Robin Blackburn and Peter Gowan

For Robin Blackburn, "Financialisation now runs the gamut from corporate strategy to personal finance. It permeates everyday life, with more products that arise from the increasing commodification of the life course, such as student debt or personal pensions, as well as with the marketing of credit cards or the arrangement of mortgages".[13]

Few writers have been as effective as Blackburn in explaining the complexities of finance to a lay readership. But his essays show relatively little engagement with the concepts traditionally associated with Marxist political economy and tend to consider the wider economic system only insomuch as it has been drawn into the financial world. As Geoff Mann points out, "The analysis of value, money and capital...are not part of Blackburn's discussion, but they remain an essential part of the political-economic stakes".[14] Blackburn has replied that he implicitly operates within a Marxist framework. But his positive statement of what this framework consists of seems to emphasise the limited capacity of workers to consume, arguing that "the root cause of the crisis was, quite simply, poverty" and increased consumption by Chinese workers could "help to lift the global economy".[15]

Often his writing gives the impression that the rise of finance comes out of finance itself: "Two processes that took hold in the 1950s and 1960s nourished financialisation—new principles of consumer credit, and the rise of institutional finance and fund management".[16] Peter Gowan,[17] another Marxist associated with the journal *New Left Review*, put an even harder case for the autonomy of finance: "An understanding of the credit crunch requires us to transcend the commonsense idea that

---

13: Blackburn, 2006, p39.

14: Mann, 2009, p120.

15: Blackburn, 2009, pp129-130. Blackburn draws on Turner, 2008, to make this argument. But while the great strength of Turner's book is to root credit bubbles in wider economic patterns, in particular wage repression, from a Marxist perspective it is also necessary to consider tendencies arising from accumulation, in particular Marx's famous law of the tendency of the rate of profit to fall. Blackburn also claims that his account is framed by the writings of the Marxist authors Robert Brenner, Andrew Glyn and Giovanni Arrighi (see, for instance, Blackburn, 2008, pp65-66) but there are important differences between these theorists precisely over questions such as the cause of the decline in profitability. So, for example, Moseley, 1999, pp132-133, contrasts the approaches of Glyn and Brenner.

16: Blackburn, 2008, p85.

17: As we were going to press we were saddened to hear of the death of Peter Gowan after his courageous battle with cancer.

change in the so-called real economy drives outcomes in a supposed financial superstructure".[18] For Gowan, financialisation was an answer to problems faced by US capitalism as a whole.[19] But he saw the growth of finance mainly as a product of changes within finance itself which were supported as a deliberate strategy by the American (and in a subordinate role the British) elite.[20] He put a powerful argument that this elite was not ignorant of the problems of financial bubbles, but that they believed that, "between blow-outs, the best way for the financial sector to make large amounts of money is to sweep away restrictions on what private actors get up to...[and] when bubbles burst and blow-outs occur, the banks, strongly aided by the actions of the state authorities, can cope with the consequences".[21]

Just how swollen has the financial system become? "As a percentage of total US corporate profits, financial sector profits rose from 14 percent in 1981 to 39 percent in 2001," writes Blackburn.[22] "In 2006, no less than 40 percent of American corporate profits accrued to the financial sector," according to Gowan.[23] This is a huge chunk of the US economy (although the US economy represents only about one quarter of the world system). But in a period characterised by a series of bubbles, profits estimated by looking at balance sheets composed of assets rising in price can be based on what Blackburn calls "fantasy valuations".[24]

What has to be explored is not just the scale of the financial sector measured in its own terms, but the effects of its growth on real accumulation. The financial sector can swell far beyond the scale justified by

---

18: Gowan, 2009, p5. He argued that this break with the "common sense" meant that "real actors" such as US homeowners were not responsible for the crisis and that "new actors" based on a "New Wall Street System" were to blame. But this seems to beg the question of whether some of the "old" capitalist actors in the wider economy (as opposed to US workers) were also to blame—Gowan, 2009, p6.

19: Panitch and Gindin, 2009, puts forwards a position similar to Gowan's: "The current economic crisis has to be understood in terms of the historical dynamics and contradictions of capitalist finance...the origins of today's US-based financial crisis are not rooted in a profitability crisis in the sphere of production." Elsewhere, these authors have argued that the development of the "New Wall Street System" effectively resolved the crisis of profitability of the 1970s. See Panitch and Gindin, 2006, and the response Callinicos, 2006.

20: Gowan, 2009, pp7-9.

21: Gowan, 2009, p21. See also Brenner, 2004, where the emerging system of "Stock Market Keynesianism", as he puts it, is explicitly seen as a response to the failure of profit rates to recover.

22: Blackburn, 2006, p39.

23: Gowan, 2009, p7.

24: Blackburn, 2008, p69.

the value created in the productive economy.[25] But this process cannot continue indefinitely. Finance in itself does not create new value, and eventually its profits must be obtained from the productive sector of the economy. In this context, crisis can be seen as "a call to order by the law of value" when the productive sphere must try to cash the cheques written by finance.[26]

Some of the accounts of financialisation risk making exaggerated claims about the changes wrought by "neoliberal" or "financialised" capitalism.[27] For Blackburn, "From the standpoint of the 'pure' investor, the corporation itself is an accidental bundle of liabilities and assets that is there to be rearranged to maximise shareholder value, which in turn reflects back the fickle enthusiasms of the investors. The corporation and its workforce are, in principle, disposable".[28] The idea that shareholder value is the central preoccupation of the ruling class as a whole is questionable, especially given the reaction to the banking crisis in which governments and central bankers have, where necessary, inflicted substantial losses on shareholders. More generally, David Harvey, in a book quite favourable to financialisation theories, argues that in recent decades "the power of the actual owners of capital, the stockholders, has been somewhat diminished" relative to those actually running companies.[29] For instance, institutional shareholders are rarely involved in the day to day running of corporations. Of course, there are tensions within the ruling class, and these are exacerbated in crises, but the short-term interests of shareholders do not always win out.

Finally, there are political implications to the financialisation arguments. According to Gowan the crisis poses a choice between two models: "A public-utility credit and banking system, geared to capital accumulation in the productive sector, versus a capitalist credit and banking system, subordinating all other economic activities to its own profit drives".[30]

Similarly, Blackburn writes, "When properly embedded in structures of social control, finance can help to allocate capital, facilitate investment and smooth demand".[31] "The solution...is not to abandon

25: By "productive economy" I mean, following Marx, the areas of the economy producing surplus value, the basis of profit and interest payments.
26: Husson, 2008, p2.
27: Harman, 2008a, is a particularly vehement rejection of such accounts.
28: Blackburn, 2006, p43. See also Lapavitsas, 2009b, p20.
29: Harvey, 2005, p33.
30: Gowan, 2009, p21.
31: Blackburn, 2008, p84.

money or finance but to embed them in a properly regulated system".[32] Geoff Mann has challenged such views: "Turning over our upside-down world requires not just the taming or grounding or redistribution of value, but its destruction. The overthrow of capitalism is the only way out. In short, it is the acceptance of the necessity, not the inevitability, of revolution that makes a Marxist adequate to Marx's analysis".[33]

Blackburn has replied that the sorts of demands he raises are "transitional measures that address the deep crisis in effective ways...which would benefit new collective and democratic institutions, in the shape of a network of social funds".[34] Demands short of revolution are certainly important. Through winning such demands workers become aware of their power to collectively transform society and confident of their strength to do so. But the relationship between these demands and the movement from below is left a little vague—with Blackburn seeing his prescriptions as measures to be brought in once a "seriously anti-capitalist government has been established" creating a system of "financial dual power".[35]

Costas Lapavitsas

Another Marxist associated with financialisation theory, Costas Lapavitsas, gives more consideration to the wider problems in accumulation, writing that "productivity growth has been problematic from the middle of the 1970s to the middle of the 1990s, most significantly in the USA".[36] But he is reluctant to root this in a long-term crisis of profitability:

> It is not so much that real accumulation does not generate enough profitable avenues for banks to lend. Rather, productive capitals can increasingly meet their financing requirements either by retaining profits or by borrowing directly in open markets... Banks have been edged out of this business, and have to seek other avenues of profitability.[37]

Lapavitsas produces figures for the percentage of corporate liabilities represented by bank loans in the US, Germany and Japan. However, shifts in these figures do not seem dramatic enough to explain a systemic transformation of capitalism—from about 12 or 13 percent in the US in the 1980s to

32: Blackburn, 2008, p106.
33: Mann, 2009, p126.
34: Blackburn, 2009, p128.
35: Blackburn, 2009, pp133, 134.
36: Lapavitsas, 2008a, p11.
37: Lapavitsas, 2008b, p19. See Lapavitsas, 2009b, pp14-19, for a more lengthy discussion.

about 10 percent through the 1990s and then falling to about 5 to 6 percent in the current decade; and remaining at above 30 percent and around 40 percent, after slight declines, in Germany and Japan respectively.[38]

The growth of consumer finance across many economies in recent decades is, however, undeniable.[39] Banks have moved into "areas that are not directly connected with the generation of value and surplus value... finance has become relatively autonomous from productive enterprises as well as growing rapidly".[40] Lapavitsas's account makes a rather abstract appeal to shifts in the "forces and relations of production" to explain the rise of finance. But this runs the risk of lapsing into a determinism that seeks to explain the trajectory of the system through recent innovations in information and communication technologies:

> The impact of new technologies on the sphere of finance has been dramatic. Finance might have become neither more efficient nor more productive in terms of intermediation per worker, but it has become capable of operations that were previously completely impossible. The changes are apparent in terms of the internal organisation of financial institutions, the speed of transactions, the feasibility of financial engineering, the links between financial markets, the techniques of pricing and risk management, and so on. Not least, finance has become technically capable of dealing with huge numbers of individual borrowers.[41]

Technological innovation can, of course, open up new areas of potential profit making. But this innovation should not be seen as an autonomous process that develops in isolation from the economy. In particular, it is necessary to account for the flows of surplus value into different areas of the economy that spur waves of restructuring and innovation.[42] An account of the long-term decline in profitability in the productive economy has the advantage of explaining why the incentive to invest in these areas declined and why finance exploded.

But whatever the causes, Lapavitsas has raised important questions about the consequences of financialisation. Traditionally Marxists

---

38: Lapavitsas, 2009a, p13.

39: Although, again, the trends are less sharp than sometimes implied. See the graphs in Lapavitsas, 2009a pp14-17.

40: Lapavitsas, 2008b, pp17-18.

41: Lapavitsas, 2009b, pp12.

42: And many of the innovations required were in place before financialisation took off. See, for instance, Panitch and Konings, 2009, p69.

have argued that the profits made by industrial capitalists and the interest earned by those who lend them money are each claims on a portion of the surplus value generated through the exploitation of workers in the productive economy.[43]

Lapavitsas has put forward the clearest alternative analysis. He has argued that banks are now involved in the "direct exploitation" of consumers to make profits. This is "direct" because it is a mechanism lying outside capitalist production, instead occurring in the sphere of circulation. It is exploitation, he argues, because finance is now seen as necessary for many workers to cover basic living costs.[44]

But exploitation in a Marxist sense has a quite specific meaning.[45] It relates to the extraction of surplus value from workers even though the commodity they supply, their labour power, is obtained by the capitalist at its value. The surplus value generated is not a "swindle" as pre-Marxist socialists had argued but a result of the gap between the new value created by labour over a given period of time and the value required to reproduce that labour power (the wage).[46] The mechanisms associated with financialisation do not generate surplus value,[47] and Lapavitsas has more recently used the less loaded phrase "financial expropriation", which he defines as a process by which financial institutions "extract profits directly and systematically out of wages and salaries".[48] As anyone with an overdraft can testify, it is undeniable that banks make profit out of personal finance. What is at stake is not whether this takes place but whether it represents a "systemic transformation of the capitalist economy".[49]

Such processes are certainly not historically novel. In the context of a discussion of the "lending" of houses to workers at usurious rates in 19th century capitalism, Marx writes:

> That the working class is also swindled in this form, and to an enormous extent, is self-evident; but this is also done by the retail dealer, who sells means of subsistence to the worker. This is secondary exploitation, which

43: Fine, 2008, p3.
44: Lapavitsas, 2008a, p15.
45: Choonara, 2009, pp29-35.
46: Marx, 1970, pp164-172.
47: Something Lapavitsas, of course, recognises—2009b, p10.
48: Lapavitsas, 2009b, p8. The term "direct exploitation" is especially confusing because Marx uses the phrase to mean exploitation of labourers in production, ie in the opposite sense to Lapavitsas—see, for instance, Marx, 1972, p244.
49: Lapavitsas, 2009b, p13.

runs parallel to the primary exploitation taking place in the production process itself. The distinction between selling and loaning is quite immaterial in this case and merely formal, and...cannot appear as essential to anyone, unless he be wholly unfamiliar with the actual nature of the problem.[50]

The analogy with price rises by retailers who sell wage goods to workers is apt. If almost 20 percent of disposable income went towards debt-servicing in the US by 2007,[51] this means that it has become more expensive for the system to reproduce labour power. To the extent that wages rise to account for this, it is a mechanism that shifts surplus value from capitalists concerned with production to those concerned with lending money, just as an arbitrary rise in the price of bread would (if wages rose correspondingly) shift surplus value to bread-producing capitalists. To the extent that wages are held down, it represents an increase in overall exploitation of workers, just as an arbitrary rise in food prices would under conditions of wage repression. And to the extent that workers default on their debts, whether credit cards or subprime mortgages, it represents a decline in a market in fictitious capital, with banks (and others) holding claims over future wage income, some of which turn out to be worthless. Whatever happens, the generation of surplus value within capitalist enterprises remains central to the system as a whole.

David McNally

Of those Marxists who offer accounts stressing wider economic processes, rather than financialisation, I intend to concentrate on those who see the period since the 1970s as one in which capitalism has been unable to resolve underlying problems in accumulation. There are, however, exceptions. A recent paper by David McNally argues that the crisis cannot be understood simply through a focus on financialisation, which is "unable to explain why this crisis has not been restricted to financial markets, or to probe its interconnection with the problems of global over-accumulation". [52] But he also rejects the notion that crisis "is just the latest manifestation of a crisis of profitability that began in the early 1970s".[53]

50: Marx, 1972, p609.

51: Lapavitsas, 2008b, p19.

52: McNally, 2008, p4.

53: McNally, 2008, p3. Jim Kincaid, 2008, has put forward a much harder version of the argument, claiming, "The basic story of the world economy over the past 25 years has been one of rising profits, and growth in output and levels of capital accumulation. Advances in productivity have not undermined profitability." I have not considered his argument here because it was developed prior to the current crisis, but see Harman, 2008b.

He substantiates this by referring to Fred Moseley's figures showing a restoration of profit rates.[54] However, there are different estimates of profitability. According to the method used by Robert Brenner, in the US the return on fixed capital has oscillated around 10.5 percent since 1974, down from an average of around 14 or 15 percent in the preceding period.[55] Other major economies such as Japan and Germany also seem to have witnessed similar falls.[56] Andrew Kilman gives average rates of profit in the US of 28.2 percent for 1941-1956, 20.4 percent for 1957-1980 and 14.2 percent for 1980-2004.[57]

The evidence suggests only a partial restoration of profitability, driven, in particular, by increased exploitation. McNally argues that this underpinned a new period of accumulation that "enabled capitalism to avoid a world crisis for 25 years"—specifically from the recession of the early 1980s through to the current crisis.[58] This accumulation was, for him, centred on East Asia up until the East Asian crisis of 1997-8. After that continued growth was premised on a bubble of credit, particularly credit supplied by the same East Asian economies, rather than rapid accumulation. In other words, McNally changes the start date for the period of financialisation and credit-driven growth from the early 1980s to 1997.

There are, however, several problems with his periodisation. First, it is not clear that the rapid accumulation in East Asia was concentrated in the period from 1981 to 1997. Chinese growth rates remained high even after 1997, a "paradox" that McNally himself recognises.[59] By contrast, Japan, the biggest East Asian economy, grew steadily in the 1980s but then stagnated after 1991, something strangely elided in his account. Second, the world system may have avoided a crisis on the scale of the current one for 25 years, but there was a serious crisis in the US in 1990-1 and another in 2000-1.

Third, McNally does not sufficiently explore the relationship between accumulation in East Asia and the larger Western economies. Is there evidence that somewhat increased profitability in the West led to a wave of investment in East Asia concentrated in the period before 1997? This certainly does not seem to hold for the 1980s when, for instance,

---

54: McNally, 2008, p4. See, for example, Moseley, 2008, p171. See Moseley, 2003, for the evolution of his account.

55: Calculated from Bureau of Economic Analysis data.

56: For this, and a careful critique of Brenners' method, see Shaikh, 1999.

57: Kliman, 2009, pp3-4.

58: McNally, 2008, p4.

59: McNally, 2008, p10.

foreign direct investment into the East Asian economies remained fairly constant and low relative to investment in the major OECD economies.[60]

Fourth, McNally's claim that "financialisation" took off after 1997 is dubious. While the East Asian economies certainly helped fuel credit growth in the US after 1997, for instance by building up large reserves of US Treasury bonds, many of the elements that would be carried to grotesque proportions in the run-up to the current meltdown were already in place. The first sharp rise in the US debt to GDP ratio was between 1981 and 1987, followed by a second sharp rise from 1997, which accelerated after 2001. The rise in the financial share of corporate profits took place in two bursts, the first in 1985-1994, the second from 2001.[61]

The Monthly Review school

Writers associated with *Monthly Review*, an influential journal of the US left, stress the stagnation of late capitalism, rather than its dynamism. The journal has regularly reported on the crisis, and a collection of recent articles by John Bellamy Foster and Fred Magdoff has been published as a short book.[62]

The authors pay serious attention to the growth of finance, providing a detailed analysis of consumer debt in the US and of mechanisms associated with financial speculation. But unlike many such accounts, this growth is seen as a result of problems faced by the wider economy and is not seen as representing a new stage: "Although the system has changed as a result of financialisation, this falls short of a whole new stage, since the basic problem of accumulation within production remains the same".[63]

This "problem of accumulation" is, for Foster and Magdoff, the one first identified by Paul Sweezy and Paul Baran in the 1960s: that post-war capitalism contains an inherent tendency towards stagnation. This was, for them, driven by the formation of monopolies that could manipulate prices, creating surplus profits that the system struggled to absorb. The result was productive overcapacity, and hence slowing investment, along with the growth of areas of "waste" spending such as arms production to absorb this

---

60: Liu, Chow and Li, 2006, p3. And even at its subsequent peak, foreign direct investment into East Asia, excluding Japan and South Korea, was substantially lower than flows into the OECD economies. See also, UNCTAD, 2006, pp39, 82.

61: See, for example, the graphs in Foster and Magdoff, 2009, pp47, 55.

62: Foster and Magdoff, 2009. Some of the essays that make up the book are available from www.monthlyreview.org

63: Foster and Magdoff, 2009, p77.

surplus.[64] The massively overblown financial system represents another such waste area.[65]

In many ways the pioneering analysis of *Monthly Review* (MR) paralleled that of *International Socialism* (IS), as developed by Tony Cliff, Mike Kidron, Chris Harman and others, and a greater interaction between these two traditions would strengthen both.[66] But the MR tradition seems to suffer from three drawbacks relative to this IS tradition. First, for MR, crisis is seen as a result of limited consumption. The roots of this go back to Paul Sweezy's writings:

> The process of production is and must remain, regardless of its historical form, a process of producing goods for human consumption...means of production are never produced except with a view to their ultimate utilisation, direct or indirect, in turning out consumption goods... The real task of an underconsumption theory is to demonstrate that capitalism has an inherent *tendency* to expand the capacity to produce consumption goods more rapidly than the demand for consumption goods.[67]

But in a Marxist framework the demand for output comes from *both* consumption *and* investment in means of production, and some of the latter will be used to produce yet more means of production, and so on—this source of demand being limited by the rate of profit. Underconsumption (or overproduction) is best viewed as a symptom of crisis rather than the cause.[68]

However, Foster and Magdoff, working in a framework that assumes monopolies manipulate prices to boost their "surplus", have little place for Marx's "law of the tendency of the rate of profit to fall".[69] Their stress on

---

64: See Foster and Magdoff, 2009, pp63-65, for a summary of this account of "monopoly capitalism".

65: Foster and Magdoff, 2009, pp83-84.

66: See Harman, 1984, for an account of the IS tradition.

67: Sweezy, 1970, pp162-186.

68: Carchedi, 1991, pp184-186; Carchedi, 2009; Fine and Harris, 1979, p79. See also Cliff, 2001, p106.

69: They do point out that in crisis capital is "devalued" boosting profitability—Foster and Magdoff, 2009, p20. They follow this up by quoting Marx, who writes, "The real barrier of capitalist production is capital itself." The passage comes from part three of the third volume of *Capital*, entitled "The Law of the Tendency of the Rate of Profit to Fall". The subsequent sentences have some bearing on the MR analysis: "Capital and its self-expansion appear as the starting and the closing point, the motive and the purpose of production; that production is only production for capital and not vice versa, the means of production are not mere means for a constant expansion of the living process of the society of producers"—Marx, 1972, p250.

limited consumption allows the authors to rely heavily on John Maynard Keynes, Michal Kalecki and subsequent left Keynesians for their general account of crisis.[70] This means, for instance, that while the IS stressed the development of waste areas such as arms spending as a means of draining surplus value away from accumulation, and so reducing the downward pressure on profit rates, Foster and Magdoff stress the role of arms spending as a boost to demand that could offset underconsumption.[71]

Second, the MR tradition can overemphasise the tendency to stagnation. Their analysis relies upon the idea that the formation of giant firms prevents the entry of potential rivals into a sector of the economy because they cannot raise the funds necessary to break into the market. But this overlooks the capacity of financial systems to draw such funds together if sufficient profits seem to be on offer—often doing so with the backing of the state, as with the rise of Japan, the "Asian Tiger" economies and then China.[72]

Faced with these challenges, even the US economy restructured to an extent after the crisis of the 1980s and again in the mid to late 1990s.[73] The MR tradition seems little interested in these forms of competitive struggle, in part because it holds a particular vision of inter-imperialist rivalry. Imperialism is seen primarily as the plunder of the Third World, rather than a system of conflict between rival national capitalisms within a system that develops unevenly.[74] Foster and Magdoff explain that they have limited the analysis in their collection of essays to US capitalism[75]—but it is impossible to explain the trajectory of the world system without taking imperialist rivalry into account.

Finally, while the MR tradition has the great strength of drawing attention to the changes in capitalism, these need to be integrated together with Marxist value theory. However, the MR tradition, in assuming late capitalism to be characterised by monopoly rather than competition, which was for Marx what enforced the law of value,[76] have relegated the role of value theory to a secondary position. As Harvey, citing Sweezy and Baran's *Monopoly Capitalism*, writes:

70: See for example, Foster and Magdoff, 2009, pp12-20.
71: Foster and Magdoff, 2009, pp42-44.
72: See Brenner, 1999, and the references therein.
73: Harman, 2007, pp151-152.
74: Foster and Magdoff, 2009, pp41, 75-76, 87.
75: Foster and Magdoff, 2009, p21.
76: Choonara, 2009, pp21, 68-70, 77.

The transition from competitive to monopoly to state monopoly forms of organisation certainly appears to represent a movement away from the "authority" of competition and therefore a movement away from the regulatory power of the law of value. Some Marxists have drawn such a conclusion. Baran and Sweezy, for example, argue: "We cannot be content with patching up and amending the competitive model which underlies [Marx's] economic theory... In an attempt to understand capitalism in its monopoly stage, we cannot abstract from monopoly or introduce it as a mere modifying factor; we must put it at the very centre of the analytical effort." The abandonment of the "competitive model" in Marx certainly does entail abandoning the law of value—which, to their credit, Baran and Sweezy are fully prepared to do. The trouble is that we cannot withdraw this, the linchpin of Marx's analysis, without seriously questioning or compromising all of the other Marxian categories.[77]

Robert Brenner

Robert Brenner is another Marxist who has looked in detail at recent empirical trends within the capitalist system. He has also, in a number of talks and articles, set out an eloquent and detailed analysis of the current crisis. He is critical of the notion that this is simply a crisis of financialisation:

> It's understandable that analysts of the crisis have made the meltdown in banking and the securities markets their point of departure. But the difficulty is that they have not gone any deeper. From Treasury secretary Paulson and Fed chair Bernanke on down, they argue that the crisis can be explained simply in terms of problems in the financial sector. At the same time, they assert that the underlying real economy is strong, the so-called fundamentals in good shape. This could not be more misleading.[78]

He sees a low level of investment since the 1970s as originating from low profit rates: "The declining economic dynamism of the advanced capitalist world is rooted in a major drop in profitability, caused primarily by a chronic tendency to overcapacity in the world manufacturing sector, going back to the late 1960s and early 1970s".[79] The slowdown in investment and

77: Harvey, 2006, p141. Sweezy claimed that he had merely "transformed" value theory, but if this is the case, he transformed it beyond recognition. See Howard and King, 1992, p120.
78: Brenner, 2009.
79: Brenner, 2008.

repression of wages as corporations attacked workers led to low levels of demand, with the gap being plugged by increasing levels of debt. A series of stock market and financial bubbles helped to keep the system moving forwards.[80] But profit rates were only partially improved: "Non-financial corporations...raised their profit rates significantly, but still not back to the already reduced levels of the 1990s".[81] So, for Brenner, the crisis we are seeing today is a deferred crisis, one that would have broken before, had not various counteracting mechanisms come into play.

There are many similarities between Brenner's framework and the IS tradition, particularly his emphasis on low rates of profit. But there are also differences. Notably, Brenner sees low profitability as rooted in overproduction and overcapacity, brought about by competition between blocs of capital with investments of fixed capital of differing age and efficiency.[82] As new capitals with more advanced and efficient fixed capital enter a sector, those with older "sunk" investment engage in price-cutting to maintain market share or suffer from excess capacity—either way the profit (the return on the *total* investment made by the capitalist) falls. Brenner concentrates on US manufacturing, where there was significant competition from Japanese and German exports from the mid-1960s, and suggests that a fall in profit rates in this area then impacted upon the wider profitability of the economy.

There are problems with such an account. For one thing, as Fred Moseley points out:

> Ironically, Brenner's theory is fundamentally the same as Baran and Sweezy's theory in *Monopoly Capital*, even though, superficially, they appear to be opposite theories. The basic assumption in both theories is that *the rate of profit is determined by the degree of competition* (inversely) or the degree of monopoly (positively) in the economy... For Marx...the degree of competition or monopoly in individual sectors affects only the distribution of the total amount of profit among those sectors; it does not affect the total amount of surplus value or the general rate of profit.[83]

In other words, even if it is the case, as Brenner argues, that

80: See, for example, Brenner, 2004.
81: Brenner, 2008.
82: He provides the most detailed account of his approach in Brenner, 2006, pp27-40. For detailed critiques of this work, see the symposium in issues 4 and 5 of *Historical Materialism*, in particular Harman, 1999; Callinicos, 1999; Moseley, 1999; Shaikh, 1999; Carchedi, 1999.
83: Moseley, 1999, p139.

intensified competition in manufacturing reduced prices in this sector, this in turn would reduce the price of inputs for capitalists who use these manufactured goods—and could be expected to raise the profit rates in other areas of the economy. To claim that a reduction of competition in manufacturing would solve capitalism's problems is wrong, even if it could redistribute some surplus value to manufacturing from other areas of the economy.[84] In addition, Anwar Shaikh has shown, in a painstaking empirical study:

> There is little evidence of any impact on relative prices from "overcompetition", and their movements do not in any case correlate with those in profitability. Equally importantly, persistent "overcapacity" cannot explain the secular fall in profit rates, because they exhibit persistent downward tendencies even when (partially) adjusted for variations in capacity utilisation... The empirical results strongly indicate that secularly falling profitability is an intrinsic feature of post-war accumulation in all three dominant capitalist countries [Germany, Japan and the US].[85]

An alternative explanation of this trend is required. For Marx, the tendency for profit rates to fall was based on a rising organic composition of capital (roughly the ratio of investment in plant, equipment and raw material to that in wages). This squeezes out the source of surplus value (what Marx calls "living labour"), relative to overall investment. Unfortunately, Brenner rejects this explanation, believing it to be paradoxical that capitalists would "adopt techniques that *decrease their own rate of profit*".[86]

But it might be perfectly logical for the first capitalist in a sector to make a productivity-raising investment, driving down the value embodied in the individual commodities they produce, because this would allow them to undercut rivals, grabbing market share and boosting profitability in the short term. It is the succeeding process in which the innovation spreads through a particular sector, driving down prices, that puts pressure on profit rates. Eventually, every capitalist in a particular sector would have to introduce the new technology, because, even though the resulting rate of profit is lower, failure to do so means that they cannot compete with rivals by

84: Moseley, 1999, p145.

85: Shaikh, 1999, p115.

86: See Brenner, 2006, pp14-15, and, in particular footnote 1 where he links his rejection of Marx's account to the "proof" by Okishio. For refutations of Okishio see Kliman, 2007; Carchedi, 1999; Shaikh, 1999.

charging the new, lower price—and the reduced profits now on offer are better than no profit at all.[87]

Having rejected this Brenner is left with a detailed narrative focusing on the rise and fall of rival blocs of capital locked into competitive struggle in a particular phase of the system's development. But what is required is both a general account of the tendencies towards crisis, based on Marx's value theory, and an account of the "specific structural forms taken by capitalism during its history", which shape how these tendencies work themselves out.[88] I will turn next to two theorists who have sought to apply Marx's law of the tendency of the rate of profit to fall to contemporary capitalism, before looking at the IS tradition's account of the historical development of the system.

Andrew Kliman

Andrew Kliman has, like Brenner, argued that the current meltdown is rooted in a long-term failure of capitalism to shrug off problems that emerged from the 1970s: "The crisis is rooted in the fact that capital was not destroyed to a sufficient degree during the global economic slump of the mid-1970s".[89] This follows Marx, who saw crisis as a mechanism through which the capitalist system can restore profitability and temporarily work out the contradictions that build up in periods of growth:

> From time to time the conflict of antagonistic agencies finds vent in crises. The crises are always but momentary and forcible solutions of the existing contradictions. They are violent eruptions which for a time restore the disturbed equilibrium.[90]

The collapse in the price of machinery, raw materials and other inputs during a crisis, along with the failure of whole companies (and attacks on wages and conditions of workers), can boost the profitability of firms that survive:

87: Shaikh, 1999, pp121-122. For an introductory elaboration of Marx's law of the tendency of the rate of profit to fall, see Choonara, 2009, pp68-78.

88: Callinicos, 1999, pp18, 25-28.

89: Kliman, 2009, p1. Earlier Kliman wrote a useful account of the developing crisis for *International Socialism* (though obviously, like all the articles penned at this stage, it has now been overtaken by events)—Kliman, 2008.

90: Marx, 1972, p249; Choonara, 2009, pp79-82.

If a business can generate $3 million in profit annually, but the value of the capital invested in the business is $100 million, its rate of profit is a mere 3 percent. But if the destruction of capital values enables new owners to acquire the business for only $10 million instead of $100 million, their rate of profit is a healthy 30 percent. That is a tremendous spur to a new boom. Thus the post-war boom which followed the massive destruction of capital that occurred during the Great Depression and World War Two came about as a result of that destruction.[91]

Kliman makes a distinction between an "observed" and an "underlying" rate of profit. He claims that the latter is a mathematical limit governed by two variables—the rate of growth of living labour and the rate at which value is accumulated—which Kliman believes are both more or less constant.[92] The observed rate will tend to fall towards this limit, before being boosted by the destruction of capital in crisis—if this destruction of capital is able to take place. Kliman's formulation is essentially a mathematical proof of the direction profit rates should move in, rather than a description of their concrete movements. There seems little reason to believe that the accumulation rate and expansion of living labour will stay constant in the short term, but Kliman believes that they may be trendless when considered over long historical periods.[93] It appears that his argument is directed against the large number of Marxist theorists who have rejected the law of the tendency of the rate of profit to fall altogether.[94] But for those who already accept this tendency, which would include most of those who have written in this journal in recent years, a focus on actual movements of the organic composition of capital, which in turn imply changes to profit rates, may be more useful.

Kliman's central point about the destruction of capital stands, whatever approach is taken and, of course, begs the question of why the

91: Kliman, 2009, p1. Brenner, 2009, also puts forward the view that "it's by way of crisis that, historically, capitalism has restored the rate of profit and established the necessary conditions for more dynamic capital accumulation... The current crisis is about that shakeout that never happened." For the role of the Second World War in the recovery from the 1930s, see Freeman, 2009.

92: The precise expression for the limit will depend on how much constant capital is fixed and how much is circulating. See the references in Kliman, 2009, for the maths.

93: Personal correspondence.

94: See Kliman, 2007, chapter 7, for a terrific defence of Marx in the face of this barrage. Carchedi, 2009, also provides a powerful vindication of Marx's explanation of why the profit rate falls.

contradictions did not work their way out of the system.[95] Kliman points to the reluctance of policy makers to allow the current crisis to destroy capital.[96] This in turn needs to be embedded in an account of the trajectory of capitalism since the Second World War, showing why this reluctance is greater than it was in previous crises, a point I shall return to below.

Anwar Shaikh

Anwar Shaikh is the Marxist theoretician who, perhaps more than any other, has stressed the centrality of the rate of profit to the dynamics of the system. For Shaikh the current crisis is a "structural crisis that had been postponed or turned into a false boom". The period since the 1970s has been one in which the amounts of profit generated by the system have risen but profit *rates* have been "essentially stagnant".

The additional point added by Shaikh's analysis is that it is necessary to look at sustained shifts in interest rates alongside profit rates in order to understand the accumulation that did take place in recent decades. "What stimulates accumulation is not the profit rate but the profit rate net of the cost of borrowing capital, ie the interest rate. If the profit rate is flat and interest rates are falling, the incentive to accumulate is kept alive, though it's kept alive artificially." The prime rate (the interest rate that businesses care about) tended to rise gradually from the end of the Second World War, with the rise accelerating sharply in the late 1970s and early 1980s, before beginning a gradual long-term decline.[97]

This created a "false boom" based on "profit of enterprise"—the term used by Marx in the third volume of *Capital* for profits net of interest payments. The long decline in interest rates also allowed consumer debt to grow for a period without, at least initially, massively increasing the debt repayments made by workers.[98]

95: Although there are debates over terminology. According to David Harvey, "Capital that is not realised is variously termed 'devalued', 'devalorised', 'depreciated' or even 'destroyed'. Marx—or his translators—seem to use these terms interchangeably and inconsistently. I shall restrict my own uses of them in the following way. The 'destruction of capital' refers to the physical loss of use-values. I shall restrict the use of the idea of 'depreciation of capital' largely in accordance with modern usage, to deal with the changing monetary valuation of assets... And I shall reserve the term 'devaluation' for situations in which the socially necessary labour time embodied in material form is lost without, necessarily, any destruction of the material form itself"—Harvey, 2006, p84.

96: Kliman, 2009, p1.

97: See, for instance, www.project.org/images/graphs/Prime_Rate_1.jpg

98: Shaikh, 2008; all quotes are my transcriptions from this recording.

Pulling the insights together

What is required is an analysis of capitalism as it ages combined with the rigour of Marx's value theory, drawing on the insights of many of the theorists I have surveyed.

Aging capitalism leads to the growth of unproductive and "waste" areas of economies. For instance, the IS tradition emphasised the role of arms spending during the long post-war boom. Military rivalry between the two Cold War superpowers, which maintained high levels of arms spending following the Second World War, created a "permanent arms economy".[99] This spending could stabilise the system as a whole by functioning as a "leak" out of the circuit of capital and thus draining off surplus value that otherwise would have been accumulated.[100]

The permanent arms economy contained the seeds of its own collapse. The boom period also saw the rise of "non-militarised state capitalisms" (notably Japan and Germany), which spent less on defence. They could invest a greater proportion of surplus value in export industries, undercutting the major arms spending economies in these areas by engaging in price competition. In the wake of the rise of these powers, and reductions in the defence budgets of the US and USSR, arms spending, though still high in absolute terms, ceased to keep pace with the growth of the world economy.[101]

Other forms of spending that are not directly productive of surplus value have also grown, and done so more evenly across the advanced capitalist economies and without subsequently declining. These include unproductive expenditures, for instance advertising.[102] There are also areas that might be described as "indirectly productive", such as public healthcare and education, which do not directly yield surplus value but which are essential to the reproduction of the kinds of labour power required in a modern capitalist economy.[103]

The rise of waste can stabilise the system but it is also a burden on the particular capitalist economy in which the waste spending takes place.

99: See, for instance, Kidron, 1970.

100: Choonara, 2009, pp134-137. Harman, 1984, chapter 3, gives a more detailed explanation of the role of arms spending.

101: For instance, US arms spending now represents between 4 and 5 percent of GDP, compared to about 10 percent in the late 1950s. World arms spending was about 2 percent of world GDP in 2007.

102: On the astonishing amounts spent on advertising in the US, see the figures in McChesney, Foster, Stole and Holleman, 2009.

103: Choonara, 2009, pp45-49.

Fred Moseley, for instance, believes that the rise of unproductive labour had as great an impact in reducing the US profit rate from the late 1940s to the mid-1970s as the rising organic composition of capital.[104]

In the post-war period the system did not grow as rapidly as it might have if all the surplus value had been accumulated in productive areas. However, nor did the ratio of investment to labour grow, or the rate of profit fall, as rapidly as it would otherwise have done. It was this that allowed the boom that followed the Second World War to extend for an unprecedented duration. When from the mid-1970s onwards crisis returned, it impacted upon a world that had been transformed during the long boom. In particular the units of capital—the firms within the system—had become larger through the processes of concentration (the gradual accumulation of capital) and centralisation (mergers and takeovers) identified by Marx.[105]

This meant that the very mechanism that clears out the system and restores it for a time to some level of health—economic crisis—had become more dangerous for the system. The collapse of one or two giant multinationals now posed the risk that profitable sections of the economy could be dragged down alongside unprofitable sections. The firms that made up the economy had also become more deeply intertwined with the state and financial system, and indeed the recent growth of finance has exacerbated the problems.[106] The growing dangers explain the recent panic over the implosion of Lehman Brothers and the way the state has intervened to manage the restructuring through bankruptcy of the US car giants GM and Chrysler.[107]

104: Moseley, 2008, pp217-218.
105: Choonara, 2009, pp90-95.
106: "The effect [of the growth of finance] was not to subordinate state capacities to market forces, but rather to make political intervention all the more necessary—not least in fighting fires sparked by financial volatility—as well as more feasible... The result was the step by step construction of a too big to fail regime, whereby intermediaries that were so large and so interconnected that their failure would bring down a significant part of the system could count on the US state, and especially the Treasury, to come to the rescue"—Panitch and Konings, 2009, p72.
107: There has been *some* "restructuring through crisis" in recent decades—Harman, 2007, pp151-152. Anwar Shaikh, 2008, makes a similar point about the crisis of the 1970s: "You had recovery in the 1980s because of job losses, because of bankruptcies, because of business failures and because of a decline in real wages...which greatly stimulated the profitability of surviving companies." Shaikh contrasts this with the crisis in Japan, which, he argues, the state prevented from sharpening through business failure and which was, consequently, a much more drawn out crisis.

The unwillingness of capitalist states to allow crisis to sweep through the system does not imply a collapse into permanent stagnation. Capitalism remains a system of competitive accumulation, along with imperialist rivalry, even if large firms have more freedom to determine prices until competitors harness the resources required to enter a market.[108] But unless there is destruction of capital on a sufficient scale, a sustained boom for the system as a whole, as opposed to temporary and localised booms, is unlikely—and periods of stagnation across areas of the system a real possibility.

As Kliman and Brenner argue, a sufficient destruction of capital certainly did not take place in the 1970s or early 1980s. Instead mechanisms came into play that deferred the crisis at the cost of generating growing contradictions that permeated the system. There was a dramatic increase in the rate of exploitation from the 1980s onwards. This is reflected, for instance, in the extension of the working year in America, to the extent that "in manufacturing the average worker put in nearly two weeks more in 2002 than in 1982".[109] The offensive on labour allowed for a partial, but only partial, restoration of profit rates.[110]

Finance, fictitious capital and real accumulation

The other mechanism deferring crisis was the growth of finance as capitalists and some states sought investment opportunities beyond the rather unprofitable productive economy. This had three effects.

The first was to prevent a crisis arising from the inability of firms to sell their output and so "realise the surplus value" embedded in the goods and services produced by the system.[111] If profit rates are high, limited consumption by workers is not a problem because there is plenty of demand for machinery, raw materials and so on. In a period of low profitability—and therefore low average levels of investment—the restriction of workers' wages can create huge problems. The growth of debt, especially personal debt in economies such as the US, allowed consumers to form a "market of last resort", providing the demand to keep capitalism in business.

The second effect was to create the illusion of profitability and dynamism through asset price bubbles. As profits sought an outlet in the world

108: Even in the most extreme version of monopolisation—bureaucratic state capitalism as practised in the USSR—in which the law of value was "partially negated", competition reasserted itself through the struggle to produce use-values, in particular weapons, enforcing a drive to accumulate—see Cliff, 1996, chapter 7.
109: Moody, 2007, p34.
110: See Harman, 2007, for a detailed discussion.
111: Marx, 1972, p244.

of finance there was a process of accumulation of what Marx calls "fictitious capital". Fictitious capital does not mean capital that does not exist, or necessarily imply fraud of some kind. Rather it is investment in "paper claims" over a share of value to be produced. The fact that fictitious capital entitles the owner to a stream of income makes it *appear* like real capital that a capitalist might throw into production to generate surplus value or loan out at the going rate of interest.

One classic example would be the bonds issued by governments, which entitle the owners to a share of future tax revenue; another would be the shares issued by companies that entitle shareholders to dividends that are a portion of the surplus value generated by the company.[112] Marx points out that, even when the paper claim "does not represent a purely fictitious capital...the capital-value of such paper is nevertheless wholly illusory". In other words, if we are dealing, for instance, in shares in a productive enterprise, the paper is merely a "title of ownership which represents this capital". Marx cautions against the illusion that the titles *are* the actual capital: "Capital does not exist twice, once as the capital-value of titles of ownership (stocks) on the one hand and on the other hand as the actual capital invested, or to be invested, in those enterprises".[113]

Fictitious capital can be traded. Indeed, Marx argues, it circulates according to "its own laws of motion", different from the laws of motion of real capital.[114] The market prices of shares might rise and fall depending on how the income flowing from them compares with that which can be obtained from other sorts of investment. Because the price of shares and other examples of fictitious capital can fluctuate in this manner, investors may also start to speculate—purchasing them in the expectation that their prices will rise and they can later be sold at a profit. In an economic "bubble" investors outbid each other in the chase after such claims and, in the process, raise their prices. So, for instance, shares in a company can be pushed well above the level represented by the actual value of the plant and equipment it owns.

The process of "fictitious accumulation" associated with rising asset prices could boost the balance sheets of the firms involved, especially financial corporations, creating the illusion of profitability.[115] In addition, although fictitious accumulation in itself produces nothing, it could spur some development of productive areas of the economy, which can add to the sense

112: These are the examples given in Marx, 1972, pp465-468.
113: Marx, 1972, p466.
114: Marx, 1972, p465.
115: Although often this was rather opaque. On the kind of financial wizardry practised in the City of London, see Lancaster, 2009.

of dynamism. (For instance, the workers who serve coffee at the Starbucks branches that have sprung up across the City of London are productive workers, even if their customers are often not.)

The third effect of the growth of finance was to further reduce the pressure for profit rates to fall. One reason for this is that the growth of the financial sector is in itself a growth of waste. The investment that goes into buildings or wages in the financial sector is unproductive—it does not lead to the generation of new surplus value and is therefore a burden on productive capital. It constitutes a "leak" from the system in much the same way as arms spending did in the post-war boom.

However, not all the money harnessed by finance represents such a leak. In the traditional Marxist picture banks gather "interest-bearing capital" which they loan to industrial capitalists, who then use it to generate surplus value, some of which then goes to the bank as interest. When this happens, "fictitious accumulation" translates into real accumulation.[116]

If, as Lapavitsas and others have argued, banks are increasingly interested in lending to workers rather than industrial capital, how does this modify the picture? The lending gives banks a claim over workers' future earnings. This has the effect of raising the rate of exploitation of the workers, unless they succeed in forcing their employer to pay higher wages, in which case the employer in effect pays for the interest on the workers' loans through a reduction in their surplus value. The bank then has the possibility of using the interest payments for productive investment.

But there is nothing automatic about finance flowing towards productive ventures, rather than speculation. For instance, mortgages and other debt have, over recent years, been repackaged as securities with names such as "collateralised debt obligations". Capitalists could then gamble on the future value of these. Derivatives called "credit default swaps" were created, which insured against people defaulting on their loans. These too became subject to speculation.[117] More generally, as a whole series of markets in fictitious capital were created or expanded, with increasingly tenuous relationships to the generation of surplus value in the wider economy, the market prices of these assets lost touch with the underlying process of value creation.[118] As long as the resulting speculative bubbles were growing, these

116: Fine, 2008, p3.

117: Ultimately it was credit derivatives issued by AIG that brought down the insurance giant. For more on the way credit default swaps were exploited by bodies such as pension funds to get round statutory requirements for them to invest only in safe concerns, see Carchedi, 2009.

118: And in some cases the assets created were so complex and unique that markets for them simply did not exist. Those who held the assets had to guess how much they were worth. This

markets could act as a temporary a "reservoir" for surplus value (as opposed to a permanent "leak" because some of this value could, in principle, find its way back into production, for instance if assets were sold and the money ploughed into a productive firm). As each bubble collapsed, another one had to be blown on an even greater scale. But crisis always threatened to force markets in fictitious capital back into line with the prospects for value production in the wider economy.

The destruction of fictitious capital goes hand in hand with the wider devaluation of capital through crisis. In principle it can help pave the way for future expansion by removing a burden on productive capital, by accelerating the processes of restructuring through crisis (for instance, by firms taking over failing rivals whose share price has collapsed) and by removing some of the claims on future value.[119] But in practice it is increasingly hard to disentangle fictitious accumulation from real accumulation. If banks that have speculated unwisely go bust, they can drag down firms that have borrowed to invest in production. If financial institutions that are seen as central to the system have lost money and are threatened with collapse, states may step in to bail them out, and they will expect either productive sectors of the economy or workers to pick up the tab.[120]

So the collapses taking place in finance are adding to the trauma of the productive sectors of the economy, even as the chronic problems afflicting these sectors for 30 years are exposed and the credit dragging the system forward is withdrawn. Financial expansion is best seen as a "counteracting tendency", deferring crisis, but one of a transitory nature. The price paid for this temporary fix was the creation of enormous imbalances within the economy—including the growth of unsustainable levels of debt, soaring financial and trade imbalances such as those between China and the US, and the formation of economic bubbles on an enormous scale. These features of the previous period help explain why, when the deferred crisis eventually broke, it did so with enormous speed, global reach and coordination, and with such terrible severity.

---

has created a situation where many banks hold assets (often off their balance sheets) that have turned out to be worth only a fraction of their "market" price. It was in this context that the recent announcements by the Bank of America of losses of $15.3 billion and Citigroup of $18.7 billion "confirmed what many experts have long suspected: the subprime losses of 2007 were a bullet that fatally wounded the banks. Many lost so much money on toxic subprime mortgage-related derivatives that they have been essentially insolvent for more than a year"—*Financial Times*, 18 January 2009.

119: See Perelman, 2008, especially pp29-31.

120: For instance, the British government admits it has *lost* at least £50 billion bailing out banks.

References

Blackburn, Robin, 2006, "Finance and the Fourth Dimension", *New Left Review 39* (May-June 2006), www.newleftreview.org/A2616

Blackburn, Robin, 2007a, "Toxic Waste in the Subprime Market", *Counterpunch*, 22 March 2007, www.counterpunch.org/blackburn03222007.html

Blackburn, Robin, 2007b, *Age Shock: How Finance is Failing Us* (Verso).

Blackburn, Robin, 2008, "The Subprime Crisis", *New Left Review 50* (March-April 2008), www.newleftreview.org/?view=2715

Blackburn, Robin, 2009, "Value Theory and the Chinese Worker: A Reply to Geoff Mann", *New Left Review 56* (March-April 2009).

Brenner, Robert, 1999, "Competition and Class", *Monthly Review*, volume 51, number 7 (December 1999), www.monthlyreview.org/1299bren.htm

Brenner, Robert, 2004, "New Boom or New Bubble?", *New Left Review 25* (January-February 2004).

Brenner, Robert, 2006 [1998], *The Economics of Global Turbulence* (Verso).

Brenner, Robert, 2008, "Devastating crisis unfolds", *Against the Current 132* (January-February 2008), www.solidarity-us.org/node/1297

Brenner, Robert, 2009, "A Way out of the Global Crisis?", interview, http://english.hani.co.kr/arti/english_edition/e_international/336766.html

Callinicos, Alex, 1999, "Capitalism, Competition and Profits", *Historical Materialism 4*.

Callinicos, Alex, 2006, "Making Sense of Imperialism: A Reply to Leo Panitch and Sam Gindin", *International Socialism 110* (spring 2006), www.isj.org.uk/?id=196

Callinicos, Alex, 2009, "An Apologist with Insights", *International Socialism 122* (spring 2009), www.isj.org.uk/?id=532

Carchedi, Guglielmo, 1991, *Frontiers of Political Economy* (Verso).

Carchedi, Guglielmo, 1999, "A Missed Opportunity: Orthodox Versus Marxist Crisis Theories", *Historical Materialism 4*.

Carchedi, Guglielmo, 2009, "The Return from the Grave, or Marx and the Current Crisis", available from http://sites.google.com/site/radicalperspectivesonthecrisis/finance-crisis/on-the-origins-of-the-crisis-beyond-finance/carchedireturnfromthegrave

Choonara, Joseph, 2008, "The value of money", *Socialist Review*, November 2008, www.socialistreview.org.uk/article.php?articlenumber=10587

Choonara, Joseph, 2009, *Unravelling Capitalism: A Guide to Marxist Political Economy* (Bookmarks).

Cliff, Tony, 1996 [1948], *State Capitalism in Russia* (Bookmarks), www.marxists.org/archive/cliff/works/1955/statecap/

Cliff, Tony, 2001 [1969], *Rosa Luxemburg*, in *Selected Works*, volume 1 (Bookmarks).

Egoavil, Michael, 2009, "Fictitious Capital and Credit Schemes", available from http://marxisthumanistinitiative.org/2009/05/06/fictitious-capital-and-credit-schemes/

Fine, Ben, 2008, "Looking at the Crisis through Marx: Or is it the Other Way About?", https://eprints.soas.ac.uk/5921/1/isrfin.doc

Fine, Ben, and Lawrence Harris, 1979, *Rereading Capital* (Macmillan).

Foster, John Bellamy, and Fred Magdoff, 2009, *The Great Financial Crisis: Causes and Consequences* (Monthly Review).

Freeman, Alan, 2009, "How Much is Enough?", http://mpra.ub.uni-muenchen.de/13262/

Gowan, Peter, 2009, "Crisis in the Heartland", *New Left Review 55* (January-February 2009), www.newleftreview.org/A2759

Harman, Chris, 1984, *Explaining the Crisis* (Bookmarks).

Harman, Chris, 1999, "Footnotes and Fallacies", *Historical Materialism 4*.

Harman, Chris, 2007, "The Rate of Profit and the World Today", *International Socialism 115* (summer 2007), www.isj.org.uk/?id=340
Harman, Chris, 2008a, "Theorising Neoliberalism", *International Socialism 117* (winter 2008), www.isj.org.uk/?id=399
Harman, Chris, 2008b, "Misreading and Misconceptions", *International Socialism 119* (summer 2008) www.isj.org.uk/?id=462
Harman, Chris, 2009, "The Slump of the 1930s and the Crisis Today", *International Socialism 121* (winter 2009), www.isj.org.uk/?id=506
Harvey, David, 2005, *A Brief History of Neoliberalism* (Oxford University).
Harvey, David, 2006 [1982], *Limits to Capital* (Verso).
Harvey, David, 2009, "Exploring the Logic of Capitalism", interview by Joseph Choonara, *Socialist Review*, April 2009, www.socialistreview.org.uk/article.php?articlenumber=10801
Howard, Michael Charles, and John Edward King, 1992, *A History of Marxian Economics, Volume II: 1929-1990* (Macmillan).
Husson, Michel, 2008, "Toxic Capitalism", *International Viewpoint 406* (November 2008), http://hussonet.free.fr/toxicapa.pdf
Kidron, Michael, 1970 [1968], *Western Capitalism Since the War* (Pelican), www.marxists.org/archive/kidron/works/1970/westcap/
Kincaid, Jim, 2008, "The World Economy—a Critical Comment", *International Socialism 119* (summer 2008) www.isj.org.uk/?id=461
Kliman, Andrew, 2007, *Reclaiming Marx's "Capital": A Refutation of the Myth of Inconsistency* (Lexington).
Kliman, Andrew, 2008, "A Crisis at the Centre of the System", *International Socialism 120* (autumn 2008), www.isj.org.uk/?id=482
Kliman, Andrew, 2009, "'The Destruction of Capital' and the Current Economic Crisis", available from http://akliman.squarespace.com/crisis-intervention/
Lancaster, John, 2009, "It's Finished", *London Review of Books*, volume 31, number 10 (28 May 2009), www.lrb.co.uk/v31/n10/lanc01_.html
Lapavitsas, Costas, 2003, "Money as Money and Money as Capital in a Capitalist Economy", in Saad-Filho, 2003.
Lapavitsas, Costas, 2008a, "Financialised Capitalism: Direct Exploitation and Periodic Bubbles", Soas, www.soas.ac.uk/economics/events/crisis/43939.pdf
Lapavitsas, Costas, 2008b, "The Credit Crunch", interview, *International Socialism 117* (winter 2008), www.isj.org.uk/?id=395
Lapavitsas, Costas, 2009a, "Financialised Capitalism: Crisis and Financial Expropriation", Soas, Research on Money and Finance working paper, 15 February 2009, available from www.soas.ac.uk/rmf
Lapavitsas, Costas, 2009b, "Financialisation or the Search for Profits in the Sphere of Circulation", Soas, Research on Money and Finance working paper, 11 May 2009, available from www.soas.ac.uk/rmf
Liu, Li-gang, Kevin Chow and Unias Li, 2006, "Determinants of Foreign Direct Investment in East Asia: Did China Crowd Out FDI from her Developing East Asian Neighbours?", Hong Kong Monetary Authority, http://www.info.gov.hk/hkma/eng/research/RM17-2006.pdf
Mann, Geoff, 2009, "Colletti on the Credit Crunch: A Response to Robin Blackburn", *New Left Review 56* (March-April 2009).
Marx, Karl, 1970 [1867], *Capital*, volume 1 (Lawrence and Witshart), www.marxists.org/archive/marx/works/1867-c1/
Marx, Karl, 1972 [1894], *Capital*, volume 3 (Lawrence and Witshart), www.marxists.org/archive/marx/works/1894-c3/

McChesney, Robert, John Bellamy Foster, Inger Stole and Hannah Holleman, 2009, "The Sales Effort and Monopoly Capitalism", *Monthly Review*, volume 60, number 11 (April 2009), http://monthlyreview.org/090406-mcchesney-foster-stole-holleman.php

McNally, David, 2008, "From Financial Crisis to World Slump: Accumulation, Financialisation and the Global Slowdown", http://sites.google.com/site/marxandthefinancialcrisis/mcnallydec2008/McNallyDec2008rev.pdf

Moody, Kim, 2007, *US Labour in Trouble and Transition* (Verso).

Moseley, Fred, 1999, "The Decline of the Rate of Profit in the Post-war United States: Due to Increased Competition or Increased Unproductive Labour?", *Historical Materialism 4*.

Moseley, Fred, 2003, "Marxian Crisis Theory and the Post-war US Economy", in Saad-Filho, 2003.

Moseley, Fred, 2008, "Some Notes on the Crunch and the Crisis", *International Socialism 119* (summer 2008), www.isj.org.uk/?id=463

Murphy, R Taggart, 2009, "Bubblenomics", *New Left Review 57* (May-June 2009).

Panitch, Leo, and Sam Gindin, 2006, "'Imperialism and Global Political Economy'—a Reply to Alex Callinicos", *International Socialism 109* (winter 2006), www.isj.org.uk/?id=175

Panitch, Leo, and Sam Gindin, 2009, "From Global Finance to the Nationalisation of the Banks: Eight Theses on the Economic Crisis", *The Bullet 189* (25 February 2009), www.socialistproject.ca/bullet/bullet189.html

Panitch, Leo, and Martijn Konings, 2009, "Myths of Neoliberal Deregulation", *New Left Review 57* (May-June 2009).

Perelman, Michael, 2008, "Fictitious Capital and Crisis Theory", available from http://michaelperelman.files.wordpress.com/2008/09/fic1.doc

Saad-Filho, Alfredo (ed), 2003, *Anti-capitalism a Marxist Introduction* (Pluto).

Shaikh, Anwar, 1999, "Explaining the Global Economic Crisis: A Critique of Brenner", *Historical Materialism 5*, available from http://homepage.newschool.edu/~ashaikh/

Shaikh, Anwar, 2008, "The Deepening Economic Disaster", speech, available from http://nyusociology.org/blogs/radical/2008/12/08/the-deepening-economic-disaster/

Sweezy, Paul, 1970 [1942], *The Theory of Capitalist Development* (Monthly Review).

Turner, Graham, 2008, *The Credit Crunch: Housing Bubbles, Globalisation and the Worldwide Economic Crisis* (Pluto).

UNCTAD, 2006, *World Investment Report 2006*, www.unctad.org/en/docs/wir2006_en.pdf

Gandhi: the man behind the myths

Talat Ahmed

"The saint has left our shores, I sincerely hope forever".[1] Jan Christiaan Smuts, a future South African prime minister, uttered these words in 1914. The saint was none other than Mohandas Karamchand Gandhi on his way home to India after 21 years in South Africa. Gandhi certainly came to personify saintliness. In 1944 the scientist Albert Einstein stated, "Generations to come, it may be, will scarce believe that such a one as this ever in flesh and blood walked upon this earth." And, of course, death sealed his iconic status. His demise at the hands of an assassin's bullet on 30 January 1948 sanctified Gandhi as the Mahatma, India's "Great Soul". King George VI described his death as "an irreparable loss for mankind". Labour prime minister Clement Atlee expressed "profound distress" and Nehru immortalised him further with the memorable words, "The light that shone in this country was no ordinary light", it was "something more than the immediate present" and would continue to "illuminate this country for many years", giving "solace to innumerable hearts".[2]

As the "father" of non-violent direct action Gandhi is credited with providing the inspiration behind Martin Luther King and the Civil Rights Movement, the peace campaigns of the Greenham Common women and today with protests over climate change and war. This veneration is

1: Quoted in Huttenback, 1971, p330.

2: Nehru, 1987, p35.

matched only by the venom that he inspired in others. Winston Churchill scorned him as a "half-naked fakir", complaining bitterly in 1931 that:

> It is alarming and nauseating to see Mr Gandhi, a seditious Middle Temple lawyer, now posing as a fakir of a type well known in the east, striding half naked up the steps of the viceregal palace, while he is still organising and conducting a campaign of civil disobedience, to parlay on equal terms with the representative of the Emperor-King.[3]

In India and elsewhere Gandhi has been criticised for being "anti-modern", a hardline traditionalist, a blackmailer who used fasting as a means of getting his way; on the left he is seen as the "mascot of the bourgeoisie" and anti working class. There are elements of truth to all these accusations but it is important to bear in mind that bourgeois nationalism is far from straightforward, much less pure, and fundamentally flawed. Indian nationalism was no exception.

Gandhi's life was one of complexities, contradictions and ironies: he was the apostle of non-violence mowed down by an assassin's bullet; a deeply religious individual who fought passionately for Hindu-Muslim unity, only to see India free but partitioned; a man who devoted much of his life to the removal of untouchability, the social uplift of women and the rights of the peasantry, who helped create an India today marked by increasing social inequality that continues to blight the lives of the poor. He was imprisoned nine times by colonial governments who saw him as a mad anarchist and yet every British viceroy from 1916 onwards had to deal with him. He never held political office and is viewed as above the grubby business of political horse-trading and yet he was a shrewd political operator who weighed every action and word in a calculated manner. This is the enigma of Gandhi: how could a London trained barrister come to dominate Indian politics in the first half of the 20th century and for much of the rest?

Childhood

Gandhi could not have been a more unlikely figure to become an icon of the Indian freedom movement. He was not from a staunch nationalist family, like that of Jawaharlal Nehru, nor was he from the professional urban elite like Muhammad Ali Jinnah. Gandhi was born in 1869 into a family of *Modh Banias*, a middle caste trading and moneylending community who had a reputation for being shrewd, wily, thrifty and good

3: Gilbert, 1976, p390.

businessmen. His birthplace was the small town of Porbandar, in a semi-independent princely state on the south west coast of Gujarat, where his father's family had for two generations been *diwans* (advisers) to the princes and kings. After primary school Gandhi was sent to be educated at the only English college in Rajkot, but growing up in a princely state resulted in him having very little contact with or experience of direct British imperial rule. This had the advantage that it instilled in him a deep conviction that Indians could and should rule themselves. But it also shielded him from the full might of the empire and its oppressive state apparatus.

London

"The home of philosophers and poets, the very centre of civilisation" is how Gandhi saw London. Coming from a conservative, small-town family, it is easy to imagine his excitement when he was sent there in 1888 to train as a barrister. In 1890 there were only 207 Indians in London and Gandhi initially found life quite solitary and perplexing. He was living alone, having to manage his own expenses, pay for lodgings, wear a new set of clothes, familiarise himself with new and strange food, and mingle with people whose mores were quite alien to him. He was not from a patrician urban background, had not been raised in a Western liberal environment, did not have the benefit of an English public schooling or Oxbridge and so did not possess the self-confidence of an upper class Nehru or Jinnah. Wearing Western suits, closed shoes and eating with cutlery were all a challenge to him, and he faced constant embarrassment over his vegetarianism and poor command of English. In order to overcome these handicaps Gandhi decided to turn himself into a typical English gentleman. He bought his clothes at the Army and Navy Store, evening suits from Bond Street, learnt to tie his ties and sported a double watch chain of gold. Not content with this he began to take lessons in dancing, French and elocution.

Acculturation aside, Gandhi was exposed to two main influences in London that would begin to shape his philosophical outlook. He eventually found a vegetarian restaurant on Farringdon Street. It was here that he came across Henry Salt's book *A Plea for Vegetarianism*. This transformed his views on diet and food. His vow of abjuring meat was no longer a vow before an illiterate mother but had become a philosophic moral principle that he had chosen. He became a member of the Vegetarian Society, the goals of which were not mere dietary concerns but to "seek the conditions necessary to reach a human ideal that valued the spiritual, physical, mental and moral aspects of human life".[4] Gandhi's membership of this society provided him entry into the middle class non-conformists and dissenters of late 19th century England. He became friends with Henry Salt who introduced him to the writings of Henry David Thoreau, author of the 1849 essay "Civil Disobedience". Thoreau was renowned for his espousal of simple living, and his opposition to the Mexican-American war and slavery led to his imprisonment for refusing to pay taxes to an unjust government. His essay would have a transformative impact on Gandhi as he became a member of the executive committee of the Vegetarian Society and made his tentative debut at public speaking, where he proved to be terribly awkward and diffident. He was more successful at writing articles on Indian vegetarians for the newspaper.[5] In these he argued that it was the "wretched custom of infant marriages and its attendant evils" that was responsible for Indian weakness.[6] He also believed that Indian weakness was the result of moral slackness that required inner regeneration. This would be a theme he would return to again and again.

The vegetarian movement was part of a larger movement of radical reformers who were anti-urban and anti-industrial in their views and critical of the commercialisation of Victorian Britain. They were bourgeois and interested in change through individual effort and moral fibre. It was this individualism and the simplicity of their message that appealed to Gandhi.

The other group important to Gandhi's evolution was the Theosophy Society. Founded in New York in 1875 by Madame Helena Petrovna Blavatsky, this group drew heavily on Hinduism and Buddhism, encouraging the reading of Sanskrit texts and seeking to reconcile new developments in Western science with organised religions. In this sense Theosophists offered a modernised reformed form of Hinduism fused with elements of Christianity and other belief systems—a sort of scientific spirituality. Thus far Gandhi had viewed religion as a series of superstitions and meaningless rituals. Reading Blavatsky's *The Key to Theosophy* disabused him "of the notion fostered by missionaries that Hinduism was rife with superstition"[7] and he was introduced to the *Bhagavad Gita* and other religious texts that he had never read before. He also came to read the Old Testament which he found nauseating but the New Testament enthralled him, especially the Sermon on the Mount. The combination of these

4: Gandhi, 2002, p52.
5: *The Vegetarian*, 7 February-14 March 1891.
6: Gandhi, 1958, p23.
7: Gandhi, 2002, p63.

texts pointed to an alternative way of being religious, one that synthesised a variety of texts and influences but simultaneously emphasised a similar message: that renunciation was the highest form of religion, the imperative of offering the other cheek and love to an opponent. This curious mixture of Christian suffering, Hindu mythology and denial would come to epitomise the adult Gandhi. The London experience demonstrates that Gandhi was not fearful of borrowing "Western" ideas and that "Gandhism", far from being a uniquely Indian creed, is a global cocktail of mysticism, nonconformism and moral indignation wrapped up in a philosophy of personal salvation—in short a variant of reformism.

On completing his law studies Gandhi was called to the bar in 1891 and set sail for home, armed with his professional qualification and Bond Street suits but also with his new found zeal. Porbandar, however, proved to be a dead end for the young barrister as he failed to secure employment to support his family. He moved to Bombay to practise Indian law but again with little success. On one occasion he called on a British agent in order to intercede in a case involving one of his brothers. In London Gandhi had enjoyed friendships and acquaintances with Europeans, including with this officer. However, now Gandhi was dismissed with the abruptness that British officials excelled in and found that "an officer on leave was not the same as an officer on duty".[8] Mortified, Gandhi was advised by his fellow barristers to "pocket the insult". There would be many more insults to pocket. Gandhi accepted an offer to act as a legal adviser to an Indian firm in South Africa and went away for what he assumed would be no more than a year.

South Africa

The scene from Richard Attenborough's 1982 film will have etched into people's minds the deep humiliation that Gandhi suffered at the hands of a ticket inspector on his way from Durban to Pretoria. This was one of numerous racist insults that Gandhi encountered. Racial segregation, discrimination and violence characterised the lives of all non-whites. Gandhi had not experienced direct racism before and it is conspicuous by its absence in his autobiography. This is not because it did not exist but because Gandhi had been accepted without prejudice in the circles in which he moved. To be treated as a "coolie" barrister disturbed Gandhi because he believed that as subjects of the empire Indians had a right to equal treatment before the law. He had developed an immense sense of pride in being Indian, believing that as a person from an ancient and proud tradition, he was the equal of

8: Gandhi, 2002, p91.

whites. But he did not extend this sympathy to the majority African population of South Africa and was initially horrified that Indians were placed on the same level as Africans. He complained that Europeans wanted to "degrade us to the level of the raw Kaffir whose occupation is hunting, and whose sole ambition is to collect a certain number of cattle to buy a wife with and, then, pass his life in indolence and nakedness".[9]

At this stage Gandhi was very much in the mould of a "Victorian" Indian who sought accommodation and acceptance into the empire. His caste background and education meant that he shared the upper class prejudices of Europeans on many issues. He had come to South Africa to provide legal advice to Indian businessmen and it was their interests that he identified with. Indians in South Africa were a heterogeneous, fragmented community with different interests. The majority of Indians had come as indentured labourers from Tamil Nadu and Bengal, working on the sugar plantations and in the mines as well as performing unskilled work in the towns. But there was a class of petty traders and merchants, professionals and white collar Indians made up of Muslims and Hindus from Gujarat and Parsis, and Christians from Bombay. The diversity of religious interests among the middle classes was something Gandhi had no difficulty in associating with. But at first he had little contact with Indian labourers, and the class and caste distinctions were new to him.

His initial campaigns were against measures in 1894 that only hit the Indian middle class—a bill to prevent extension of parliamentary franchise beyond the mere 300 Indians already enjoying it and another stipulating that "no person of Asiatic race, birth or descent" could take out a licence to trade. But an amendment to immigration laws in 1895 signalled an assault on all Indians in Natal, the Orange Free State and Transvaal. It stipulated that every free Indian had to be re-indentured for a further two years or pay an extra annual tax if they were not being returned to India.

Gandhi helped to form the Natal Indian National Congress and wrote letters to parliamentarians in London. He returned to India twice, in 1896 and 1899, to meet with nationalist leaders and publicise the plight of Indians. He travelled to London in 1906 and 1909, again to petition on behalf of "his Majesty's subjects". His initial campaigns used methods that suited middle class politics such as letter writing, emphasising that their campaign was not for equality of all Indians but for equality of the "respectable" classes. Gandhi even accepted that the "coolies" had unsanitary habits that needed reform! His feeling that the policies of discrimination were

9: Gandhi, 1958, p410.

alien to "the values of the empire" led him to mobilise over 1,000 people for the ambulance corps on the side of the British in the 1899 Boer War.

His attitudes began to change when he read Leo Tolstoy's *The Kingdom of God is Within You* in 1894 at the age of 25, which turned his attention to the concept of non-violence. "Before the...profound morality and the truthfulness of this book", he later wrote, "all the books...seemed to pale into insignificance". His reading of John Ruskin's *Unto this Last* made him "determined to change my life",[10] influencing his concept of "soul-force" as a substitute for physical force. He learnt from it that "the good of the individual is contained in the good of all...the lawyer's work has the same value as the barber's...a life of labour, ie, the life of a tiller of the soil and the handicraftsman, is the life worth living."

He writes that he "arose with the dawn, ready to reduce these principles to practice".[11] His literary readings about the worth of manual labour led him to think about the way the Indian middle classes treated their fellow indentured countrymen. He found their condescension and loathing of this community to be contemptible. Equally important in influencing his thinking was the paltry state of Indian political organisation. Gandhi was the chief organiser and tactician of the merchant and professional Indian community from 1894 to 1906. However, merchant politics was conservative and this prevented issues being raised that could build and retain a broad base of support. Gandhi saw that businessmen were incapable of seeing beyond their narrow, selfish interests and this was the result of a kind of "moral degradation". He began to rethink his views, not only on caste, class and race, but also on tactics.

In 1906 the Transvaal government passed a law making it compulsory for Indians over eight years of age to carry a pass bearing their thumbprint. This caused outrage among the Indian population and a 3,000-strong mass gathering decided that no Indian would apply for registration, meeting attempts to enforce the law with passive resistance. This represented a major shift from protest centred on lobbying to that based on mass action. By the end of January 1908, 2,000 Indians had been jailed. But many key figures in the movement fled the colony rather than be arrested and eventually Gandhi reached agreement with Jan Smuts, the Afrikaner politician who was then colonial secretary, whereby the act would be repealed if everyone registered voluntarily. He faced severe criticism for the compromise and offered to be the first to register, but Smuts denied he had made any promises and Gandhi was arrested and assaulted on his way to the registration

10: Gandhi, 2002, p274.
11: Gandhi, 2002, p275.

office. It was from this point onwards that he began to break with the elitist and narrow interests of the business community.

A new £3 tax imposed on ex-indentured Indians led to a new campaign in 1913, beginning in Newcastle, Natal. Gandhi worked with Thambi Naidoo, leader of the Johannesburg based Tamil Benefit Society, to gain the support of both the working classes and the Newcastle merchants. A strike supported by railway workers and miners began in mid-October, and by the end of the month between 4,000 and 5,000 miners had downed their tools. Gandhi began leading strikers over the provincial border into Transvaal on 29 October 1913, but his attempt at courting mass arrests failed as Smuts, now the key man in the South African government, opted instead to wait. Most strikers were ready to return to work when a spontaneous strike in Natal altered the situation radically. Violent confrontation with the police resulted in several strikers being killed and injured but more protesters joined. By the end of November the produce markets of Durban and Pietermaritzburg were paralysed, sugar mills were closed and hotels, restaurants and homes were left without domestic workers. The coalfields were also affected and whole fields of sugar cane were burned. Reports of the arrest of Gandhi and police brutality caused uproar in India and the British government intervened to bring about an agreement with the strikers. Gandhi was released in order to negotiate with Smuts, resulting in the 1914 Indian Relief Bill. This scrapped the hated £3 tax and relaxed provisions preventing wives joining their husbands in South Africa. Restrictions on trade and movement from province to province for Indians remained but Gandhi was welcomed as a hero, the Mahatma, when he returned to India in 1915.

Back in India

The leaders of the major national political force, the Indian National Congress, were desperate for mass influence and even more for the colonial state to take them seriously. They hoped that some of Gandhi's magic would rub off on them. Gandhi was uncomfortable with this hero status, finding Indian nationalist politics to be extremely patrician, elitist and wedded to a constitutional approach. So he decided to tour the length and breadth of the country. Travelling third class on trains, stubborn in his refusal to take cars or *tongas* (light horse-drawn carriages), he walked everywhere, spoke Hindustani, though his native tongue was Gujarati, and even more importantly, discarded his Western suits for the simple *dhoti*. This paraphernalia came to symbolise the tiny figure as he toured India meeting peasants, and low caste and tribal communities in the scores of villages and hamlets that were home to India's masses. Gandhi, already 45 years old, had never before "seen" India and this experience was to have a deep and lasting impact on him

Indian Nationalism

The Indian National Congress that dominated the political scene had been established in 1885 as an association representing the interests of upper class Indian men to the state. It was the brainchild of two British civil servants in the Raj who felt that Indians had a right to expect some representation. It was a highly select, exclusive club, drawing in such notables as Gopal Krishna Gokhale, a Bombay leader and close associate of Gandhi, Dadabhai Naoroji, a Parsi intellectual and cotton trader who became a Liberal MP for Finsbury Central in 1892, and Romesh Chandra Dutt, an economic historian and writer from Calcutta. It also included Motilal Nehru, the father of India's first prime minister, Jawaharlal Nehru, and, initially, Muhammad Ali Jinnah, who was to become the first leader of Pakistan. Congress's goals and strategy were defined by the social milieu of the upper class, liberal minded would-be parliamentarians at its core. Initially the organisation did not demand independence, instead lobbying for consultation and representation.

The "moderate" wing of Congress was challenged by the "extremists" centred on the fiery nationalism of the Maharashtra based Brahmin Bal Gangadhar Tilak and the Bengali nationalist leader Aurobindo Ghose. They demanded outright independence and were prepared to use violence to achieve this. In spite of obvious differences in goals and tactics the common element in both wings of nationalism was their elitism and substitutionism. Congress leaders believed that the enlightened and educated, ie themselves, should speak for the masses; the colonial regime could placate them with vague talk of reform and future consultation. Those espousing an armed revolutionary assault saw change as coming from a dedicated minority brave enough to carry out a revolution on behalf of the majority. The might of the colonial state was able to marginalise and outmanoeuvre them through arrest, assassination and deportation. In both instances the absence of a mass movement was the fundamental weakness. It was Gandhi's intervention at this juncture that was decisive in shifting the goals and parameters of the freedom movement.

Gandhi and mass action

Gandhi's travels through India had made him acutely aware of the poverty and humiliations that afflicted the vast majority of Indians—the peasants. On 6 February 1916 he made a speech at the opening of the Benares Hindu

University lambasting the use of English at public meetings, deriding the Indian rich and princes for their lack of concern for the poor, and even seeming to condone the use of violence.[12] The next year he initiated campaigns based on mass action that would fundamentally change the character of the nationalist movement.

Gandhi visited the village of Champaran in the north eastern province of Bihar in April 1917. Here, as in many villages, peasants were at the mercy of ruthless, greedy plantation owners (mostly European) who forced cultivators to grow indigo on a portion of their land—a practice known as the *tinkathia* system. This insistence on cash crops as opposed to food crops resulted in poor diets and was compounded further by punitive taxes. The daily routine of peasant life was further blighted by poor sanitation, ignorance, stifling caste oppression and imposed purdah for women. Sporadic rebellions in 1914 were effectively crushed by militias working for landlords. Gandhi instituted a campaign of recording peasant grievances and drawing up a charge sheet against the plantation owners, effectively establishing his own court to plead on behalf of cultivators. He eventually got a commission of inquiry, on which he sat, which negotiated a settlement that abolished the century old *tinkathia* system and reduced the revenue paid to the planters by 20 to 25 percent. This seemed like a spectacular victory in the face of intransigent planters and the provincial government.

Word of this victory quickly spread as Gandhi's magic seemed vindicated on Indian soil. He led a *satyagraha* (non-violent protest) a year later in the Kheda district outside Ahmedabad for peasants who, in the grips of a desperate famine arising from crop failure, faced a demand from colonial officials that they pay not only full taxes but also a 23 percent increase. Peasants started a payment boycott under Gandhi's leadership. Some 3,000 signed a pledge not to pay the taxes and to conduct themselves as *satyagrahis* (non-violent protesters). The revolt was astounding in terms of discipline and unity. In spite of government provocation, and the seizure of property and cattle by hired thugs, the majority of peasants did not resist arrest or retaliate violently. After five months the provincial commissioner ordered a settlement forfeiting the government's right to collect taxes for one year. Again Gandhi appeared to be a "just" and effective taciticián, and a champion whose non-violent creed could be used effectively in an Indian setting.

As if to prove that *satyagraha* was not confined to rural cases, Gandhi had been asked to intervene in an industrial dispute on behalf of mill workers at a textile factory in Ahmedabad in March 1918 before going

12: Gandhi, 1965a, pp148-155.

to Kheda. Here workers demanded a 35 percent wage increase but the mill owner would only countenance 20 percent. Gandhi sanctioned a strike after the owners refused to go to arbitration but only on certain conditions: no violence, no intimidation of scabs, no begging and no yielding. At a mass meeting workers voted overwhelmingly to pledge themselves to these conditions. The employers imposed a lockout for two weeks and then said they would allow back to work those who accepted the initial 20 percent wage rise. A fortnight with no income and no prospect of one caused some workers to relent. Frustration blew up against strikebreakers but also against Gandhi: a striker commented bitterly that Gandhi and his associate Anasuyaben Sarabhai[13] "come and go in their car", "eat elegant food" and could not understand the agonies of the starving.[14] As violence threatened, Gandhi began his first political fast, stating, "I cannot tolerate for a minute that you break your pledge. I shall not take any food nor use a car till you get a 35 percent increase".[15] He broke his fast after three days when the strikers voted to continue their pledge and the mill owners agreed to go to arbitration, which led to the workers finally being awarded 35 percent. These three experiences came to epitomise Gandhi's tactics and propel him to national leadership. In each instance his version of peaceful "mass action" by ordinary people appeared to win the day.

Gandhi's first national test

In addition to Gandhi's tactics, objective circumstances played a significant role. The 1919 Government of India Act had introduced a limited system of Indian representation at provincial council level for agriculture, health and education. However, state governance was still dominated by British officials and there was no provision for home rule, let alone complete independence. Disappointment with government reforms was compounded by the introduction of the Rowlatt Act, which maintained wartime emergency powers to arrest and imprison people without trial for conspiracy, sedition and terrorism. It was used to suppress radical literature, and prevent newspapers from reporting items seen as incompatible with public order as well as prohibiting public assembly.

One of the most serious challenges took place in Amritsar. A protest outside the residence of the deputy commissioner demanded the release of two popular nationalist leaders, Satya Pal and Saifuddin Kitchlew. Military

13: She was the sister of Ambalal Sarabhai, Ahmedabad's leading mill owner.
14: Quoted in Rajmohan Gandhi, 2007, p199.
15: Gandhi, 1965b, p364.

police opened fire, killing several protesters. In response banks, the town hall and the railway station were attacked and set on fire, culminating in the deaths of at least five Europeans with repeated retaliatory firing on the crowd from the military killing a further eight people. The British government placed most of Punjab under martial law. On 13 April thousands of people gathered in the Jallianwala Bagh park. Brigadier Reginald Dyer marched a group of 90 British Indian Army soldiers into the park accompanied by two armoured cars carrying machine guns. He ordered the troops to open fire without warning and to direct fire towards the densest sections of the crowd. The firing continued until all the ammunition—approximately 1,400 rounds—was exhausted. Official records put the figures for those killed at 379 (337 men, 41 boys and a six week old baby) and those injured at 200, though the actual figure, likely much higher, is unknown to this day.

Popular outrage led Gandhi to launch his first national *satyagraha* on 1 August 1920, after the expiry notice that he had given the viceroy, asserting the right recognised "from time immemorial of the subject to refuse to assist a ruler who misrules". Gandhi's programme involved the surrender of titles and offices, resignation from posts on local bodies, a boycott of British courts, refusal to attend government functions, the use of *swadeshi* (Indian-made) cloth only, withdrawal of children from schools and colleges, and the establishment of national schools and colleges. Truth and non-violence were to be strictly observed by non-cooperators. The most successful item of the programme was the boycott of foreign cloth. The value of cloth imports fell from Rs 102 crore (1,020 million rupees) in 1920-1 to Rs 57 crore in 1921-2.

In July 1921 a new challenge was thrown to the government. The journalist and Muslim League activist Mohammad Ali was arrested along with other leaders for holding the view that it was "religiously unlawful for the Muslims to continue in the British army". Ali's campaign was part of the Khilafat movement, a protest at the British and French recognition of Kemal Attaturk's abolition of the caliphate based in Istanbul. Gandhi and Congress supported Mohammad Ali, so the non-cooperation movement brought together the "Sikh" wrong of Amritsar and the "Muslim" wrong of Khilafat with the three elements of *swaraj*, *ahimsa* and *swadeshi* (independence, non-violence and home-grown).

Gandhi's stature was so great that he had assumed the effective leadership of Congress, serving as its president from 1924 to 1929. The freedom struggle assumed an all-India character under his leadership and on 26 January 1930 Congress, led by Gandhi and Jawaharlal Nehru, publicly issued the Declaration of Independence which boldly declared, "India must sever the British connection and attain *Purna Swaraj* or complete independence".[16]

Gandhi used his mixture of nationalism and mass action in the civil disobedience movement from 1930 to 1934. This included the famous 1930 salt march when he walked 240 miles from Ahmedabad to the coastal town of Dandi with 78 male volunteers. The British had a monopoly on the collection and manufacture of salt, levying a tax that all had to pay. Upon arrival at Dandi, Gandhi issued a statement to the world's press saying that, although the government had not interfered with the march, "the wanton disregard shown by them to popular feeling and their high-handed action leave no room for doubt that the policy of heartless exploitation of India is to be persisted in at any cost". The only interpretation he could put on the non-interference in the march was that "the British Government, powerful though it is, is sensitive to world opinion" which would "not tolerate repression" of civil disobedience "so long as disobedience remains civil and therefore necessarily non-violent". He would now test whether the government would "tolerate the actual breach of the salt laws by countless people".[17]

The following day Gandhi picked up a lump of muddy salt and declared, "With this, I am shaking the foundations of the British Empire".[18] After boiling it in seawater to produce illegal salt he implored his followers to do likewise "wherever it is convenient".[19] The effect was dramatic. Mass civil disobedience spread throughout India as millions broke the salt laws by making salt or buying illegal salt. As protests spread they generalised to wider opposition to British rule. Unpopular forest laws were defied in Maharashtra, Karnataka and the Central Provinces. Gujarati peasants refused to pay tax in Midnapore and Bengal.[20] In Peshawar *satyagraha* was led by a Muslim Pashtoo disciple of Gandhi, Ghaffar Khan (known as the Frontier Gandhi), who had trained a 50,000-member army of non-violent activists.[21] On 23 April 1930 Khan was arrested. A crowd gathered in Peshawar's *Kissa Khawani* (storytellers) Bazaar. The British ordered troops to open fire with machine guns on the unarmed crowd, killing an estimated 200 to 250. The Pashtun *satyagrahis*, in accord with their non-violent training, willingly faced bullets as troops fired on them. One British Indian Army regiment

16: Quoted in Wolpert, 1999, p204.
17: Gandhi, 1994, pp238-239.
18: Gandhi, 1996, p72.
19: Gandhi, 1994, p240.
20: Habib, 1997, p57.
21: Habib, 1997, p55.

refused to fire and the entire platoon was arrested, many receiving heavy penalties, including life imprisonment.[22]

The British responded with more laws, including censorship of correspondence and declaring the Congress and its associate organisations illegal, and incarcerated over 60,000 people by the end of April. None of those measures slowed the movement as middle class women joined the ranks of civil disobedients manufacturing and selling salt throughout India. Usha Mehta, an early Gandhian activist, remarked, "Even our old aunts and great-aunts and grandmothers used to bring pitchers of salt water to their houses and manufacture illegal salt. And then they would shout at the top of their voices, 'We have broken the salt law!' ".[23]

The symbolism of salt was not lost on Gandhi. It was a basic necessity and the idea of an alien power taxing an indigenous product was too good an issue to pass up. He included the salt issue as part of his 11-point programme for this *satyagraha*, which also demanded a reduction of land revenue assessments, cutting military spending, and a tariff on foreign cloth. Gandhi planned a raid on the Dharasana Salt Works in his native Gujarat but was arrested and held without trial near Pune. The raid went ahead led by a 76 year old retired judge and Gandhi's wife, Kasturba. Both were arrested and sentenced to three months in prison. Sarojini Naidu, a woman poet and freedom fighter, took over and marched the protesters to the factory. As she insisted, "You will be beaten, but you must not resist: you must not even raise a hand to ward off blows," soldiers began clubbing protesters with steel tipped *lathis* (canes). The United Press correspondent Webb Miller reported:

> Not one of the marchers even raised an arm to fend off the blows. They went down like ten-pins. From where I stood I heard the sickening whacks of the clubs on unprotected skulls. The waiting crowd of watchers groaned and sucked in their breaths in sympathetic pain at every blow. Those struck down fell sprawling, unconscious or writhing in pain with fractured skulls or broken shoulders... The survivors without breaking ranks silently and doggedly marched on until struck down.[24]

The campaign seemed to work and civil disobedience continued until early 1931, when Gandhi was finally released from prison to hold talks with the viceroy, Lord Irwin.

22: Habib, 1997, p56.

23: Quoted in Hardiman, 2003, p113.

24: Miller's report from 21 May 1930, quoted in Martin, 2006, p38.

In every instance Gandhi initiated mass action and in every case this propelled the freedom movement forward as it became larger, broader and deepened as activists radicalised. This is how thousands of young people were drawn to Gandhi. As CLR James noted:

> That Gandhi has the rich and middle class Hindu with him is not surprising. But that the agricultural labourer in remote villages, the slum dwellers in the towns, should all be ready to face hardships, imprisonment, death; should understand and practise so successfully ideals as difficult as non-cooperation and non-violence, all this is something which to me is as miraculous as anything I have ever read.[25]

This is what marks his intervention as seminal in the inter-war years. But it was also the case that at each stage the momentum was ahead of Gandhi. As the movement grew more militant the weakness of his politics and limitations of his strategy became all too obvious. Just as he instigated and led from the front, he quickly backtracked and called a halt to activity when he felt it was veering off course. So he had called off non-cooperation in February 1922 after 22 policemen were burned alive when an angry crowd set fire to a police station in Chauri Chaura in the United Provinces in retaliation for the police shooting three unarmed protesters dead. Gandhi not only called an end to the movement but also fasted as a penance for the killings.

Similarly, he brought the magnificent momentum of the salt march and civil disobedience to an end in early 1931, when he was finally released from prison to hold talks with Lord Irwin. Though the British eventually agreed that individual families could procure salt for domestic purposes, the British offered no progress towards self-rule, no significant gains were made on the other points of Gandhi's 11-point programme and even the salt law remained in place. Within Congress Jawaharlal Nehru and Subhas Chandra Bose protested over the calling off of the movement but Gandhi, who was talking to the viceroy as an equal for the first time, firmly believed in a "peace with honour"—just as when he negotiated with Smuts in South Africa. Compromise was the hallmark of Gandhi's tactics. To make sense of this we have to examine the specifics and peculiarities of "Gandhian" philosophy.

Gandhi's ideas

Gandhi was influenced by a range of religious and political ideas, as we have seen. In 1908 he wrote *Hind Swaraj or Indian Home Rule*. Less than

25: James, 1931, p19.

100 pages long, it is cast in the form of a dialogue between Gandhi, who is "The Editor", and his interlocutor, "The Reader". Though Gandhi still had another 40 years to live, this document represents the closest thing to a personal manifesto penned by him. Despite its many ambiguities and contradictions, and notwithstanding historical controversy as to its reliability, it constitutes his thinking on a range of ideas that he would return to at various stages of his life. It also allows us to understand how Gandhi could command sufficient authority and popularity to catapult him to national prominence.

The most striking aspect of *Hind Swaraj* is how critical Gandhi is of Western style industrial development and his scathing observations on "modern civilisation" as the only path to progress. He chastises Britain as "a civilisation in name only". He castigates the trappings of modern capitalism with its factories and mines and believes the fate of workers "is worse than that of beasts" as they are "enslaved by temptation of the luxuries that money can buy". A "degraded and ruined" nation like Britain could rule India not because they had conquered it by physical and mental superiority or meat eating but because "we gave it to them. They are not in India because of their strength, but because we keep them". Again on modernisation he complained that railways, lawyers and doctors have impoverished the country, claiming "medicine to be a 'European' science designed to keep Indians enslaved through reliance on conventional drugs". He firmly believed that individuals became lawyers "not in order to help others out of their miseries, but to enrich themselves...they gladden when men have disputes". He was merciless towards those who believed that India should follow British style parliamentary representation, holding "the mother of all parliaments" to be "a sterile woman" comparing it to "a prostitute because it is under the control of ministers who change from time to time". He warns the national movement against "English rule without Englishman... you would make India English. And when it becomes English it will be called not Hindustan but Englishtan. This is not the *Swaraj* that I want".[26]

Swaraj should not be the mere replacement of British colonial rule for the rule of the brown *sahibs*. For Gandhi self-rule meant a complete mental and psychological break with existing society. This was the power of his analysis. He was labelled an "anarchist" by the British and Indians alike for his unorthodox views on modernisation and industry. But his opinions were not simple lunacy as some would have us believe. He had seen the ugly side of industrialisation, with people being harnessed to machines in London and South Africa. The squalor of Victorian cities, the slums of African townships

26: Gandhi, 1938, pp36, 38, 58-60, 55, 31, 30.

and the poverty that blighted urban life convinced Gandhi that industrial development could not be equated with progress. Drawn towards what he perceived as the simplicity and cohesion of rural life as it had been, he believed India's future lay in self-sufficient village communities. He preferred a society composed of rights and responsibilities, with individuals fulfilling their respective economic and social roles to the benefit of all, to avoid the social conflicts and tensions that marred advanced industrial societies. He gained a hearing precisely because of his ferocious attacks on Western society as devoid of meaning and substance, and his championing of an ancient India before the advent of Europe. This refusal to accept Europe as superior won Gandhi an audience and authority that other Congress leaders could not match.

Contradictions

Yet Gandhi's philosophy was imbued with paradoxes. He may have denounced modern conveniences but he made full use of the trappings of modern civilisation—for instance, press and media outlets were a constant feature of his campaigning, whether promoting his epic salt march of 1930 or the protests in South Africa. He was against industrialisation but he made alliances with Indian capitalists. His campaigns were made possible by drawing from the vast financial resources of the industrialist GD Birla. Birla has been described as a devotee of Gandhi but he benefited from the social and religious prestige which his association with Gandhi brought him. Additionally, Gandhi gave his blessing to Birla's abundant wealth with his teaching on trusteeship, asserting the right of the rich to accumulate and maintain wealth as long as it was used to benefit society.

His championing of an ancient Indian civilisation, though a necessary corrective to British imperial arrogance, has all the hallmarks of invention and imagining a pre-capitalist community without recognising class as a central dynamic of society. Elevating "spiritualism" over "materialism" leads to an "exaltation of purely spiritual values, etc, to passivity, to non-resistance, and to cooperation—but in reality, it is a debilitating and diluted form of resistance, the mattress against the bullet".[27]

His attitude to the masses was contradictory. He would champion peasants' demands and organise them on condition that they remained peaceful, respectful of landowners and obedient to Gandhi's tactics. If they had the temerity to demand the confiscation of private property, they were deemed to be ungrateful, unruly and unworthy. The orientation on simple farming and an apparent "equilibrium" of peasant life

27: Gramsci, 2007, p61.

underestimated the degree of social and economic exploitation inherent in rural communities.

Similarly, with workers and employers Gandhi's tactics had all the hallmarks of compromise and conciliation. The notion of trusteeship was used to dissipate workers' anger and prevent them from fighting as workers. The emphasis was on rights but also responsibilities. So although Gandhi could claim, "What the two hands of the labourer could achieve, the capitalist would never get with all his gold and silver", he could also insist that "capitalists are amenable to conversion".[28] Gandhi was enormously suspicious of socialists for their atheism and but also because he held communism to be "evil" and "unnatural" because it demanded abolition of private property. He once stated, "I can no more tolerate the yoke of Bolshevism than of capitalism."

It is for this reason that the British Indian Marxist Palme Dutt referred to Gandhi as the "mascot of the bourgeoisie" and the founder of the Communist Party of India, Manabendra Nath Roy, held Gandhism to be the most important ideology of class collaboration within the nationalist movement. In describing the movement's contradictions Roy argued, "One need not be a sentimental humanitarian, nor a religious fanatic in order to denounce the present order of society in the countries where capitalism rules." Roy understood that Gandhi identified the "latent discontent" of the masses but did not want it to "burst out in fatal physical revolt or revolution... This was the true inwardness of his campaign".[29]

The Indian left understood that pacifism and compromise were inadequate but was unable to offer a sustained pole of attraction to rival Gandhi's mass action. In the 1930s Communists worked with Socialists inside Congress and their activists enjoyed influence in the textile mills of Bombay and among some workers, students and intellectuals, and peasant unions across north India, Bengal and Kerala. However, they faced problems. For one thing, many leaders came from privileged urban English speaking backgrounds. This is not a problem in itself, but Gandhi had the capacity to articulate the concerns, albeit in convoluted, moral sentiments, of the ordinary Indian. To be fair to the Communists, for most of the 1920s and 1930s they were a proscribed organisation with many cadres in jail. The best opportunity for the left came in 1937 when Nehru launched a mass contact campaign to appeal to Hindus and Muslims in the United Provinces as workers and peasants. Leading Communists took the initiative in this as they organised meetings,

---

28: Tendulkar, 1960, pp33, 159.

29: Quoted in Chakrabarty, 2006, pp88-89.

published leaflets and distributed newspapers in Urdu and Hindi. Gandhi had withdrawn from national politics in the late 1930s, and both Congress and the Muslim League were obsessed with parliamentary elections. The embryonic movement presented a small window of opportunity to put forward an alternative type of mass activity based on a grassroots approach to mass mobilisation basing itself on workers and peasants.

Tragically, the campaign was wound up after a few months due to pressure from the right wing of Congress, reflecting the hostility of middle caste and middle class Hindu interests. This section was totally opposed to any initiative that paid special attention to Muslims. Nehru was not prepared to challenge this right wing, fearing his own lack of authority and social weight inside Congress. And the Communist Party was not prepared to break from Nehru and challenge his "top-down" style of politics. Tied to the Comintern (the Communist International that was now dominated by Stalinism), which at this point was pushing for the formation of broad "popular fronts", the Communists were incapable of launching a viable political alternative. The same political problems applied in the Quit India movement, where the Communist Party refused to support the insurgency, and again after the war when, under Stalin's guidance, the party supported the notion of distinct nationalities in India, providing a left gloss for Jinnah's view of a two-nation theory with separate Hindu and Muslim states.

The paradoxes and inconsistencies are sharper when we consider Gandhi's attitudes towards women, untouchables and Hindu-Muslim unity. Gandhi was mercilessly hostile to discrimination and oppression of any group. He castigated men for their repression of women:

> Of all the evils for which man has made himself responsible, none is so degrading, so shocking or so brutal as his abuse of the better half of humanity—to me, the female sex, not the weaker sex. It is the nobler of the two, for it is even today the embodiment of sacrifice, silent suffering, humility, faith and knowledge.[30]

He attacked the commodification of women and insisted that "wives should not be dolls and objects of indulgence", and he appealed to the men in Congress to "see that women became equal partners in the fight for *swaraj*".[31] He opposed child marriage and championed the rights of widows to control their own fate. Compared to most of his contemporaries these statements

30: Gandhi, 1967a, p225.
31: Gandhi, 1992, pp363-364.

were a positive endorsement of women's liberation. His campaigns provided space for women to be visibly active and engaged in the fight for freedom.

However, the role that Gandhi assigned for women was as "a true helpmate of man in the mission of service".[32] Service is the operative word. For Gandhi women symbolised the "honour" and "virtue" of the nation. He believed that men and women possessed distinct qualities as a result of biology. Men were naturally aggressive and selfish, and women were passive, self-sacrificing and pure. So women were more suited to the domestic sphere, particularly family life and motherhood. His models for women lay in the Hindu goddesses Sita and Draupadi, who epitomised courage and strength but also service to the community. In the non-cooperation and civil disobedience movements women's activity was primarily confined to picketing wine shops and boycotting foreign cloth. And at major protests women were to nurse the male *stayagrahis* when they were struck down by police charges. He had nothing but contempt for the tactics of suffragettes in Britian, not only for the use of violence but because their activity entailed the questioning of traditional roles and the demand for complete equality. Gandhi's views were embedded in a deep social conservatism that was underpinned by self-righteousness. He was not so much concerned with changing the material conditions for women's emancipation as their "moral" condition.

Hindu-Muslim unity was the crux of Gandhi's whole national project. His own religiosity meant that he held all faiths to be equal, stating that they were different paths to the one god and salvation. But he was acutely conscious of the fact that Muslims were a minority, whose grievances and discrimination had to be addressed. His championing of the Khilafat movement was crucial to aiding Hindu-Muslim unity and forcing the nationalist movement to politically identify with a "Muslim" cause. On partition and to those who espoused the removal of Muslims from India Gandhi retorted, "Death for me would be a glorious deliverance rather than that I should be a helpless witness of the destruction of India, Hinduism, Sikhism, and Islam".[33]

Every fibre of Gandhi's body spoke Hindu-Muslim unity but some of his pronouncements and actions caused anxiety in Muslim communities. So Gandhi could hold killing cows to be "sinful", declaring, "When I see a cow, it is not an animal to eat; it is a poem of pity for me and I worship it and I shall defend its worship against the whole world".[34] Statements such as this only provided succour to Hindu chauvinists for whom cow slaughter

---

32: Gandhi, 1992, pp363-364.

33: Gandhi, 1992, pp408-409.

34: Gandhi, 1967b, p459.

was (and continues to be) a stick with which to beat Muslims. In spite of Gandhi's personal convictions he presented himself first and foremost as a "Hindu" figure. And, as if to underscore this ambiguity, he argued in relation to Muslims:

> I find no parallel in history for a body of converts and their descendants claiming to be a nation apart from their parent stock. If India was one nation before the advent of Islam, it must remain one in spite of the change of faith of a very large body of her children.[35]

This did not enhance his claim to represent all Indians. It provided the Muslim League with further ammunition to claim to be the sole leadership of India's Muslims and spurred on Hindu extremists in their fervour to "Hinduise" India.

As a caste Hindu, Gandhi was a defender of the caste system. But by the late 1920s he was adamantly opposed to caste discrimination and the mistreatment of untouchables at the hands of caste Hindus. He held untouchability to be a "rotten part or an excrescence", "no integral part of Hinduism",[36] and a "blight" that had to be eradicated. Gandhi led a campaign for dalit[37] rights in the 1930s, undertaking a nine-month tour of some 12,500 miles in 1933, campaigning for the opening up of wells, temples and roads to dalits. He carried a begging bowl to raise money and cleaned latrines with *bhangis*, the lowest untouchable category. For a short time this appeared to have a remarkable impact. In cities, small towns and rural areas Brahmin Hindus were observed embracing untouchables on street corners, allowing them access to restricted wells and talking up the Gandhi mantra that untouchables were *harijans* (children of god). But Gandhi also encountered much resistance from orthodox caste Hindus. They disrupted his meetings and in June 1933 a bomb was thrown at him in Pune.

However, his treatment of untouchables was not without ambiguity. The term he gave for untouchables, *harijan*, was patronising. His temple entry bill only called for the lifting of restrictions formalised under colonial rule, not for the enforcement of entry. His campaign called for untouchables to go around the temple and not into it, and he admonished them for their lack of hygiene, poor sanitation and the "impure" habits of meat eating and drinking alcohol. As with other issues, Gandhi's concern was with moral

35: Gandhi, 1979, p101.

36: Tendulkar, 1960, p183.

37: This is the political term used by untouchables to describe themselves.

indignation and limited social reform without connecting this to any systematic analysis of the structures of power and class. So opposing untouchability did not mean advocating the abolition of caste. Gandhi wanted caste Hindus to acknowledge untouchables and accept them into the wider fold of Hinduism. This is why he clashed with Ambedkar, the great dalit leader of the 1930s. Ambedkar campaigned for separate electorates for untouchables and persuaded the British to agree to this after 1931. Gandhi saw this as "the vivisection" of the Hindu community and he embarked upon a fast unto death to have it revoked, forcing Ambedkar to buckle under the weight of emotional and political blackmail after just three hours of the fast. As with many forms of social inequality Gandhi held the caste system to be a productive and harmonious means of social organisation—not because he wished to propagate inequality but because he was not a revolutionary. His Hinduism emphasised the "equality" of souls and an organic social order whereby every individual had a role to fulfil.

Gandhi's ambiguities were at the core of his appeal, his relative successes and his limitations. His ideas had the power and capacity to lead mass action that elite groups—whether national constitutionalists or terrorists—did not. As such he was able to advance the freedom movement and bring into its orbit several constituents that established leaders were impervious to. But the movement also corresponded to the interests of the Indian bourgeoisie and middle classes, who were drawn to Gandhi's message of opposition to colonialism, and of self-reliance, social reform and class collaboration. This ensured that political activity would be firmly within the limits of non-violence and also remain non-revolutionary.

Gandhi's tragedy

The tragic consequences of this were shown at three decisive moments towards the end of Gandhi's life. Firstly, there was the Quit India movement in 1942 when, in spite of himself, he called mass action that went beyond his control. Gandhi introduced the Quit India resolution at the All-India Congress Committee held in Bombay on 8 August 1942, stipulating, "Every Indian who desires freedom and strives for it must be his own guide urging him all along the hard road where there is no resting place and which leads ultimately to the independence and deliverance of India".[38]

In addition he uttered the famous mantra, *karenge ya marenge* (Do or die). This was taken as a marked departure from his pacifist teachings. The next day the entire Congress leadership was arrested. The spirit of the Free

38: Quoted in *Modern Review*, September 1942 (Calcutta), pp197-198.

India movement was Gandhian but its tactics went far beyond that framework. Lord Linlithgow, the viceroy, described what followed as by far the most serious rebellion since the 1857 mutiny.[39]

For the month of August some areas of north India were virtually under parallel governments as a younger generation of activists took the lead and unleashed protests and strikes, which cut off essential supplies, and sabotaged administration buildings. Some 208 police outposts, 332 railway stations and 945 post offices were destroyed or damaged and there were 664 bomb explosions. State repression was quick and brutal. Over 90,000 people had been arrested by the end of 1943, free use was made of public floggings and of torture such as pushing rulers up the rectums of captured protesters, with Linlithgow ordering aerial bombing of crowds disrupting communication networks in Patna Bihar. Resistance had been quelled by the middle of 1944. From the Aga Khan jail, his place of detention, Gandhi issued a call to end the disruption and asked leaders to stop the sabotage and protests. Along with arrests this further dissipated the movement. A further twist to this tragedy was that the Communist Party refused to endorse the Quit India resolution and supported the British war effort in line with Stalin's policy of "people's war", leaving the largest left force completely disarmed and impotent during the protests. In fact in areas where the party had a base its members actively worked to defuse strikes, demonstrations and walkouts. This meant that the bourgeois leaderships of Congress and the Muslim League could emerge intact and strengthened after the war.

The second decisive moment came straight after the war ended. Britain emerged from the war a considerably weakened power. This, along with the successive waves of mass action that had taken place, severely diminished its resolve to hold on to its empire. The push for independence was irresistible. In November 1945 the weakened but vindictive imperial power placed three soldiers of the Indian National Army (INA) that had fought alongside Japan in Burma on trial: a Muslim, a Hindu and a Sikh. Nehru was part of their defence counsel. They were found guilty of "waging war against the emperor" and sentenced to transportation for life. Popular outcry forced the British to accede to demands for their release as national heroes. This galvanised nationalist feeling and on 18 February 1946 Indian sailors of the Royal Indian Navy on board ship and in shore establishments in Bombay struck and then mutinied. From here the mutiny spread throughout British India, from Karachi to Calcutta and Madras with the slogans "Strike for Bombay", "Release 11,000 INA prisoners" and "*Jai*

39: Quoted in Ghosh, 1995.

Hind" (Long live India). It came to involve 78 ships, 20 shore establishments and 20,000 sailors, uniting Hindus and Muslims whose grievances entailed poor food rations, lack of career advancement but also racism at the hands of navy personnel.

Such was the feeling that even the Gurkhas in Karachi refused to fire on striking sailors. The mutineers hoisted the flags of the Congress, Muslim League and Communist Party onto their ships in a symbolic display of national unity. Tragically, Gandhi condemned the mutiny, criticising the strikers for mutinying without the call of a "prepared revolutionary party" and without the "guidance and intervention" of "political leaders of their choice".[40] He further criticised a local Congress leader, one of the few prominent political leaders of the time to offer her support for the mutineers, who had stated she would rather unite Hindus and Muslims on the barricades than on the constitutional front. And in spite of his reservations about constitutional methods earlier, Gandhi betrayed his true views on the mutiny by declaring, "If the union at the barricade is honest then there must be union also at the constitutional front".[41]

The leaders of Congress and the Muslim League also refused to back the mutineers and effectively sabotaged the strike by sending their representatives to broker an agreement. Not only was the mutiny called off but none of its demands were met and, to add insult to injury, none of the dismissed mutineers were ever admitted into the Indian or Pakistani navies after independence. The shortcomings of Gandhi's mass action and his version of nationalism, based as it was on an appeal to the religiosity of individuals, were woefully inadequate when tested at a crucial juncture. The magnificent unity on display during the mutiny was not to be nurtured by national leaders vying for territory and power in the run-up to the final transfer of power as August 1947 approached.

Gandhi's final tragedy was his complete inability to prevent the partition of India and the communal frenzy that accompanied it. He travelled to Noakali in Bengal to see the horror of hundreds and thousands of dead Muslims and Hindus following the Muslim Day of Action in August 1946. When partition was announced Gandhi stayed away from the "celebrations" of national independence, stating, "Let posterity know Gandhi was not party to the vivisection of India." In September 1947 he went to Calcutta and stayed in the home of a Muslim, in the face of arch opposition by Hindu extremists. Here he began a fast unto death to stop the

---

40: Chandra and others, 1989, p485.

41: Chandra and others, 1989, p486.

communal killing that followed the division of Bengal. After five days, with Gandhi a stone and half lighter, all violence stopped. Gandhi was able to use his stature, but also his fragility and the emotional toll of partition to bring a halt to the killing for a short while. But he had not been able to stop the tragedy of partition. To achieve that would have required the vision and strategy employed by the naval mutineers to redirect politics in a class direction. The biggest irony of Gandhi's life was perhaps that partition and independence gave birth to a capitalist state like any other, or in fact two states, with the capitalist features he detested—immense poverty and obscene wealth, wars and nuclear weapons.

Conclusion

If one reads Gandhi as a waif-like figure wandering around India in a loincloth with a staff, it does seem remarkable that he could bring the might of the British Empire to its knees. If, however, we remember that Gandhi was a British trained barrister, with ample experience of political activity, accustomed to bargaining, what emerges is a figure who was shrewd, calculating and extremely clever.

This does not mean he was insincere. Far from it. Gandhi was totally committed to a united, independent India. He wanted an end to the callous treatment meted out to dalits and low caste groups. He wanted women to be treated with respect, free to marry or not and to have financial independence, and he desperately wanted Hindu-Muslim unity to be the defining feature of a composite Indian nationhood. However, he was a reformer, not a revolutionary. This was a reformism rooted in social conservatism that did not seek the overthrow of capitalism but its taming. In this sense the enigma of Gandhi is not so perplexing or extraordinary. In relation to conservative, elite social forces Gandhi did offer a programme of mass action and political activity that drew in wider layers of activists. But in relation to achieving the world of social harmony without inequality that he aspired to, his strategy proved sorely lacking in failing to understand how to direct the mass action he helped to initiate.

References

Chakrabarty, Bidyut, 2006, *Social and Political Thought of Mahatma Gandhi* (Routledge).

Chandra, Bipan, and others, 1989, *India's Struggle for Independence, 1857-1947* (Penguin).

Gandhi, Mohandas Karamchand, 1938, *Hind Swaraj or Indian Home Rule* (Navajivan Trust).

Gandhi, Mohandas Karamchand, 1958, *Collected Works of Mahatma Gandhi*, volume 1 (Ministry of Information and Broadcasting, India), www.gandhiserve.org/cwmg/VOL001.PDF

Gandhi, Mohandas Karamchand, 1965a, *Collected Works of Mahatma Gandhi*, volume 15 (Ministry of Information and Broadcasting, India), www.gandhiserve.org/cwmg/VOL015.PDF

Gandhi, Mohandas Karamchand, 1965b, *Collected Works of Mahatma Gandhi*, volume 16 (Ministry of Information and Broadcasting, India), www.gandhiserve.org/cwmg/VOL016.PDF

Gandhi, Mohandas Karamchand, 1967a, *Collected Works of Mahatma Gandhi*, volume 24 (Ministry of Information and Broadcasting, India), www.gandhiserve.org/cwmg/VOL024.PDF

Gandhi, Mohandas Karamchand, 1967b, *Collected Works of Mahatma Gandhi*, volume 25 (Ministry of Information and Broadcasting, India), www.gandhiserve.org/cwmg/VOL025.PDF

Gandhi, Mohandas Karamchand, 1979, *Collected Works of Mahatma Gandhi*, volume 77 (Ministry of Information and Broadcasting, India), www.gandhiserve.org/cwmg/VOL077.PDF

Gandhi, Mohandas Karamchand, 1980, *Collected Works of Mahatma Gandhi*, volume 81 (Ministry of Information and Broadcasting, India), www.gandhiserve.org/cwmg/VOL081.PDF

Gandhi, Mohandas Karamchand, 1992, *Collected Works of Mahatma Gandhi*, volume 90 (Ministry of Information and Broadcasting, India), www.gandhiserve.org/cwmg/VOL090.PDF

Gandhi, Mohandas Karamchand, 1994, *The Gandhi Reader: A Sourcebook of His Life and Writings* (Grove).

Gandhi, Mohandas Karamchand, 1996, *Selected Political Writings* (Hackett).

Gandhi, Mohandas Karamchand, 2002, *An Autobiography or the Story of My Experiments with Truth* (Navijan Trust), www.forget-me.net/en/Gandhi/autobiography.pdf

Gandhi, Rajmohan, 2007, *Gandhi: The Man, his People and the Empire* (Haus).

Ghosh, Suniti Kumar, 1995, *India and the Raj 1919-1947*, volume 2 (Research Unit for Political Economy, Bombay).

Gilbert, Martin, 1976, *Winston Churchill*, volume 5 (Heinemann).

Gramsci, Antonio, 2007, *Prison Notebooks*, volume 3 (Columbia University).

Habib, Irfan, 1997, "Civil Disobedience 1930-31", *Social Scientist*, volume 25, numbers 9–10.

Hardiman, David, 2003, *Gandhi in His Time and Ours: The Global Legacy of His Ideas* (Columbia University).

Huttenback, Robert, 1971, *Gandhi in South Africa: British Imperialism and the Indian Question, 1860-1914* (Cornell University).

James, CLR. 1931, "Review of *Gandhi: His Own Story*", *The Beacon*, volume 1, number 5 (August 1931).

Martin, Brian, 2006, *Justice Ignited* (Rowman & Littlefield).

Nehru, Jawaharlal, 1987, *Selected Works* (New Delhi).

Tendulkar, Dinanath Gopal, 1960, *Mahatma: Life of Mohandas Karamchand Gandhi* (New Delhi).

Wolpert, Stanley, 1999, *India* (University of California).

Capitalism, class, health and medicine

Mike Haynes

Over the past 30 years—during all the time we have been told that class is dead—something strange has been happening in the study of health. A generation of epidemiologists who study patterns of death (mortality) and illnesses (morbidity) have been obsessing about social inequality. Journals such as the *Lancet* and the *British Medical Journal* have published pieces presenting the latest research that talks about the most basic inequalities and social structures. The concern has been to map the link between health and inequality in a descriptive sense: to show that those with a higher social situation suffer less ill health than those with a lower one.

Stand outside any doctor's surgery and you will see people carried there by inequalities. Their illnesses, major and minor, physical and mental, are markers of where they stand in society. When it comes to ill health, less is always more—the less your situation, the more likely you are to have a health problem. It is a short step from here to pointing to the use of class as an explanatory category: your class position causes you to be more or less sick, to live more or less long. And from here it is only another short step, though one more establishment researchers are understandably loath to take, to argue that, since capitalism is at the root of class society, it is capitalism that makes you more or less ill. If health problems are the product of social organisation, and if we want to really address them, we have to focus on the social conditions and social organisation that give rise to them. As Sir Michael Marmot, the leading epidemiologist in the UK puts it,

"Inequalities in health between and within countries are avoidable".[1]

Premature death arises from three sources: infectious or communicable diseases such as typhus, typhoid, smallpox, cholera, Aids, etc; non-communicable diseases such as heart disease, cancer, nutritional diseases; and violence. In the past infectious diseases played a much larger part than they do today. It is not that non-communicable diseases did not exist but that infectious diseases carried people off first. The shift towards a predominance of death from non-communicable diseases (and violence) is called the "epidemiological transition". Infectious diseases have not gone away. In poorer parts of the world such diseases continue to play a crucial role—Aids is one example, alongside diseases of poverty that flow from dirty water, inadequate sanitation and the like. But only in Africa is infectious disease still the major cause of premature death: "Of the 45 million deaths among adults age 15 years and older in 2002, 32 million were due to non-communicable disease and a further 4.5 million to violent causes".[2]

Not every disease and cause of death shows a clear socio-economic pattern but the most common diseases and causes of death do. Death does not strike randomly. There has always been a general understanding of this. What is different now is the focus on the systematic process of causation and the need to connect up different elements of an explanation of health and ill health, to seek out what has been called "the cause of the cause". It is this that takes us to the problem of social class and health, and to a view of capitalism as a toxic form of human society.

The way that health is closely moulded by inequality and unequal power and control was set out in 1980 in the UK in *The Black Report.* Originally sponsored by the 1970s Labour government it was politically sidelined by the first Thatcher government.[3] The opponents of the social approach to health then tried to explain away the evidence of the link between health and inequality. They attacked the reliability of the data, focusing on what is called the "health selection effect". Causation might run not from society to health but from health to society. For example, as unemployment rises we know that the unemployed will register more illness than the employed. So does unemployment make you sick or does being sick mean that you are more likely to be unemployed? The attempts to focus on health selection, however, have failed. In most instances the causation *does* flow from society to health: "There is no evidence to support health selection as an explanation

1: Marmot, 2005, p1103.
2: Marmot, 2005, pp1100, 1101.
3: Townsend and Davidson, 1982.

of broader social inequalities in health," wrote Marmot in 1994 and the evidence against the health selection hypothesis has grown.[4]

In 2003 the World Health Organisation published the second edition of a document edited by Marmot and Richard Wilkinson called, *The Solid Facts*.[5] This attempted to quash such arguments and finally establish that there is a strong "social gradient" of health and ill health. Social conditions mould people's early lives, their work and leisure, their patterns of consumption, friendship groups, etc, and this can then explain, at the group level, patterns of disease and death to quite an astonishing degree. Wilkinson and Kate Pickett reiterate this same argument in a recent book, *The Spirit Level*. In rich societies, as the level of inequality rises, so average life expectancy falls and the rates of physical and mental illness rise. Inequality can also help predict levels of obesity, teenage pregnancy, illiteracy, crime, murder, people in prison, happiness—the connections seem almost endless.[6] Greater inequality produces a situation where the same health risks produce different outcomes depending on who you are. Take a group of senior civil servants who smoke and compare them with a lower grade group who also smoke. Which will have the higher death rate? This is the type of question asked in the "Whitehall Studies", led by Marmot, which tracked ill health among civil servants in the UK for many years and whose results have inspired countless other studies. Here is the answer in Marmot's words:

> An administrator who smokes 20 cigarettes a day has a lower risk of dying from lung cancer than does a lower grade civil servant who smokes the same amount even after pack years (packs per years times the number of years the person has smoked), tar content and the gradient in mortality from coronary heart diseases among non-smokers are taken into account.[7]

To see how this happens we need to go on a journey into the relationship between class, capitalism, health and medicine.

Class society and the health issue

Humans have not always lived in class societies. For tens of thousands of years our ancestors lived in small mobile groups, which survived by gathering and

4: Marmot, 1994, 2003. If causation flowed the other way it would not make "selection" acceptable—merely the process of ill health different. And there is now considerable evidence to show that poor health results from an accumulation of disadvantage that begins in the womb.

5: Marmot and Wilkinson, 2003.

6: Wilkinson and Pickett, 2009.

7: Marmot, 1994.

hunting. We know little about how these groups functioned save that their lifestyles were based on a basic equality and a communal reciprocity which leads to them being called "primitive communist". For some commentators the result was lives that were nasty, brutish and short. Infanticide, for instance, was practised to make sure that supplies were sufficient to feed the number of mouths. Others suggest that life was more comfortable and that social deprivation was limited—there was a greater degree of ease than we can easily imagine, even a kind of primitive "affluence" in the satisfaction of basic wants and the absence of modern style artificially constructed needs.

What is more important from our point of view is that, once settled human societies begin to emerge from 10,000 BC to 6,000 BC, class organisation also developed with them. The ruling groups seized control of the social surplus, consuming more of it and also organising society to perpetuate their rule and their control. The paradox of the development of class society is that, although in the long run it develops the material wealth of society, it does so in such a way that the benefits go disproportionately to the few. This led to inequality being marked not only in differing life expectancies but in the degree to which lives are marked by disease.

To make sense of this we need some basic demographic concepts. *Infant mortality* refers to deaths under the age of one, *child mortality* to deaths under the age of five and *adult mortality* to deaths over the age of 15. The fourth crucial concept is *life expectancy*. This is usually measured from birth. It is an average of the length of time those born live, so if life expectancy is low this does not necessarily mean that there are no old people. Rather life expectancy will be pulled down if large numbers die in the first years of life.

With the development of class society new social forces emerged which moulded the patterns of life and death. Access to material resources now became unequal, along the lines of the class nature of society. This was true of normal times but it was even more true in years of famine. The regularity of famine reflected the interaction between nature and the economic and social systems, and the way that these determined the nature of agricultural production. Malnourishment was extensive. You could often determine a person's place in society by how they looked physically. As Wilkinson puts it, "The rich were fat and the poor were thin".[8]

The concentration of population in urban centres, albeit on a scale incomparably smaller than today, created a new vulnerability to infectious disease agents. In the towns not only were social conditions often bad, but also the water supply was polluted, sanitation systems were primitive and the

8: Wilkinson, 1994.

air foul. The result was epidemic diseases such as typhus, typhoid, smallpox and endemic diseases (there all the time) such as tuberculosis. And every so often there was a good chance of pandemic diseases such as plague.

In these settled societies violence now became more organised, whether it was the violence within societies or the violence between societies. War became a regular feature of social development and in its wake came not only death and destruction on the battlefield but social immiseration in the areas through which armies marched and fought.[9]

With low productivity and diseases rife, population grew slowly for thousands of years, as is apparent in table 1.

Table 1: World population and percentage urban share

Source: www.census.gov/ipc/www/worldhis.html early urban estimates Kingsley Davis, UN World Urbanisation Prospects. The 2005 Revision; The 2007 Revision.

	Population (billions)	**Percentage urban**
10,000 BC	0.005	-
1,000 BC	0.050	-
1 AD	0.285	1
1000	0.300	1
1500	0.500	1-2
1800	0.978	2.4
1900	1.69	13
1950	2.52	29
1975	4.07	37.2
2000	6.09	46.7
2030	8.01	57.5
2050	9.19	69.6

The key issue here was the combination of material deprivation, infectious diseases and weakened bodily resistance. The social effects of this were uneven. The rich who ate better could hope to live better. "Countries in which access to nutritious food varies by social class for whatever reasons tend to show class gradients in height and health status," write two modern researchers.[10] But the rich could not escape from the patterns of infectious disease. In an urban environment epidemic diseases easily jumped from a

9: Haynes, 2008.

10: Frank and Mustard, 1994.

poor house to a richer one, and both houses might draw on the same water supplies or buy food in the same markets. In 1694 Queen Mary died of smallpox, one of a long line of European monarchs to go this way. Almost 170 years later, in 1861, Prince Albert, the husband of Queen Victoria, was carried off by typhoid. Similarly, lack of knowledge of how to deal with the complications of childbirth could kill rich women as easily as it could poor and in the early weeks all babies were vulnerable.

This helps to explain the fact that, although lifestyles differed considerably between classes, when it comes to measuring mortality rates the class differences were less than might be imagined.

Capitalism

In Western Europe capitalism began to emerge from feudalism in the 16th century, and as it did so it began to change the pattern of disease. But the really dramatic shifts came with the industrial revolution and the development of industrial capitalism at the turn of the 19th century. Technological change and increased production created a larger surplus, which allowed societies to begin the "demographic transition". They shifted from a pattern of high birth rates and high death rates to low birth rates and low death rates. In this transition, however, the death rate initially fell faster than the birth rate. The result was that rapid population growth occurred before a new balance was reached. Table 1 shows how world population has grown and its projected new equilibrium at around nine to ten billion (despite the fears of Thomas Malthus who believed that population growth would outrun the food supply).

In the first instance urban and industrial growth intensified health and mortality problems, not least in the big cities. Britain led the way, becoming in 1851 the first urban state with more than half its population in towns. Others followed in the 20th century. Today on a global scale half the world's population is now urban, as can also be seen from table 1.

Over time the falling death rate led to an increase in life expectancy. This fall in the death rate is commonly thought to have been bound up with medical advance but this was *not* the case. Some specific diseases like smallpox were reduced because of medical advance, but until the mid-20th century medical knowledge was so slight (and often mistaken) that it had a limited impact on population growth. Critics like the early 18th century essayist Joseph Addison could comment that "we may lay it down as a maxim, that when a nation abounds of physicians, it grows thin of people".[11]

There are four genuine causes of the improvement in life expectancy.

11: Shorter, 2006, p109; Wootton, 2006.

The first was the increase in the standard of living. Where this occurred better nutrition led to healthier bodies. Height and weight grew, and so did resistance to disease. The second, closely related, was the possibility of better standards of public hygiene. The third was the improvements in public health that came with the development of clean water systems, sewage systems and measures to deal with pollution. It should never be forgotten that one of the greatest killers of infants throughout history is dehydration brought on by diarrhoea. In 19th century England, for example, diarrhoea is reckoned to have killed as many infants every two years as all the 19th century cholera outbreaks put together.[12] Today diarrhoea is still estimated to be the second biggest killer of children worldwide, overwhelmingly in poor countries. The fourth factor worth noting is that some diseases may have mutated into less virulent strains.

These four elements help to explain the ways in which infectious diseases eventually came to be contained by rich countries. The result has been the shift to a pattern of ill health and death from non-communicable diseases to the so-called "diseases of affluence", except that these now began to fall disproportionately on the lower classes in wealthier societies. Capitalism's potential to solve humanity's problems is not and cannot be realised because of the ways in which the system also traps us into putting human need second to profit and competition. To see this we have only to look at the patterns of mortality that exist in the world today.

The first thing to note is the huge gaps in life expectancy that still exist between countries. In 2004 life expectancy in Japan was 82 years; in Sierra Leone it was only 34. This is not because there is a lack of food and other basics. The world today produces more than enough to go round. For decades now global food supplies have risen ahead of population growth. In 1961 there were 2255 calories available per head of world population. By 2000 the figure was 2,805, a 25 percent increase despite the huge growth in numbers.[13] The resources exist then to create the basis for a healthy life for everyone—the problem is that they are not used this way. In this situation the most vulnerable continue to be the youngest. Infant mortality in Sierra Leone is 316 per 1,000 live births, whereas in countries like Japan and Finland it is only 4.5 per 1,000.

The second element is the size of the differentials in mortality that exist within countries and the fact that, despite improvements in health, such gaps have been widening in key countries. This is not least the case in the

12: Wootton, 2006.

13: Fogel, 2004. There was an 11 percent increase in calories per head in the developed world and a 39 percent in the developing world in this period.

UK and the US. These gaps can be measured in the pattern of infant and child mortality, adult deaths and life expectancy. To illustrate this table 2 shows life expectancy gaps in the UK using the official social classification.

Table 2: Changing male life expectancy at birth in the UK
Source: ONS, news release, "Variations Persist in Life Expectancy by Social Class", 27 October 2007.

	1972-6	1987-91	2002-5
Professional	71.9	76.2	80.0
Managerial	71.9	75.0	79.4
Skilled non-manual	69.5	74.4	78.4
Skilled manual	70.0	72.7	76.5
Semi-skilled	68.3	70.8	75.7
Unskilled	66.5	66.7	73.8

There is good reason to think that per capita income (in today's values) of around $10,000 is sufficient to solve the material problems underpinning health inequality. At this level there is enough go around and enough to provide the resources for adequate public health. What separates societies, therefore, is less the per capita income over this level (in the UK/US case we are looking at roughly three times this) than the degree to which it is unequally distributed, and the scale of relative deprivation between different social groups. The greater the degree of inequality, the greater the health gaps. As Wilkinson has put it, "People in a country can be twice as well off on average as those in another country without benefit to their mortality rates" if the distribution of income and wealth is unequal.[14]

This is explained by a third element, which is the way that capitalism not only generates material inequality, but also social mechanisms, that lead to ill health. The problem is both the material pressures on human beings—our basic work security, the environment, pollution, etc—and the uneven social and psychological means we have for dealing with the unequal outcomes that follow.

This leads to a fourth element, which is that when these patterns are revealed the system can also encourage perverse responses. If society makes you ill, the obvious solution is to deal with the diseases of ill health at the societal level. But the temptation is often to push resources into dealing with the consequences. If the procedures to deal with consequences are

14: Wilkinson, 1994.

themselves a source of profit, then the temptation will be to bend further discussion away from causes and social solutions towards a self-perpetuating pattern focused on medical technologies, drugs, therapies and the like.

Fortunately capitalism also creates a fifth element: the knowledge base to understand the real relationship along with groups of people, those at the bottom and "professionals", who should better understand the situation and can join together to demand change. However, the extent to which this will happen is a political issue. For a century now the medical profession has been divided between what have been called *mercenaries*, seeking to exploit ill health for gain, and *missionaries*, who are concerned to remove its social causes.[15] But the mercenaries have now been supplemented by the *managers* who have benefited from the commercialisation and privatisation of health and who tell us that the way forward is health markets that they can run jointly with the mercenaries.

Class society makes you ill

"I ask myself how, as a physician, I find myself up to my ears with the problems of society," writes Michael Marmot. It is a question that committed doctors have been asking for several generations as they try to explain and cope with the way that illness is moulded by society.[16] Evidence for the social gradient is astonishingly widespread. It affects us all. It is not just about the contrast between the rich and poor but is so "fine grained" that if we graph illness against some indicator of relative position we see that as relative position improves so does health. Wilkinson calculated that 50 to 75 percent of the differences in average life expectancy in rich countries are now determined by differences bound up in the distribution of income and related factors. Table 3 shows how this is reflected in the pattern of key illnesses in the UK.

Why should this be? Material need cannot be ignored. Income poverty is not the basis for a good life, and societies with the greatest levels of inequality will also have the largest numbers of poor people. But it is relative poverty and position that matter most. So what is going on? The biomedical answer seems to be that vulnerability and susceptibility to illness and death are related to the degree of adversity in our lives. Some exercise is good for you but relentless physical demands in circumstances over which you have no control drain the body. Similarly, some stress is good for you but relentless worrying about job, home, family, etc not only drains you emotionally but feeds back into physical and mental ill health:

15: Widgery, 1979

16: Marmot, 2003, p8.

> The relationship among the nervous system, the endocrine system, and the immune system is emerging as the pathway that can help our understanding of the changes in health which are associated with changing social and economic conditions.[17]

In other words, although illness arises from bodily processes it is really a product of social organisation. And—this is crucial—because health follows the social gradient it is not just about improving the conditions of the poorest. In health terms it is in our collective and individual interest to tackle the problem more systematically. As Marmot puts it:

> Much of the discussion about social inequities in heath has focused on the health disadvantage of the lower class. This is analogous to seeing social problems as particular to a disadvantaged minority, rather than a problem for society as a whole.[18]

Table 3: The UK disease pattern by social group 1991-3, standardised rates per 100,000 for men aged 20-64.
Source: Acheson, 1997.

	Lung cancer	Coronary heart disease	Stroke	Accidents, poisonings violence	Suicide
Professional	17	81	14	13	13
Managerial	24	92	13	13	14
Skilled non-manual	34	136	19	17	20
Skilled manual	54	159	24	24	21
Semi-skilled	52	156	25	24	23
Unskilled	82	235	43	52	47

Marmot's argument here is partly a reformulation of RH Tawney's famous comment that "what thoughtful rich people call the problem of poverty, thoughtful poor people call with equal justice the problem of riches" but it is more. The steeper the social gradient, not only the bigger the health gap between those at the top and those at the bottom, but also the lower

17: Frank and Mustard, 1994.
18: Marmot, 1994.

the average position of all. "The countries with the longest life expectancy are not the wealthiest but those with the smallest spread of income and the smallest proportion of the population in relative poverty." There is therefore a problem with thinking that because I am near the top in UK terms (and the level of inequality in the UK is one of the highest) I will live longer than someone at the bottom or in the middle. This is true. But it is also true that you would live longer still if society were more equal. It was realised in the 1990s that "the mortality rate for the lowest social class in Sweden [with less inequality] is less than that for the top social class in the United Kingdom".[19]

The narrow biomedical mechanism that produces this has three elements. The first is the psycho-social impact of pressure on bodily processes. This is socially determined. The second is our health behaviour and how we respond in terms of what we eat, whether we smoke and drink, take exercise, etc. This too is socially determined. The third is how supportive our family, friends and social networks are. This is also socially determined. Only then does the fourth issue, healthcare, become a central issue and, when it does, it too is socially determined.

If we look at our lifestyles as a whole, their patterns reflect either the accumulation of advantage or disadvantage. The story starts in the womb with fetal development, it is manifest in the early years, at primary and secondary school. It is then compounded by what type of job we get and how precarious our employment is, and so on. But why can this not be explained by people at the top choosing wisely and those at the bottom choosing badly?

The really interesting aspect of the social approach to health is how careful the analysis is of what conditions our behaviour. The cleverness of the Whitehall Studies of UK civil servants is a good example. The researchers took a large group in which the members appeared to be similar and apparently had some more positive elements in their work conditions. They then designed a study of how work, position, life, social situation, etc interacted and combined. This analysis allowed them to nail the myth that top managers are prone to more heart attacks because of "pressure". They are not and we now know why. With responsibility comes status, power, control, means to relieve stress (membership of the gym, a night at the opera, a holiday villa) often arranged by your secretary and so on. As you move lower down, so people's lives become more bound up with lower status, less control and the need to battle and juggle a host of other commitments. It is the harassed worker on the shopfloor or in the office who is more at risk of a heart attack and, beneath them, the cleaner doing two jobs on the minimum wage. This

19: Wilkinson, 1994.

also explains negative health behaviours and why these should give rise to different incidences of disease when the same immediate causal factors, eg smoking, appear to be present.

But some readers may be puzzling about a theoretical problem in the link between social class and the health gradient. Those who insist that we live in a class society have to defend themselves not only against those who deny the reality of class but also those who want to define it simply in terms of hierarchy. It is here that we run up against the fundamental weakness of the argument about social gradients in health. It is clear that they exist, but what causes them? What is the "cause of the cause"? To solve this problem we have to look behind the gradients and explore what determines the different incomes, jobs and degree of control that people have over their lives. This means that the central thing has to be class analysis and showing how any gradient is structured by ownership and control and not least, in capitalism, by ownership and control of the means of production.

Here several related concepts are absolutely central—alienation, exploitation, class and class conflict. Inequalities are a consequence of how these interact and it is from this that social gradients and gradients of ill health flow. Marmot makes occasional gestures towards this but they are weak and inconsistent. The same is true of Wilkinson even though he has a more systematic grasp of the social side. To insist on the importance of this is not just about adding an additional layer of possibly superfluous explanation. It makes the argument stronger in terms of its logic and explanatory power, and it gives it a clearer political thrust because it also forces us to consistently address the political economy of both health causation and the limits of reform within the system.

Alienation, for example, is fundamental to explaining both our loss of control of social processes and the way that they are turned against us, and our resulting inability to relate to one another as proper human beings.[20] Exploitation gives us the possibility of understanding how and why the rewards go to the few who make so little contribution to our real wealth. And class and class conflict help us to understand the resulting texture of social relationships and their antagonisms.[21]

We can make these arguments work in a more precise fashion too. As organisations have become more powerful the argument arises about who has effective disposition of capital and labour within them. The key social argument here is that the more your position gives you control over

20: See Yuill, 2005; Crinson and Yuill, 2008.

21: See Muntaner and Lynch, 1999; Muntaner and others, 2003.

capital and labour, control over yourself, your work, the work and lives of others, the lower the levels of ill health. The more your life is controlled by others the less the level of health. The social gradient is not simply about "who has what" but the capacity to command people and resources—the very issue that is at the centre of class analysis.

But to take this analysis further we need people whose expertise is the analysis of capitalism's social structures to link up with the people whose expertise is in health and illness. One of the most creative ways of making the connection was set out nearly three decades ago by Eric Olin Wright. Wright took on the argument that class was disappearing in modern society because of the alleged explosion of groups in the middle. These groups appeared to stand between capital and labour; they had what he called "contradictory class locations". He then devised a way of mapping these contradictions, focusing crucially on how much control of capital and labour they had. It becomes obvious in his analysis that these intermediate groups often have little and are therefore closer to labour than capital. This reflects what many of us understand intuitively: the badge may say manager but we all know that in reality it means some low grade supervisory responsibilities that do not preclude trade union membership and even militancy.

Using these ideas to map how capitalism really operates and divides us has an obvious attraction for those seeking to more systematically underpin the analysis of health gradients, and some researchers have already looked in this direction. But here's the problem. Almost immediately Wright had set out this argument he retreated under the pressure of the anti-class theorists. This has meant that it has fallen to others to defend this extension of class analysis as a way to understand capitalism.[22] But it has also acted as a disincentive to use the argument to tighten the theoretical and empirical links between class and health.

Medical myths and medical madness

But this argument raises other political issues and not least for the medical establishment. Prevention, as everyone knows, is better than cure. "The most sophisticated and effective healthcare in the world cannot produce results as good as simply remaining healthy in the first place." But "creating healthy societies and individuals largely results from action outside the health sector".[23] Healthcare can never remove the gradients in causation, only deal with some of the consequences.

22: See Callinicos and Harman, 1987.

23: Evans 1994; Marmot, 1994.

This type of argument is difficult to make. We are rightly appalled by inadequacies in healthcare but we tend to take for granted the inequalities in health causation. It is awful that when Julie had her heart attack in her fifties she had to wait 30 minutes for an ambulance; then there was the four-hour wait in accident & emergency and the dirty wards on which she eventually died. But the prior question is why she had a heart attack in her fifties and why Jane, who worked as a cleaner in the same office, had one a couple of years later and died before help could get there?

We need to take any argument about the role of medicine in health in two stages. The first is to stress the absolute importance of what is called primary prevention and not to fall into the trap of thinking that we can leave the causes of illness alone and focus on better treatment. Primary prevention saves lives but primary prevention may not involve medical measures in the narrow sense at all. Only three out of the 39 proposals made by the 1997 *Acheson Report of the Inquiry into Inequalities in Health* related directly to health service provision.[24] If the problem is a choice between a worse treatment and a better one, we should obviously demand the better one. But the issue should not be about whether we can afford treatments but whether we can afford people to be ill. It is often said that medical costs will always rise. This is an absurd argument in itself because it ignores the way in which the drive for profit is behind the cost rises that exist. But even if it were true, reducing the numbers of ill people in the first place would reduce the cost problems. The less people that you have to treat, the more you can afford to spend on making those who have the genuine misfortune (and not the socially determined one) to fall ill. The real problem then is to alter the fundamentals of the generation of illness caused by class society.

Primary prevention is therefore politically challenging. There has always been a minority tendency in the medical establishment that links health improvement to real social reform, and within this group a smaller one still who continue to insist that so long as capitalism and class society exist we will remain trapped in unequal lives and unequal deaths.[25] But many health professionals also see the immediate attraction of the medical fix. And so do we as patients once we get trapped in ill health. Even the

24: Marmot, 2004, pp260, 267-276.

25: In the UK the Socialist Health Association is a good example. Its website contains a mass of valuable material but, associated with the Labour Party, it oscillates between radicalism one day and bland commentary the next. See www.sochealth.co.uk. Julian Tudor Hart, associated for many years with the Communist Party, has been a doctor and key individual researcher for half a century pushing for a more consistently radical position see—www.juliantudorhart.org. The Politics of Health group has some excellent material. See www.pohg.org.uk

members of the team that produced the original *Black Report* were split on this issue. According to Sir Douglas Black:

> We were all agreed that education and preventative measures, specifically directed towards the socially deprived, were necessary. But the sociological members of the group...considered that the consequent expenditure should be obtained by diversion from acute services. On the other hand the medical members...felt that the acute services played a vital role in the prevention of chronic disability and could not be further cut back without serious effects on emergency care, on the training of doctors for both hospital work and for family practice and on the length of waiting lists. We spent a long time, without real success trying to resolve this matter.[26]

This fudge is not enough. Consider the problem of mental ill health. Its burden continues to rise in the advanced world. There is a big question over whether the medical fix actually works. But suppose the evidence was clearer that it did. It would still not be enough for three reasons. First, "it is inconceivable that enough professionals could be trained and employed to treat the many millions of causalities of our psychologically toxic social environment one at a time". Second, if the problem is the toxic environment then once people are returned to it their symptoms are likely to recur. Third, this approach does nothing to stop new cases appearing.[27] But the same logic applies to other areas. Britain, for example, is acknowledged to have one of the poorest records in the advanced world for longer-term survival after major incidents like cancer and heart attacks. You can now guess that there may be two explanations for this. One is medical—the weaknesses of early identification, treatment and follow up. The other is inequality. If inequality increases your chances of getting a life threatening disease, then however good the medical fix the pressure will be on again once you return to the environment that helped to cause the illness in the first place.

At this point, however, many take fright. It seems easier to imagine that the way forward is to work on medical solutions to ill health and demand more resources for these. But this takes us to the second issue of whether a health system run for profit can ever rationally answer human need. The answer is an unequivocal no. The first simple rule of healthcare is Tudor Hart's "inverse care law", which says that "the availability of good medical care tends to vary inversely with the need for the population served [and

26: Townsend and Davidson, 1982.

27: Fryer, 2000.

this] operates more completely where medical care is most exposed to market forces".[28] A national health system has to be based on principles of comprehensiveness, universality and equitability. "Supply and demand", internal and external markets, subvert these principles and undermine the capacity of rational health planning. They even undermine the very sources of information which would make such planning possible. The result is variation in the coverage of basic services. With this comes a huge loss in real efficiency.

A second simple rule of healthcare then emerges: *the more the logic of capitalism determines the supply of healthcare, the higher the costs, the larger the management layer, and the greater the diversion of resources away from treatment and care and into private hands.* With this level of irrationality in the system we can then move to a third simple rule of healthcare: *the more the logic of capitalism determines the supply of healthcare, the more the healthcare system itself may become a threat to social health.*

A genuine national health system would seek to minimise the causes of ill health in society at large and to maximise the coverage, comprehensiveness and efficiency of healthcare when it was needed. The focus on "bringing the market in" does just the opposite. It helps to maximise the stresses that produce poor health and it fatally compromises the ability of any healthcare system to rationally deal with the resulting patterns of ill health. In the 1990s attention in the UK was for a time focused on Dr Harold Shipman who turned out to be a doctor who was also a serial killer, dispatching his older patients. But the real story of the last decades is that the biggest serial killer in the health system is the market, and in the dock alongside Shipman should have been all those who pushed it and the consequent break up of the NHS. Sadly, if this sounds like rhetoric, it is supported by a grotesque trail of evidence, and not least in the statistics of lives lost and the stories of grieving relatives, of how healthcare is failing in market driven systems.

In the UK the NHS that was built up after the Second Word War had serious faults and these were not helped by systematic underfunding. But it was based on a developing sense of comprehensiveness, universality and equity, and in comparative terms it was one of the most, if not the most, efficient healthcare systems in the world. Its dismantling through the development of first internal, and then external, markets—the creation of what Allyson Pollock calls the *NHS PLC*—has broken this and begun to reproduce some of the worst irrationalities of private healthcare systems and their scandals. Worse, although this process began under the Tories, if

28: Tudor Hart, 1971.

anything it proceeded faster under New Labour.[29]

It is true that over time more money has been pushed into health but the market-based health reforms have also created more routes by which this money could be devoted to non-health outcomes and into private pockets. Part of the systematic underfunding of the NHS in the past has been reflected in low pay in its lower levels, and nobody could object to this being improved. But additional resources have also been sucked to the top and out of the system by the market privatisation process, building better offices for the likes of global accountancy and consultancy firms such as KPMG or PriceWaterhouseCoopers, rather than providing more hospital beds. Health is big business. In Europe the health service consumes around 8 to 10 percent of output. In the US it is nearer to 15 percent. Add in all other forms of healthcare and we are nearer to 10 to 20 percent. This is such a huge amount that the pressure is to grab as much as possible for privatised control and private profit. Any number of examples could be given but it will be sufficient to sketch the perverse consequences in terms of the pharmaceutical industry. It is not the case, as is sometimes argued, that "big pharma" has no interest in cures. Of course it does. The problem is the way it operates under capitalism systematically compromises a rational allocation of resources to meet human need.

First note the scale and interlocking character of this industry—not just the huge drug companies but also biotech, the food supplement manufacturers, the vitamin producers, even homeopathy, far from being "alternative", are big business. Few in number, these companies are diversified global giants in their own right but they are far from averse to underhand linkages. The biggest corporate criminal fine in history was of $1.5 billion levied by the US government against the "vitamin cartel" for price fixing.[30] But it is easy to see the attraction of fleecing the market.

29: Pollock, 2005; Shaw and others, 2005a, 2005b; Player and Leys, 2008.

30: The vitamin cartel included some of the top pharmaceutical companies. For all its faults, the US enforcement agency can be quite blunt: "The international vitamin cartel, which affected over $5 billion in US commerce, was the most harmful and elaborate conspiracy ever uncovered by the Antitrust Division. The members of the vitamin cartel reached agreements on everything from how much product each company would produce, to how much they would charge, to which customers they would sell. The victims who purchased directly from the cartel members included companies with household names such as General Mills, Kellogg, Coca-Cola, Tyson Foods and Proctor & Gamble. However, these companies were just the first to feel the effects of this conspiracy. In the end, for nearly a decade, every American consumer—anyone who took a vitamin, drank a glass of milk, or had a bowl of cereal—ended up paying more so that the conspirators could reap hundreds of millions of dollars in additional revenues"— www.usdoj.gov/atr/public/4523e.htm

Medical drug sales alone in the UK work out at £200 per person anually or over 1 percent of national income—a huge amount. In the US the figure is nearer 2 percent of national income.

Getting as much of this income as possible means big profits. This helps to explain the fact that the pharmaceutical industry spends only around 14 percent of income on research and development but 30 percent plus on marketing and administration. It also helps to explain the startling fact that 10 percent of the world's health burden gets 90 percent of the research and development. Money follows the patients and the systems with spending power. Ninety percent of the human health burden gets a mere 10 percent of R&D, and even more grotesquely this is probably less than the amount now spent to provide better drugs for pets in rich countries. Plus all this research is now becoming less effective. In the middle decades of the previous century there were major medical advances in drugs, techniques and treatments but in recent decades the rate of real improvement has declined. That means that companies now have to push copycat, "me too", drugs that barely differ from one another, or encourage us to believe in new diseases for which they can then sell us old cures. In this battle patents are crucial. Eighty percent of drug expenditure is on patented drugs in advanced countries. Patents keep prices high and allow profits to be squeezed even if the drug could be lifesaving for those who cannot afford it. These same pressures then lead on to the systematic undermining of ethical standards in research as companies pressure researchers into exaggerating the efficacy of their copycat drug over someone else's.

But the pressure of these big companies is also highly political. They are a formidable lobby, spending billions, and leaning on governments and international organisations. They practise a revolving door system whereby politicians, regulators and top health service people are regularly invited to join them and effectively rewarded for their past compromises. They subvert the health debate. Systematic bribery is practised in the health trade with all sorts of inducements to prescribe one product over another. Front organisations are set up. Some patient groups have stupidly allowed themselves to be compromised by accepting drug company money and becoming advocates demanding costly drugs whose real benefits are doubtful. And if all else fails, these companies follow the trail pioneered by the tobacco industry of sowing doubt where there should be none and intimidating their critics.[31]

This is not a pretty picture. But it is made worse by the way that the drive towards more markets and privatisation in health service provision

31: Widgery, 1979; Goldacre 2008.

further sideline real solutions. This is perhaps best seen as an attempt to enable the private sector to plunder the state by means of legalised corruption—the private finance initiative disaster in the UK is the best example. Of course the ideological preference for markets reflects something more than the veniality of the pocket but it is important to stress how much material interest there is in profiting from health privatisation.

What cements this is the managerialisation of state health provision. In Britain this now permeates all levels of the NHS, co-opting medical staff, but the most obvious indicator is the rise in the number of people who are specifically employed as "managers and senior managers". In 1998 there were 22,000 of them; by 2008 there were 40,000. This has led to a fall in the number of staff per "manager" from 48:1 to 34:1.[32] And presiding over them all, the NHS board at the very top had eight people in 2004-5 and cost £1.2 million. By 2008 it had 24 and cost £3.5 million.[33] And alongside these are a huge army of management and IT consultants so that the NHS alone vies with UK manufacturing each year for the title of the fourth largest funder of UK consultancy firms.[34] While this may make little sense in its own terms, it is a necessary step in enabling a more systematic distortion of healthcare, leading towards the creation of a "medico-industrial complex".

But the most disturbing issue is the extent to which healthcare itself can become a source of ill health—indirectly though the diversion of resources and directly through the systematic failure to offer patients the cures that they expect and, on occasion, even giving them new illnesses.

In the previous century enormous progress was finally made in developing medicine that had some hope of curing some patients. But the limitations of medicine are still more serious than is often imagined. Not the least of these is that treatment can have unintended consequences. Cases of adverse drug reaction are well known and these often received huge publicity. But there are bigger issues. Even in the best systems, all hospitals, anywhere in the world, are unsafe places. You can make them better or worse but the problems will never be removed completely, so the best approach is to reduce the numbers needing their services. In the UK, for example, the National Audit Office estimates that as many as one in 12 to one in ten patients will experience an adverse incident. These can range from negative reactions to treatment to mistakes, care and neglect problems

32: Calculated from NHS Information Centre, 2009. The full-time equivalent fall was from a ratio of 39:1 to one of 30:1.

33: *Independent*, 14 November 2008.

34: Every autumn *Accountancy Age* reports on the fees of UK Management consultancy.

and, most serious of all in terms of large numbers, cross-infection. This can lead to illness, disability and death. Unnecessary deaths in NHS hospitals have been as high as 34,000 a year but the government report which gave this figure added that "in reality the NHS simply does not know".[35]

Most attention has been focused on "superbugs", such as MRSA and clostridium difficile, to which the weak and elderly are especially vulnerable. The rise of this type of infection appears to be in part a consequence of new antibiotic-resistant strains. But more immediate causes appear to be at work. One is ward cleanliness—what those in the trade call "the mop and matron" problem, looking back to an age when matrons reputedly directly supervised nurse and ancillary staff performance. The second is rates of bed occupancy that are the highest in the advanced world.[36] The third is insufficient appreciation of the danger of cross-infection by medical staff and visitors and therefore their lack of care in contact. The first and second issues are unambiguously related to the NHS profit/target driven culture. And if the three issues were properly addressed in the short term, they could cut cross-infection and death but the threat would still be there. Although better hospital design adds a further long-term element, it seems that we will have to live for the foreseeable future with a greater degree of cross-infection risk. On top of this we can then add poor case management. Again this can unambiguously be related to the profit/target culture, as was revealed in the notorious case in Staffordshire where managers manipulated patients to hit targets, leading to an estimated 400 to 1,200 unnecessary deaths. But as critics pointed out, Staffordshire is only the tip of the iceberg and the practices here, albeit perhaps pursued more systematically, are apparent across the NHS.

The case for radical change

In how radical a direction do these arguments really push us? Since inequality varies between countries it cannot be the case that there is no space within capitalism to improve things. Reducing the levels of inequality in the US and the UK to those in Sweden is clearly compatible with the continued existence of capitalism since Sweden is a capitalist country. Moreover this would dramatically improve the lives of people in the US and the UK. This is the obvious case for reform and this is the immediate punch of the inequality argument and the argument of those who appeal to the self-interest of governments in facilitating change. But this is too easy, for even in Sweden the gaps and the inequalities, although less, are real.

35: National Audit Office, 2005.

36: Orendi, 2008.

In economic terms Sweden is actually a very unequal society. We can measure inequality before and after transfer spending. Transfers are taxes that are paid and then redirected as welfare, social and health spending. A country such as Sweden combines a high pre-tax inequality with a low one after tax and transfers. It allows the basic inequalities of capitalism but offers a "compensating mechanism". In the rich countries levels of social expenditure run at just over 20 percent of total output. In Sweden they are about 30 percent of output. The result is evident in the comparative poverty statistics. According to one set, before transfers the poverty rate in the UK was 28.8 percent, higher than even the US at 23 percent. Sweden was almost as high as the UK at 28.3 percent. Welfare spending of all kinds transformed this situation. The US poverty rate fell to 18.6 percent, the UK to 16.4 percent but the Swedish to just 3.3 percent.[37] In comparative terms this is an enormous difference. But the big point in terms of the health argument is that the Swedish system is still built around very significant core inequalities and therefore the social processes that generate unequal health. What Sweden is much better at is using welfare and social policies to limit some of the consequences but not, crucially, eliminating them, as workers in Sweden know to their cost.

We know, for example, that the massive rise in unemployment will damage people's health through its financial and psychological effects. The impact will be worse in a country like the UK where benefits are low, means tested and stigmatising compared to a country such as Sweden where the welfare state is more comprehensive and generous in funding and attitudes. But all the care in the world can only take second place as a solution to not losing your job in the first place and knowing that you can rely on having decent work and a decent life. The best solution to the problem of unemployment leading to ill health is therefore a system which does not put your heath at risk by putting your job at risk in the first place.

In addition, we must not make the mistake of assuming that progress in the longer term will always be positive. Although there have been widespread increases in life expectancy during the past two to three decades, a significant minority of countries have gone backwards. Since the 1990s 16 countries have experienced sharp falls in life expectancy—mostly in Africa but also in the states of the former Soviet bloc. This has been catastrophic for the countries concerned and it is no exaggeration to say that lives shortened and lost run into many millions.[38]

37: Bryant and Raphael, 2005.

38: Haynes and Husan, 2003.

And the recent pressures across the globe, including in countries such as Sweden, have been towards weakening both people's economic positions and the systems available to deal with the consequences. The extent of real labour market "flexibility" and of precarious work is a matter of dispute, and we should be the last people to exaggerate it. Fear can weaken people's resolve to defend what they have and a strongly organised labour force is likely to be a healthier one. But we cannot ignore the pressures to undermine past achievements and the attrition that is still ongoing. This is the lesson in the UK of two decades of Labour and Tory commitment to the market, whatever its health costs.[39] State policies to bolster the strength of capital, however they are presented, are not simply based on intellectual errors and misunderstandings. They reflect the intrinsic need of the state to support capitalism. And this is taken to a whole new level during a crisis.

Crisis, by reducing economic activity, cuts some causes of death such as accidents at work and on the road, but it increases others as the pressure of the crisis is felt. The focus on profit now leads to mass unemployment, and governments panic over how much to spend and how much to cut. The pressure of crisis undermines the possibility of making an appeal to enlightened self-interest. The bosses who jump ship or practise crisis management by slash and burn are hardly likely to slow down in the face of appeals about the human misery that will follow. If you are closing a plant at a day or even a few hours notice, the issue of a "fair" redundancy process and the availability of counselling for redundant or surviving workers is unlikely to be a priority. Nor should we imagine that because there has been a catastrophic failure of global capitalism this will in itself prompt a systematic rethinking. Without a fight it will not even necessarily undermine the influence of those who brought about the crisis. It should never be forgotten that the economic crisis of 1929 did not lead to a radical change in establishment ideas. The people running the system in the 1930s were the same as those in charge in the 1920s, or their subordinates or worse. This helps explain why the greatest crisis that capitalism produced what W H Auden dismissed as "a low dishonest decade". Without a radical alternative we risk the same scenario for ourselves.

This points to the need to understand that the balance of class forces is not only crucial to patterns of ill health and death but also to the solution. We know from history, for example, that war and revolution can radically change patterns of health, illness and health service delivery, and often in a remarkably short time. Problems which are deep rooted do not disappear

39: Shaw and others, 1999, 2005a, 2005b.

overnight but they can be confronted in new ways. For instance, in the UK in the Second World War, despite the conflict, civilian health improved as radical changes had a dramatic short-term effect and health delivery was shifted towards a new basis. Elsewhere more rapid political change has had the same effect. It acts this way because it challenges the whole basis on which society is run and resources are allocated, and in so doing leads to a more fundamental questioning of the mechanisms that produce ill health and are supposed to lead to its solution. Not least, it leads to people being able to see themselves less as isolated, alienated and exploited victims than as part of a more collective solution.

The real solution then has to be a radical one and it has to raise the nature of capitalism as a system. But this cannot be achieved by shouting from the sidelines. A battle against the inequalities of the system and the crisis has to be fought at all levels: to sustain and improve conditions in the workplace; to oppose redundancies; to resist budget cuts; to fight against housing repossessions. Those who will be most useful, resilient and successful will be those who understand that not only are such campaigns important in their own right but make best sense if they link up and become part of an argument for a general change. This can then lay the basis of a decent society that will also be a healthy one—one in which social inequality will no longer give rise to unequal lives and unequal deaths.

References

Acheson, Donald, 1998, *Independent Inquiry into Inequalities in Health* (The Stationary Office).

Bryant, Toba, and Dennis Raphael, 2005, "Politics, Public Policy and Population Health in the United Kingdom", in Politics of Health Group, *UK Health Watch 2005. The Experience of Health in an Unequal Society*, www.pohg.org.uk/support/downloads/ukhealthwatch-2005.pdf

Callinicos, Alex, and Chris Harman, 1987, *The Changing Working Class: Essays on Class Structure Today* (Bookmarks).

Crinson, Ian, and Chris Yuill, 2008, "What can Alienation Theory Contribute to an Understanding of Social Inequalities in Health?", *International Journal of Health Services*, volume 38, number 3.

Evans, Robert, 1994, "Health Care as a Threat to Health: Defense, Opulence, and the Social Environment", *Daedalus*, volume 123, number 4 (autumn 1994).

Floud, Roderick, and others, 1990, *Height, Health and History: Nutritional Status in the United Kingdom, 1750-1980* (Cambridge University).

Fogel, Robert, 2004, "Health, Nutrition and Economic Growth", *Economic Development and Cultural Change*, volume 52, number 3.

Frank, John, and J Fraser Mustard, 1994, "The Determinants of Health from a Historical Perspective", *Daedalus*, volume 123, number 4 (autumn 1994).

Fryer, David, 2000, "The Future of Primary Prevention", *The Journal of Primary Prevention*, volume 21, number 2.
Goldacre, Ben, 2008, *Bad Science*, (Fourth Estate).
Haynes, Michael, 2008, "The Comparative Accountancy of Death in War", *History Teaching Review Yearbook*, volume 22, http://pers-www.wlv.ac.uk/~le1958/war.pdf
Haynes, Michael, and Rumy Husan, 2003, *A Century of State Murder? Death and Public Policy in Russia* (Pluto Press).
Marmot, Michael, 1994, "Social Differentials in Health Within and Between Populations", *Daedalus*, volume 123, number 4 (autumn 1994).
Marmot, Michael, 2003, *Status Syndrome* (Bloomsbury).
Marmot, Michael, 2005, "Social Determinants of Health Inequalities", *Lancet*, volume 365, issue 1099, 19 March 2005.
Marmot, Michael, and Richard Wilkinson, 2003, *The Solid Facts* (second edition), World Health Organisation, www.euro.who.int/document/e81384.pdf
Muntaner, Carles, and John Lynch, 1999, "Income Inequality, Social Cohesion and Class Relations: A Critique of Wilkinson's Neo-Durkheimian Research Program", *International Journal of Health Services*, volume 29, number 1, pp59-81.
Muntaner, Carles, and others, 2003, "The Associations of Social Class and Social Stratification with Patterns of General and Mental Health in a Spanish Population", *International Journal of Epidemiology*, volume 32.
National Audit Office, 2005, *A Safe Place for Patients: Leaning to Improve Patient Safety*, www.publications.parliament.uk/pa/cm200506/cmselect/cmpubacc/831/831.pdf
Orendi, Jeorge, 2008, "Health-care Organisation, Hospital-bed Occupancy and MRSA", *Lancet*, volume 371, issue 9622, 26 April 2008.
Player, Stewart, and Colin Leys, 2008, *Confuse and Conceal: The NHS and Independent Sector Treatment Centres* (Merlin).
Pollock, Allyson, 2005, *NHS PLC: The Privatisation of Our Healthcare* (Verso).
Shaw, Mary, Dorling Danny, Mitchell Richard and George Davey Smith, 1999, *The Widening Gap: Health Inequalities and Policies in Britain* (Policy Press).
Shaw, Mary, Dorling Danny, Mitchell Richard and George Davey Smith, 2005a, "Health Inequalities and New Labour: How the Promises Compare with Real Progress", *British Medical Journal*, volume 330, 30 April 2005.
Shaw, Mary, Dorling Danny, Mitchell Richard and George Davey Smith, 2005b, "Labour's 'Black Report' Moment?", *British Medical Journal*, volume 331, 10 September 2005.
Shorter, Edward, 2006, "Primary Care", in Roy Porter (ed), *The Cambridge History of Medicine* (Cambridge University).
Townsend, Peter, and Nick Davidson, 1982, *Inequalities in Health: The Black report* (Penguin).
Tudor Hart, Julian, 1971, "The Inverse Care Law", *Lancet*, 27 February 1971.
Widgery, David, 1979, *Health in Danger* (Macmillan).
Wilkinson, Richard, 1994, "The Epidemiological Transition: From Material Scarcity to Social Disadvantage", *Daedalus*, volume 123, number 4 (autumn 1994).
Wilkinson, Richard, and Kate Pickett, 2009, *The Spirit Level: Why More Equal Societies Almost Always Do Better* (Penguin).
Wootton, David, 2006, *Bad Medicine. Doctors doing Harm since Hippocrates* (Oxford University).
Yuill, Chris, 2005, "Marx: Capitalism, Alienation and Health", *Social Theory and Health*, volume 3.

The full story: on Marxism and religion

Roland Boer

"Religion is the main cause of wars and conflicts through history." How often do we hear that old idealist argument used in our day of renewed global conflict? In an earlier issue of this journal John Molyneux wrote a useful response to that position.[1] I would like to offer a critical reply to Molyneux, pointing out where he falls short but also developing one or two points further.

Molyneux's article offers a Marxist analysis of the so-called "return to religion" in today's geopolitical context. We see it in the Islamist opposition to Western imperialism, in the strident criticism of religion by the likes of Richard Dawkins and Christopher Hitchens, in the strange recovery of some Christian identity by some countries (especially European) that have been deeply secular for some time, in the claims that we are returning to age-old ideological conflicts between Christianity and Islam, and even in the increasing number of us on the left who are reassessing Marxist approaches to religion. Molyneux also points out that economic realities have determined that Islam would be the focus of much hostility in the West. The reason is simply that oil and Muslim-majority states happen to be in the same areas. In a global capitalist system addicted to oil those regions have become a contested zone. He then offers a brief survey of Marx's approach to religion, arguing that the key is not dismissal (in light of the reality of material

1: Molyneux, 2008.

circumstances) but explanation of religion. From there he assesses Richard Dawkins's *The God Delusion*, Christopher Hitchens's *God is Not Great* and Terry Eagleton's review of Dawkins's book in *The London Review of Books*.[2] He might have added others such as Daniel Dennett or Sam Harris, but there are more than enough books that say basically the same thing—religion is bad for you.[3] Finally, Molyneux goes on to show how a Marxist analysis might provide some guidelines for assessing religion in light of opposition to exploitation and oppression. To my mind, this is the most interesting part of his article, so I will have a few more things to say about it later.

What I like about Molyneux's argument is the way he punctures the idealist assumptions behind the argument that religion is the cause of all that is bad in the world. His point that Muslim opposition arises from a long history of capitalist imperialism is well taken but not particularly new. However, the suggestion that Muslim-majority countries happen to be located where there is oil is astute. If that crucial source of cheap energy happened to be in some other part of the world where Buddhism were the dominant religion (Molyneux's example), then any concerted opposition to overdeveloped capitalist exploitation would be viewed as a hostile response by an evil and militant Buddhism. Further, his attacks on Dawkins and Hitchens are well made, especially against Hitchens who used to be a fellow-traveller on the left. Molyneux doesn't fall for the standard response to these neo-atheists by saying they really don't understand religion properly. Instead he uncovers the reactionary idealism at the heart of their works. In many respects, we may as well be back in 18th century France with characters such as Voltaire, or perhaps 19th century Germany when the likes of David Strauss, Max Stirner and Bruno Bauer felt that the most radical thing to do was attack Christianity. I would add to that the crass materialism which creeps around the edges of these works: science proves that god doesn't exist. I'm surprised they don't invoke the so-called "god gene" proposed by the geneticist Gene Harmer, who argues that some of us are genetically and psychologically predisposed to religious belief and others not.[4]

While all these criticisms are well made, Molyneux's discussion of Marx is more interesting, as is his final argument for what can be called a politics of alliance between the secular and religious left. I would like to look at both in more detail. The section on Marx is as interesting for what it doesn't say as for what it does. Molyneux focuses on the famous

2: Dawkins, 2006; Hitchens, 2007; Eagleton, 2006.

3: Dennett, 2007; Harris, 2005, 2006.

4: Harmer, 2005.

few pages in Marx's "Introduction" to his *Contribution to the Critique of Hegel's Philosophy of Law*.[5] This is where we find Marx's observations that in Germany the criticism of religion is complete, that the criticism of theology should become the criticism of politics, the criticism of heaven become the criticism of earth, and that religion is the theory of this world and the "opium of the people". While justly famous and the subject of endless analysis, there is far, far more in Marx and Engels's collected works. In fact, what I would like to do is bring Engels back into the discussion, since he is more important that many of us realise.

Most of Marx's discussions of religion appear in his earlier works, especially *The Leading Article in No 179 of the* Kölnische Zeitung, *Debates on Freedom of the Press and Publication of the Proceedings of the Assembly of the Estates*, *Contribution to the Critique of Hegel's Philosophy of Law* (and the separate introduction) and the *Theses on Feuerbach*.[6] Written during his early years of journalism and research, these are only the most substantial. Many of his other works contain comments and observations, but if I listed them here, it would fill up the rest of the article. *Capital*, for example, is peppered with comments, allusions and references (even to Luther). By contrast, Engels wrote a number of key texts on religion over his lifetime, including *Letters from Wuppertal*, observations on religious life in Bremen while he was living there, three essays on Schelling's lectures in Berlin, a delightful satirical poem on the Bible, extended correspondence with his friends the Graeber brothers on matters theological and biblical, and then a series of major works: *The Peasant War in Germany*, *Bruno Bauer and Early Christianity*, *The Book of Revelation* and, towards the end of his life, the influential *On the History of Early Christianity*.[7] Engels never lost the habit of alluding to or quoting a Bible verse in the midst of his polemic to hammer home a point. These number in the hundreds if not thousands in his works. Two other joint texts are also steeped in religious matters, namely *The Holy Family* and *The German Ideology*.[8] Some, but by no means all, of these works have been gathered in various collections over time.[9]

Apart from a rather rationalist approach to religion in his home and the use of allusions in his early poetry (which is not very good), Marx never

5: Marx 1975a.

6: Marx, 1975b, 1975c, 1975a, 1975d, 1976a.

7: Engels, 1975a, 1975b, 1975c, 1975d, 1975e, 1975f, 1975g, 1975h, 1975i, 1975j, 1975k, 1975l, 1975m, 1975n, 1975o, 1975p, 1975q, 1975r, 1975s, 1975t, 1975u, 1975v, 1975w, 1975x, 1975y, 1978, 1989, 1990a, 1990b.

8: Marx and Engels, 1975, 1976a.

9: Marx, 2002; Marx and Engels, 1976b.

had any religious commitment, finding the dirty little relationship between church and the powers that be obnoxious from an early stage. At university he fell under the sway of Bruno Bauer's radical critique of religion. Bauer was a biblical scholar and Marx studied the book of Isaiah with him in Berlin (Marx's doctoral thesis shows the influence of Bauer). By contrast, Engels grew up in a pious Calvinist household in Wuppertal. Through great struggle he eventually broke with this background as he read for himself the critical literature on the Bible by the likes of David Strauss and Ludwig Feuerbach, but not before it had left him with a deep knowledge of the Bible and a lifelong interest in matters biblical and religious.

Religion and politics in 19th century Germany

As Molyneux points out, the most well known and influential argument of Marx and Engels is that religion must be explained in terms of its social and economic conditions. While Marx tended to view religion as the expression of alienation, Engels was more prepared to grant it a liberating dimension. Yet there is far more to their views on religion than this argument. Religion appears in the work of Marx and Engels in three ways: the context in which they first developed historical materialism, the use they made of religion in developing their own arguments, and explicit arguments concerning religion.

Beginning with the context, for a number of historical reasons the various German states dealt with a whole range of modern issues through religion, which really means Christianity and the Bible.[10] While France had the radical atheistic criticism of Voltaire and company and while England had the deists, in Germany the debate was restricted to the nature of the Bible. Given the inseparable nature of religion and politics in the "Christian state" (as the Prussian king, Friedrich Wilhelm IV, called it), to attack the Bible or Christianity was to attack the political status quo. So we find that the most controversial works in the early part of the 19th century were David Strauss's *Das Leben Jesu*, where he argues that the accounts of Jesus in the Gospels are purely mythological,[11] or the arguments of the atheistic biblical critic Bruno Bauer against the oppressive particularism of religion and for a democratic self-consciousness,[12] or Ludwig Feuerbach's argument that religion is actually the projection of what is best in human beings, a projection that leads us to create an

10: See especially Breckman, 1999.
11: Strauss, 1835.
12: Bauer, 1838, 1840, 1841, 1842.

entity called "God".[13] Through these theological and biblical works all of the central questions were debated, such as democracy, individual rights, freedom (of the press), reason, republicanism, parliamentary representation and so on. I can't stress enough that these debates took place above all on the territory of the Bible and theology. It was there that Marx and Engels began their philosophical and political work.

Developing a system

In order to develop their own system of thought Marx and Engels had to distinguish themselves from the overwhelming theological frame in which German thought operated in the 1830s and 1840s. For a time Marx counted himself as a friend of Bruno Bauer, hoping for a university appointment under his patronage. For his part, Engels identified closely with the Young Hegelians in Berlin, especially during his year of military service (1842). His works on Schelling and the satirical poem, *The Insolently Threatened Yet Miraculously Rescued Bible*, come from this period.[14] However, as their collaborative work progressed, they had to come to terms with the major Young Hegelians, especially in the two joint works *The Holy Family* and *The German Ideology*.

Alongside Strauss's *Life of Jesus*, Feuerbach's *The Essence of Christianity* was one of the most significant texts of the time.[15] Marx saw the idea that religion and the gods were projections of human beings as a huge breakthrough. He used and extended what may be called the "Feuerbachian inversion" at a number of points in his own work. Feuerbach's idea is an inversion since it argues that previous thought about religion began at the wrong point, namely in the middle. God is not a pre-existing being who determines human existence; rather, human beings determine god's existence.

Marx took this argument and claimed that it marked the end of the criticism of religion: "For Germany the *criticism of religion* is in the main complete, and criticism of religion is the premise of all criticism".[16] He went on to suggest that the first great phase of criticism—the criticism of religion—began with Luther and ended with Feuerbach. The next revolutionary phase had already begun with Feuerbach and Marx saw himself as part of that new phase.

13: Feuerbach, 1986, 1989.

14: Engels, 1975g, 1975h, 1975i, 1975j.

15: Feuerbach 1986.

16: Marx, 1975a, p175; 1976b, p378.

For Marx, Feuerbach was the last word on religion. A statement such as the following (a text that Molyneux quotes) is pure Feuerbach:

> Religion is the general theory of this world, its encyclopaedic compendium, its logic in popular form, its spiritual *point d'honneur*, its enthusiasm, its moral sanction, its solemn complement, and its universal basis of consolation and justification. It is the *fantastic realisation* of the human essence since the *human essence* has not acquired any true reality.[17]

As Molyneux points out, Marx also wanted to go beyond Feuerbach on two counts. First, since human beings project religion from within themselves, the place to begin analysis is not in the heavens, but here on earth with flesh and blood people. Second, the fact that people do make such projections is a signal that something is wrong here on earth. If they place their hopes and dreams elsewhere, that means they could not be realised here and now. So the presence of religion becomes a sign of alienation, of economic and social oppression. *That* needs to be fixed. This theme occurs strongly in the famous *Theses on Feuerbach*, especially the fourth and eleventh theses:

> Feuerbach starts out from the fact of religious self-estrangement, of the duplication of the world into a religious world and a secular one. His work consists in resolving the religious world into its secular basis. But that the secular basis lifts off from itself and establishes itself as an independent realm in the clouds can only be explained by the inner strife and intrinsic contradictoriness of this secular basis. The latter must, therefore, itself be both understood in its contradiction and revolutionised in practice. Thus, for instance, once the earthly family is discovered to be the secret of the holy family, the former must then itself be destroyed in theory and in practice.
>
> The philosophers have only *interpreted* the world in various ways; the point is to *change* it.[18]

Marx would go on to use his own adaptation of the "Feuerbachian inversion" in a number of ways, not least to argue that Hegel's position on the state was exactly the same as theology: it began with abstracted ideas

---

17: Marx, 1975a, p175; 1976b, p378.
18: Marx 1976a, pp4-5.

such as state, sovereignty, constitution and tried to make human beings fit.[19] Much later on, in 1886, Engels would fill this picture out in his lucid prose and show why Feuerbach was so important for the development of historical materialism.

Bruno Bauer's a-theology

Given Feuerbach's importance, it is not for nothing that the first section of *The German Ideology* should be devoted to his work. There is also a section given over to Bruno Bauer. In a number of writings Marx would come back to Bauer, initially to defend him but then later to attack him mercilessly.[20] Even so, many years later they kept in touch and met up frequently in London when Bauer was there. But why attack Bauer? The basic reason was that Bauer achieved a radical republican and democratic position through his biblical criticism and theology. Marx in particular was thoroughly opposed to such a possibility: theology dealt with heaven and was not concerned with earth—*that* was the task of the new historical materialism. For Marx, Bauer was far too much under the influence of Hegel's idealist method and in many respects Marx's distancing from Bauer was an effort to come to terms with Hegel. So we find the repeated and often heavily satirical criticism that "Saint Bruno" Bauer left matters in the realm of theology and thereby stunted his critical work.

Marx was also excising the influence of someone who had been a close friend, first as a fellow member of the Young Hegelian *Doktorklub* from 1837, later as a teacher of the Book of Isaiah at the University of Berlin in 1839 and as one who might have gained Marx a position. The problem was that Bauer was removed from Berlin to Bonn in 1839 and then eventually lost his job in Bonn for his radical theological and political positions. He argued that the church was ossified and dogmatic, for it claimed universal status for a particular person and group. In the same way that we find a struggle in the Bible between free self-consciousness and religious dogmatism, so also in Bauer's own time the religious dogmatism of the church needed to be overthrown. In its place Bauer argued for atheism, democracy and republicanism.

Max Stirner's world history

So we find Marx and Engels at the point where Feuerbach's inversion has enabled them to step beyond the criticism of religion and focus on the criticism of the earthly conditions of human struggle, and Bauer's

---

19: See Marx, 1975d.

20: Marx, 1975e, 1975f.

radical theology had to be negated since religion cannot provide one with a radical critique. The engagement with Max Stirner is a little different. Most don't bother with the endless pages of *The German Ideology* given over to a detailed refutation of Stirner's *The Ego and His Own*,[21] preferring to stop after the first part with the early description of the new historical materialist method.

However, the Stirner section is crucial because Marx and Engels develop the first coherent statement of historical materialism in response to Stirner's world history. In other words, Marx and Engels offer an alternative theory of the workings of world history as they develop their critique of Stirner. The way they wrote the manuscript (which was never published in their lifetime) is important: as they wrote sections on Stirner they found that increasingly coherent statements of an alternative position began emerging in their own thought. Some of these statements remain in the Stirner section, while others were moved to the beginning of the manuscript and placed in the Feuerbach chapter (especially sections II and III). What we find is that, in contrast to Stirner's radical focus on the individual, Marx and Engels develop a collective focus. Instead of Stirner's use of Jesus as the first great individual human ego, they sought an approach that was very much of this world. Above all, Stirner wanted to provide a schema of world history that was pitched against Hegel. The reason why Marx and Engels devoted so much attention to him is that they too wanted a schema of world history that overturned Hegel. The difference is that while Stirner mades that lever of history the radical individual ego modelled on a very human Jesus, Marx and Engels located the lever with the internal contradictions of class, economics and modes of production. The long struggle with Stirner was an effort to overcome this residual religious influence. One only has to look at the structure of Marx and Engels's criticism, moving through the major books of the Bible and quoting the Bible *ad nauseam*, criticising Stirner's prophetic role and theological dabbling, to see that what is at stake is religion. Out of that intense struggle with Stirner the first clear statement of historical materialism arose.

Idols and fetishes

So far I have dealt with a number of arguments from religion that Marx transformed into his own approach, particularly with Feuerbach's inversion and Stirner's effort to rewrite world history from scratch. There is one other idea that fascinated Marx—fetishism. One of the most read sections

21: Stirner, 2005.

of Marx's *Capital* is the one called "The Fetishism of Commodities and the Secret Thereof".[22] Here Marx traces the way commodities seem to gain a life of their own and begin to interact with one another as though they were social beings. At the same time, human social relations seem to suffer since they have become like the relations between things. It as though commodities and human beings have swapped roles. Yet this is by no means the first time Marx has made such an argument. It derives ultimately from the study of religion. Marx offers the following hint at the opening of this section in *Capital*:

> A commodity appears, at first sight, a very trivial thing, and easily understood. Its analysis shows that it is, in reality, a very queer thing, abounding in metaphysical subtleties and theological niceties.[23]

So let us follow his hint and see where it leads. The first stop is with the emerging study of world religions, where data and studies were becoming available. In the early 1840s Marx read a book by Charles de Brosses called *Du culte des dieux fétiches ou Parallèle de l'ancienne religion de l'Egypte avec la religion actuelle de Nigritie*.[24] A pioneering work in ethno-anthropology and the history of religion, it coined the word "fetish", by which de Brosses meant an object attributed with superhuman and magical powers and thereby worshipped (in other words, an idol). With subsequent elaboration the term fetish has claimed a permanent seat for itself in the study of the history of religions. As for Marx, in preparation for his lost study on Christian art he read several works on comparative religion, including a German translation (by Pistorius) of de Brosses's book.

This is by no means the last time Marx dealt with the religious origins of fetishism. Close to the end of his life, he made some reading notes that are now called *The Ethnological Notebooks*.[25] It is a collection of notes and comments on the anthropologists LH Morgan (the basis for Engels's *Origin of the Family*), John B Phear, Henry Maine and John Lubbock. These notebooks are an extraordinary read, with sentences that jump around between German, English and French, good slabs of Greek and Latin and occasional terms from Russian, Sanskrit, Ojibwa and other languages, endless abbreviations, unfinished sentences, slang, vulgar terms,

---

22: Marx, 1996, pp81-94.
23: Marx, 1996, p81.
24: Brosses, 1760.
25: Marx, 1972.

exclamations and references to current affairs. The most interesting pages are the last few on John Lubbock. Here Marx deals explicitly with the religious side of fetishism. Marx can't stand that "civilised ass" Lubbock, but what these notes show is that Marx never lost sight of the religious element of the term fetish.

In between his reading of de Brosses and Lubbock, Marx kept adapting the idea of fetishism. He used it for political polemic, but above all it comes into service in his economic arguments, including the categories of money, labour, commodities and capitalism itself. As an example of political polemic, there is an early piece criticising the various decisions by the Rhine Province Assembly (a gathering of nobles) back in 1839. Marx accuses the Rhineland nobles of having a fetish for wood and hares, since they wished to punish the peasants who helped themselves to fallen wood and hares.[26] A little later (1844) Marx would develop the argument that money as a mediator of exchange is analogous to Christ the mediator. Christ is projected by human beings as the ideal mediator, whom we must worship, from whom we have our being, without whom we are worthless, and above all as the one who mediates between us and god and enables our salvation. So also does money become a quasi-divine mediator: before it too we must kneel, we gain our worth from money, its pursuit becomes our goal in life, and it mediates between objects and us.[27]

When we get to his critique of labour and commodities, Marx extends the idea of fetishistic transference: fetishism is the transference of human social characteristics to objects and vice versa. With labour, the more the worker puts into the product he or she is making, the less the worker becomes. In the end, the product becomes hostile, alien and independent at the expense of the worker.[28] Or in terms of the commodity-form, the relation between commodities takes on the appearance of relations between human beings, while human beings seem to relate like objects: it is a "mysterious thing, simply because the social character of men's labour appears to them as an objective character stamped upon the product of that labour; because the relation of the producers to the sum total of their own labour is presented to them as a social relation, existing not between themselves,

---

26: Marx, 1975c, pp262-263.

27: Marx, 1975g, p212.

28: Marx 1975g, p272. Similarly, "Every self-estrangement of man, from himself and from nature, appears in the relation in which he places himself and nature to men other than and differentiated from himself. For this reason religious self-estrangement necessarily appears in the relationship of the layman to the priest, or again to a mediator, etc, since we are here dealing with the intellectual world" (p279).

but between the products of their labour".[29] It is important to note here that Marx doesn't say this actually happens. It is, like religion and fetishism, an illusion (he continually uses religion as an example). And it is an illusion that belongs above all to the political economists he is criticising.

This is especially so with capital itself. In a delightful passage towards the end of the extraordinary and endless *Economic Manuscript of 1861-63* Marx traces the mystification of capital. Here we find exactly the same logic: what appear to be forces and powers beyond the worker are in fact produced by free labour. But now he supplies a huge list of all the things that are fetishised: the capitalist as a personification of capital, the productive powers of capital, use-value and exchange-value, the application of forces of nature and science, the products of labour in the form of machinery, and so on. They all appear as an alien, objective presence in advance that rules over the worker. In short, capital itself becomes a power before which the worker is powerless: all these items "stand on their hind legs vis a vis the worker and confront him as capital".[30] It seems that one of the problems with money, commodities and capital itself is that in the eyes of the economists who worship them they are illusory items that obscure and abstract from the process of human labour and social interaction.

The two sides of opium: the ambivalence of religion

So we can see that some of the key elements of historical materialism were developed in response to religious positions. Now I would like to shift focus to what we can call the political ambivalence of religion. This is one part of Molyneux's argument, but he doesn't go far enough to show that it actually comes right out of the heart of Marx and Engels's work.

Try the following game: begin a discussion on religion and then after a while mention Marx; then ask for the first word that comes into people's heads. Invariably the answer will be "opium". The key passage, over which much ink has been spilled, is as follows:

> *Religious* suffering is, at one and the same time, the *expression* of real suffering and a *protest* against real suffering. Religion is the sigh of the oppressed creature, the heart of a heartless world, and the soul of soulless conditions. It is the *opium* of the people.[31]

29: Marx, 1996, pp82-83.
30: Marx, 1994, pp457-458.
31: Marx, 1975a, p175; 1976b, p378.

Too often we assume that Marx felt that he (or rather Feuerbach) had put the last nail in the coffin of religion. And too often we assume that he did not hear the knocking from the inside of the coffin. However, Marx was a little more astute than that, as Molyneux points out. Here there is a hint of the ambivalence of religion. Religious suffering may be an expression of real suffering and religion may be the sigh, heart and soul of a heartless and soulless world. But it is also a protest against that suffering. That point has been made often enough but there is an ambivalence in the most well known of Marx's phrases: it is the opium of the people. In an excellent article McKinnon points out that the role of opium was ambiguous in 19th century Europe.[32] In contrast to our own associations of opium with drugs, altered states, addicts, organised crime, wily Taliban insurgents, and desperate farmers making a living the only way they can, attitudes to opium were, in Marx's day, much more ambivalent. Widely regarded as a beneficial, useful and cheap medicine at the beginning of the century, it was increasingly vilified by a coalition of medical and religious forces. In between debates raged. McKinnon traces in detail how opium was the centre of debates, defences and parliamentary inquiries, how it was used for all manner of ills and to calm children, how the opium trade was immensely profitable, how it was one of the only medicines available for the working poor, albeit often adulterated, how it was a source of utopian visions for artists and poets, and how it was increasingly stigmatised as a source of addiction and illness. In effect, it ran all the way from blessed medicine to recreational curse.

Marx himself was a regular user of opium, along with arsenic and creosote. As he followed a punishing schedule of too much writing, too little sleep and an inadequate diet, Marx would use it for his carbuncles, toothaches, liver problems, bronchial coughs and so on. As his wife Jenny wrote in a letter to Engels in 1857:

> Dear Mr Engels, One invalid is writing for another by *ordre du mufti*. Chaley's head hurts him almost everywhere, terrible tooth-ache, pains in the ears, head, eyes, throat and god knows what else. Neither opium pills nor creosote do any good. The tooth has got to come out and he jibs at the idea.[33]

For Marx, opium was an ambiguous and multidimensional metaphor. That is why he chose it as the key metaphor for religion.

32: McKinnon, 2006.

33: Jenny Marx, 1983, p563.

The biblical temptations of Engels

While Marx hinted at the political ambivalence of religion, Engels brought it out with his characteristic clarity. Engels grew up in a very pious Calvinist household and was clearly committed until his late teens or early twenties. In the process he came to know his Bible very well, could read the New Testament in Greek and could quote almost any verse at will. His path to liberal Christianity and then atheism turned on the question of biblical contradictions. If the Bible is the word of god, how then do we deal with its myriad contradictions? In his letters to the Graeber brothers and his poem, *The Insolently Threatened Yet Miraculously Rescued Bible*, he struggles with this issue, shifting position all the time—liberal, pantheist, Hegelian, agnostic—until he finally decides that Christianity will never change and that it is irretrievable.[34]

Yet for all his staunch atheism in his later years, he was never quite able to excise the Bible from his thought. There is one biblical book to which he kept returning: the Book of Revelation. In his early texts Engels often made use of the scene of the final judgment at the end of history, whether playfully, in critical satire or in order to express his own sense of the times. So we find him characterising his close friend Friedrich Graeber (a minister in the church) playing cards oblivious to the final battle of good and evil that rages around him.[35] Then there are his mock depictions of the battles between the orthodox theologians and "The Free", as the Young Hegelians of Berlin called themselves.[36] And then at the close of his booklet *Schelling and Revelation*, he makes a very different use of the Book of Revelation. Flushed and excited with the new discoveries, having just read Feuerbach's *The Essence of Christianity* and feeling the shackles of his old, narrow belief structure snapping open, Engels celebrates with a rousing image of the final battle between free thought and obscurantism, all of which ends with the arrival of a New Jerusalem.[37]

Later in life Engels came back to the Book of Revelation to make use of the newly established historical criticism of the Bible.[38] The purpose was to defuse the wild speculation and excitement the biblical book had generated over time by showing that the lurid imagery actually had a mundane historical reference point in the Roman Empire, for it refers to the expected

34: Engels, 1975l, 1975m, 1975k, 1975n, 1975o, 1975p, 1975q, 1975r, 1975s, 1975t, 1975u, 1975v, 1975w, 1975x, 1975y, 1975j.

35: Engels, 1975l.

36: Engels, 1975v, 1975j.

37: Engels, 1975h.

38: Engels, 1990a. See also Engels, 1989.

return of Nero and his defeat by god's forces. But there is one feature of this essay on the Book of Revelation that is vitally important: he points out that Christianity has at various moments been the ideology of revolutionary movements. This argument would become the centrepiece in two final works of his to be considered here, *On the Early History of Christianity* and *The Peasant War in Germany*.

While *The Peasant War in Germany* is mostly concerned with Engels's great love, namely tracing out battle plans, troop movements and assessing tactics, it also has a curious argument concerning Thomas Müntzer. The latter was the leading theologian of the revolt and war in 1525. A reformer who was deeply influenced by Luther, he took Luther's position to its logical conclusion, threw in the need for constant contact with god through dreams and visions, and predicted that the final battle of Armageddon would come soon. Needless to say he met a swift end against the heavy armour of the nobility. While many write Münzer off as a crackpot, Engels wanted to give him his due. Müntzer was, argued Engels, expressing through theological and biblical language the grievances of class oppression and conflict. Religious language was the only way he knew how to express such grievances. If he had lived in Engels's own day the language would have been very different. Indeed, Engels gives his argument a strange twist, suggesting that the closer Müntzer gets to economic and class analysis, the more atheistic he becomes. Despite this odd move, the text gained a life of its own and the better parts of the argument were expanded by the likes of Karl Kautsky and Ernst Bloch.[39]

What Engels had managed to with this piece on the Peasant War was point to a revolutionary side of Christianity. Forty three years later, two years before his death, he wrote *On the History of Early Christianity*, where he argued that Christianity was originally a revolutionary movement. It is a text that influences biblical studies to this day. In his essay Engels relied on the relatively new critical approach to the Bible. Dispensing with dogmatic positions and seeking only what was historically verifiable, such critical readings of the Bible challenged many of the assumptions about the authorship, formation and nature of biblical literature. From this scholarship Engels drew upon conclusions concerning the Gospels and the impossibility of knowing anything much about Jesus (here he relied on Bruno Bauer, who by this time Engels admired) and repeated his earlier observations about the Book of Revelation.

The basic argument is that early Christianity was as close as one could get to a socialist movement in the ancient world. In response to the social,

39: Kautsky, 2002; Bloch, 1969.

cultural and economic breakdown of the Hellenistic world, Christianity offered a solution. Unfortunately that solution was a heavenly rather than earthly one. At this point Engels was ambivalent: even though it offered an other-worldly solution, he also argued that it was revolutionary in practice. It was, he said, the socialism of its day. In this respect it has a number of parallels with the socialism of Engels's own time—appeal to the downtrodden masses, sectarian splits, false prophets, rapid expansion and communism in living.

Conclusion: the politics of alliance

For Marx and especially Engels, a religion like Christianity is politically ambivalent. All too often it sides with the rich and powerful and turns a blind eye to oppression and suffering. But every now and then it also gives voice to rebellion and revolution. This point brings us to Molyneux's call for a politics of alliance. Molyneux argues that activists on the left shouldn't dismiss a comrade who works for the same cause if he or she happens to have a religious belief. He gives the following example: "To put the matter as starkly as possible: from the standpoint of Marxism and international socialism an illiterate, conservative, superstitious Muslim Palestinian peasant who supports Hamas is more progressive than an educated liberal atheist Israeli who supports Zionism (even critically)." He also draws on Lenin to support his position. It seems to me that this position comes out of the heart of the writings of Marx and Engels on religion. Marx's hints concerning the ambivalence of religion were taken much further by Engels who ended up arguing that early Christianity was a proto-socialist movement.

Let me finish with a couple of points. First, the old antagonism between the left and radical currents within religion, once seemingly set in cement, should be a thing of the past. We can well understand how those antagonisms came to be, for religion, power and wealth have all too often been in bed together. The history of the opposition between some types of communism and religion has not helped either. It used to be the case that if a Christian declared she or he had become a socialist, then the assumption was that that person had lost his or her faith. It does not help matters when the major churches also declare Communism to be "godless". But these are, or at least should be, things of the past. Indeed, those who do believe are not necessarily reactionary or fundamentalist. The 200,000 members of the International League of Religious Socialists put the lie to that assumption, as does the movement of Christian Communists. Both the secular and religious left have more in common than they might think.

Further, a politics of alliance recognises the diversity and pluralism of the left. Rather than the long tradition of one small group on the left feeling as though it is the keeper of the grail, spending all its energy condemning other groups as revisionists, deviationists or heretics, the sheer diversity of the left is one of its great achievements. Within this diversity, a religious left has a legitimate and crucial role to play. For example, at the protests against the World Economic Forum in Melbourne in 2000 and then again at the G20 meeting in 2006, we found anarchists, environmentalists, socialists, feminists, various elements of the loopy left, and some religious groups for whom the protests were perfectly consistent with their religious positions.

References

Bauer, Bruno, 1838, *Kritik der Geschichte der Offenbarung: Die Religion des alten Testaments in der geschichtlichen Entwicklung ihrer Prinzipien dargestellt* (Ferdinand Dümmler).

Bauer, Bruno, 1840, *Kritik der evangelischen Geschichte des Johannes* (Karl Schünemann), http://books.google.com/books?id=47OUAAAAYAAJ

Bauer, Bruno, 1841, *Kritik der evangelischen Geschichte der Synoptiker*, 2 volumes, (Otto Wigand), http://books.google.com/books?id=cScWAAAAYAAJ and http://books.google.com/books?id=_SUWAAAAYAAJ

Bauer, Bruno 1842, *Kritik der evangelischen Geschichte der Synoptiker und des Johannes, Dritter und letzter Band* (Fr Otto).

Bloch, Ernst, 1969, *Thomas Münzer als Theologe der Revolution*, in *Werkausgabe*, volume 2 (Suhrkamp).

Breckman, Warren, 1999, *Marx, the Young Hegelians, and the Origins of Radical Social Theory* (Cambridge University).

Brosses, Charles de, 1760, *Du culte des dieux fétiches ou Parallèle de l'ancienne religion de l'Egypte* (Paris), http://books.google.com/books?id=CfcWAAAAYAAJ

Dawkins, Richard, 2006, *The God Delusion* (Houghton Mifflin).

Dennett, Daniel C, 2007, *Breaking the Spell: Religion as a Natural Phenomenon* (Penguin).

Eagleton, Terry, 2006, "Lunging, Flailing, Mispunching", *London Review of Books*, 19 October 2006, www.lrb.co.uk/v28/n20/

Engels, Frederick, 1975a [1839], *Letters from Wuppertal*, in Karl Marx and Frederick Engels, *Collected Works*, volume 2 (Progress).

Engels, Frederick, 1975b [1839], *FW Krummacher's Sermon on Joshua*, in Karl Marx and Frederick Engels, *Collected Works*, volume 2 (Progress), www.marxists.org/archive/marx/works/1839/05/telegraph.htm

Engels, Frederick, 1975c [1840], *Reports from Bremen: Theatre. Publishing Festival*, in Karl Marx and Frederick Engels, *Collected Works*, volume 2 (Progress), www.marxists.org/archive/marx/works/1840/07/bremen.htm

Engels, Frederick, 1975d [1840], *Two Sermons by FW Krummacher*, in Karl Marx and Frederick Engels, *Collected Works*, volume 2 (Progress), www.marxists.org/archive/marx/works/1840/09/sermons.htm

Engels, Frederick, 1975e [1840], *Reports from Bremen: Rationalism and Pietism*, in Karl Marx and Frederick Engels, *Collected Works*, volume 2 (Progress), www.marxists.org/archive/marx/works/1840/07/bremen.htm

Engels, Frederick, 1975f [1841], *Reports from Bremen: Ecclesiastical Controversy*, in Karl Marx and Frederick Engels, *Collected Works*, volume 2 (Progress), www.marxists.org/archive/marx/works/1840/07/bremen.htm

Engels, Frederick, 1975g [1841], *Schelling on Hegel*, in Karl Marx and Frederick Engels, *Collected Works*, volume 2 (Progress), www.marxists.org/archive/marx/works/1841/anti-schelling/ch01.htm

Engels, Frederick 1975h [1842], *Schelling and Revelation: Critique of the Latest Attempt of Reaction Against the Free Philosophy*, in Karl Marx and Frederick Engels, *Collected Works*, volume 2 (Progress), www.marxists.org/archive/marx/works/1841/anti-schelling/ch02.htm

Engels, Frederick 1975i [1842], *Schelling, Philosopher in Christ, or the Transfiguration of Worldly Wisdom into Divine Wisdom: For Believing Christians Who Do Not Know the Language of Philosophy*, in Karl Marx and Frederick Engels, *Collected Works*, volume 2 (Progress), www.marxists.org/archive/marx/works/1841/anti-schelling/ch06.htm

Engels, Frederick 1975j [1842], *The Insolently Threatened Yet Miraculously Rescued Bible or: The Triumph of Faith, To Wit, the Terrible, Yet True and Salutary History of the Erstwhile Licentiate Bruno Bauer; How the Same, Seduced by the Devil, Fallen from the True Faith, Became Chief Devil, and Was Well and Truly Ousted in the End: A Christian Epic in Four Cantos* in *Marx and Engels Collected Works*, in Karl Marx and Frederick Engels, *Collected Works*, volume 2 (Progress), www.marxists.org/archive/marx/works/1842/cantos/

Engels, Frederick, 1975k [1839], *To Friedrich Graeber in Berlin, Bremen, about 23 April-1 May 1839*, in Karl Marx and Frederick Engels, *Collected Works*, volume 2 (Progress), www.marxists.org/archive/marx/works/1839/letters/39_04_23.htm

Engels, Frederick, 1975l [1839], *To Friedrich Graeber, Bremen, 19 February 1839*, in Karl Marx and Frederick Engels, *Collected Works*, volume 2 (Progress), www.marxists.org/archive/marx/works/1839/letters/39_02_19.htm

Engels, Frederick, 1975m [1839], *To Friedrich Graeber, Bremen, 8 April 1839*, in Karl Marx and Frederick Engels, *Collected Works*, volume 2 (Progress), www.marxists.org/archive/marx/works/1839/letters/39_04_08.htm

Engels, Frederick, 1975n [1839], *To Wilhelm Graeber in Berlin, Bremen, about 28-30 April 1839* , in Karl Marx and Frederick Engels, *Collected Works*, volume 2 (Progress), www.marxists.org/archive/marx/works/1839/letters/39_04_30.htm

Engels, Frederick, 1975o [1839], *To Wilhelm Graeber in Berlin, Bremen, 24 May-15 June 1839* , in Karl Marx and Frederick Engels, *Collected Works*, volume 2 (Progress), www.marxists.org/archive/marx/works/1839/letters/39_05_24.htm

Engels, Frederick, 1975p [1839], *To Friedrich Graeber in Berlin, Bremen, 15 June 1839*, in Karl Marx and Frederick Engels, *Collected Works*, volume 2 (Progress), www.marxists.org/archive/marx/works/1839/letters/39_06_15.htm

Engels, Frederick, 1975q [1839], *To Friedrich Graeber in Berlin, Bremen, 12-27 July 1839*, in Karl Marx and Frederick Engels, *Collected Works*, volume 2 (Progress), www.marxists.org/archive/marx/works/1839/letters/39_07_12.htm

Engels, Frederick, 1975r [1839], *To Wilhelm Graeber in Berlin, Bremen, 30 July 1839*, in Karl Marx and Frederick Engels, *Collected Works*, volume 2 (Progress), www.marxists.org/archive/marx/works/1839/letters/39_07_30.htm

Engels, Frederick, 1975s [1839], *To Wilhelm Graeber in Berlin, Bremen, 8 October 1839*, in Karl Marx and Frederick Engels, *Collected Works*, volume 2 (Progress), www.marxists.org/archive/marx/works/1839/letters/39_10_08.htm

Engels, Frederick, 1975t [1839], *To Wilhelm Graeber in Berlin, Bremen, 20-21 October 1839*, in Karl Marx and Frederick Engels, *Collected Works*, volume 2 (Progress), www.marxists.org/archive/marx/works/1839/letters/39_10_20.htm

Engels, Frederick, 1975u [1839], *To Friedrich Graeber, Bremen, 29 October 1839*, in Karl Marx and Frederick Engels, *Collected Works*, volume 2 (Progress), www.marxists.org/archive/marx/works/1839/letters/39_10_29.htm

Engels, Frederick. 1975v [1839], *To Wilhelm Graeber in Berlin, Bremen, 13-20 November 1839*, in Karl Marx and Frederick Engels, *Collected Works*, volume 2 (Progress), www.marxists.org/archive/marx/works/1839/letters/39_11_13.htm

Engels, Frederick, 1975w [1839], *To Friedrich Graeber in Berlin, Bremen, 9 December 1839-5 February 1840*, in Karl Marx and Frederick Engels, *Collected Works*, volume 2 (Progress), www.marxists.org/archive/marx/works/1839/letters/39_12_09.htm

Engels, Frederick, 1975x [1840], *To Wilhelm Graeber in Barmen, Bremen, 20 November 1840*, in Karl Marx and Frederick Engels, *Collected Works*, volume 2 (Progress), www.marxists.org/archive/marx/works/1840/letters/40_11_20.htm

Engels, Frederick, 1975y [1841], *To Friedrich Graeber, 22 February 1841*, in Karl Marx and Frederick Engels, *Collected Works*, volume 2 (Progress), www.marxists.org/archive/marx/works/1841/letters/41_02_22.htm

Engels, Frederick, 1978 [1850], *The Peasant War in Germany*, in Karl Marx and Frederick Engels, *Collected Works*, volume 10 (Progress), www.marxists.org/archive/marx/works/1850/peasant-war-germany/

Engels, Frederick, 1989 [1882], *Bruno Bauer and Early Christianity*, in Karl Marx and Frederick Engels, *Collected Works*, volume 24 (Progress), www.marxists.org/archive/marx/works/1882/05/bauer.htm

Engels, Frederick, 1990a [1883], *The Book of Revelation*, in Karl Marx and Frederick Engels, *Collected Works*, volume 26 (Progress).

Engels, Frederick 1990b [1894], *On the History of Early Christianity*, in Karl Marx and Frederick Engels, *Collected Works*, volume 27 (Progress), www.marxists.org/archive/marx/works/1894/early-christianity/

Feuerbach, Ludwig, 1986 [1841], *Das Wesen des Christentums* (Reclam, Ditzingen).

Feuerbach, Ludwig, 1989, *The Essence of Christianity* (Prometheus).

Harmer, Dean, 2005, *The God Gene: How Faith Is Hardwired Into Our Genes* (Anchor).

Harris, Sam, 2005, *The End of Faith: Religion, Terror and the Future of Reason* (W W Norton).

Harris, Sam, 2006, *Letter to a Christian Nation* (Knopf).

Hitchens, Christopher, 2007, *God Is Not Great: How Religion Poisons Everything* (Twelve Books).

Kautsky, Karl, 2002 [1897], *Communism in Central Europe in the Time of the Reformation* (Fisher and Unwin), www.marxists.org/archive/kautsky/1897/europe/

Marx, Jenny, 1983, *Jenny Marx to Engels in Manchester, London, about 12 April 1857*, in Karl Marx and Frederick Engels, *Collected Works*, volume 40 (Progress), www.marxists.org/archive/marx/letters/jenny/57_04_12.htm

Marx, Karl, 1972, *The Ethnological Notebooks of Karl Marx* (Van Gorcum).

Marx, Karl, 1975a [1844], *Contribution to the Critique of Hegel's Philosophy of Law: Introduction*, in Karl Marx and Frederick Engels, *Collected Works*, volume 3 (Progress), www.marxists.org/archive/marx/works/1843/critique-hpr/intro.htm

Marx, Karl, 1975b [1842], *The Leading Article in Number 179 of the* Kölnische Zeitung, in Karl Marx and Frederick Engels, *Collected Works*, volume 1 (Progress), www.marxists.org/archive/marx/works/1842/07/10.htm

Marx, Karl, 1975c [1842], *Proceedings of the Sixth Rhine Province Assembly. First Article: Debates on Freedom of the Press and Publication of the Proceedings of the Assembly of the Estates*, in Karl Marx and Frederick Engels, *Collected Works*, volume 1 (Progress), www.marxists.org/archive/marx/works/1842/free-press/

Marx, Karl, 1975d [1844], *Contribution to the Critique of Hegel's Philosophy of Law*, in Karl Marx and Frederick Engels, *Collected Works*, volume 3 (Progress), www.marxists.org/archive/marx/works/1843/critique-hpr/

Marx, Karl, 1975e [1842], *Yet Another Word on "Bruno Bauer und die Akademische Lehrfreiheit" by Dr O F Gruppe, Berlin, 1842*, in Karl Marx and Frederick Engels, *Collected Works*, volume 1 (Progress), www.marxists.org/archive/marx/works/1842/11/16.htm

Marx, Karl, 1975f [1844], *On the Jewish Question*, in Karl Marx and Frederick Engels, *Collected Works*, volume 3 (Progress), www.marxists.org/archive/marx/works/1844/jewish-question/

Marx, Karl, 1975g [1844], *Economic and Philosophic Manuscripts of 1844*, in Karl Marx and Frederick Engels, *Collected Works*, volume 3 (Progress), www.marxists.org/archive/marx/works/1844/manuscripts/preface.htm

Marx, Karl, 1976a, [1845], *Theses on Feuerbach (original version)*, in Karl Marx and Frederick Engels, *Collected Works*, volume 4 (Progress).

Marx, Karl, 1976b [1844], *Zur Kritik der Hegelschen Rechtsphilosophie. Einleitung*, in Karl Marx and Frederick Engels, *Werke*, volume 1 (Dietz).

Marx, Karl, 1994, *Economic Manuscripts of 1861-1863 (conclusion): A Contribution to the Critique of Political Economy*, in Karl Marx and Frederick Engels, *Collected Works*, volume 34 (Progress).

Marx, Karl, 1996 [1867], *Capital*, volume 1, in Karl Marx and Frederick Engels, *Collected Works*, volume 35 (Progress), www.marxists.org/archive/marx/works/1867-c1/

Marx, Karl, 2002, *Marx on Religion* (Temple University).

Marx, Karl, and Frederick Engels, 1975 [1845], *The Holy Family, or Critique of Critical Criticism*, in *Collected Works*, volume 4 (Progress), www.marxists.org/archive/marx/works/1845/holy-family/

Marx, Karl and Frederick Engels 1976a [1845], *The German Ideology: Critique of Modern German Philosophy According to Its Representatives Feuerbach, B. Bauer and Stirner, and of German Socialism According to Its various Prophets* in *Collected Works*, volume 5 (Progress), www.marxists.org/archive/marx/works/1845/german-ideology/

Marx, Karl, and Frederick Engels, 1976b, *On Religion* (Progress).

McKinnon, Andrew M, 2006, "Opium as Dialectics of Religion: Metaphor, Expression and Protest", in Warren S Goldstein (ed), *Marx, Critical Theory and Religion: A Critique of Rational Choice* (Brill).

Molyneux, John, 2008, "More Than Opium: Marxism and Religion", *International Socialism 119*. www.isj.org.uk/?id=456

Stirner, Max, 2005 [1845], *The Ego and His Own: The Case of the Individual Against Authority* (Dover Publications), http://flag.blackened.net/daver/anarchism/stirner/theego0.html

Strauss, David Friedrich, 1835, *Das Leben Jesu, kritisch bearbeitet* (CF Osiander), http://books.google.com/books?id=gssrAAAAYAAJ

The NPA: a space for rebuilding

Denis Godard

The New Anticapitalist Party (Nouveau Parti Anticapitaliste, NPA) is an exciting political development because it responds to a need arising from the struggle in France over the past few years. Marxist revolutionaries were at the heart of its creation, and at a time when the crisis of global capitalism is accelerating the NPA opens up for them the prospect of active intervention in an advanced capitalist country on a scale unprecedented outside a revolutionary period. This is what makes the debate between François Sabado and Alex Callinicos so significant.[1] At a time when revolutionaries have an increased opportunity to learn from concrete experience and a duty to rid themselves of the burden of sectarianism, the open tone of the debate is not the least of its merits.

The rationale common to both Sabado and Callinicos in their discussion is that the crisis of the traditional leaderships of the workers' movement has opened up a space "to the left of the reformist left" that needs filling. Their disagreements turn on the question of the programmatic delimitations of the organisation that seeks to fill this space—whether it should be revolutionary and whether there should be restrictions upon Marxists within its ranks.

In his latest intervention Callinicos acknowledges that, for reasons specific to France, Sabado is correct to argue that the NPA can be not only an anti-capitalist organisation but even a revolutionary one in the broad sense. But Callinicos also insists that the approach to other situations requires

1: Callinicos, 2008; Sabado, 2009; Garganas, 2009; Callinicos, 2009.

greater flexibility. To read Callinicos is without doubt to see that grasping the nature of reformism—that is, understanding the contradictions that run through class consciousness and understanding the dynamics of its evolution—is for him the most important factor in arming the political revival and defining appropriate strategies and tactics. I share his preoccupation.

Debate about the NPA should not centre in the first instance on programmatic delimitations, however, but on how well it can organise some kind of formal or informal leadership, emerging from the process of struggle, how well it can influence the movement—and even lead and rebuild it on a class basis. For that to happen, the revolutionary current in the NPA must possess clarity and coherence. The claimed revolutionary delimitations for an organisation of this kind are not only an illusion; they weaken the coherence of the revolutionary current and become an obstacle to building the common anti-capitalist strategy this party needs.

The limits of the debate between Sabado and Callinicos seem to me to stem from the fact that the space they speak of is not just a space "to be filled". This is no mere "party"[2] or narrowly political space. Its nature is ideological, social and political. To a large extent the space must be rebuilt.

The coming together, following their own rhythms, of changes in the capitalist mode of production and therefore structure of the working class, of economic crisis and the return of struggle has created a historically new political situation, one characterised by Stathis Kouvélakis as a prolonged crisis of hegemony: "Precisely because its character is fundamentally destructive of the previous social compromise, neoliberalism has only been able to emerge victorious over it on the basis of defeating the dominated classes and forcing them to retreat. It has won solely by default, in the absence of an alternative perspective. It has not succeeded in creating majority popular support. In Gramscian terms, this is domination without hegemony".[3]

One element in this crisis of hegemony is the crisis of the traditional leaderships of the working class. This is not simply because ideologically they have "swung to the right". Changes in the working class have largely weakened the bastions on which these leaderships rested and in some cases have destroyed them. At the same time new sectors have developed. The entire structuring of the "world of work" is in crisis (every traditional class organisation, together with its reference points and "culture", has been

2: In this respect at least, this shares Olivier Nachtwey's criticism of the concept of social liberalism as "concentrating too much on the ideological orientation of the new social democracy and leaving class representation in the shade"—Nachtwey, 2009.

3: Kouvélakis, 2009.

weakened). Beyond that, so too is the influence the workers' movement might have over the whole of society. The crisis of the workers' movement has indeed weakened workers' ability to resist the neoliberal offensive. Kouvélakis is right to underline that this is as much a condition as an effect. But we must not lose sight of the way the domination of the traditional leaderships in the workers' movement, the (bureaucratic) structuring of the workers' movement and its culture, used to be one factor in the dominant hegemony in the previous period. From this point of view, it is correct to speak of a space opening up.

Relevance of a paradox

In a 1970 interview Tony Cliff astonished a journalist from the *International Idiot* by talking more of the struggle to be carried out within the working class than of the struggle against the ruling class. Domination by a capitalist minority is in reality only possible because generally the vast majority of workers "incorporate" this domination within their ideas and practices. Reformism is no straightforward "manipulation of consciousness". It is an expression of what Gramsci calls the "contradictory consciousness" of workers—their acceptance of dominant ideas and the way in which the expression of their real interests enters into contradiction with these dominant ideas.

The basis for challenging dominant ideas develops through the experience of even limited resistance to exploitation or more generally of resistance to injustice. But this challenge is always partial and heterogeneous within the class as a whole. Thus, if concrete struggle against the ruling class is necessary for the working class to develop itself as a class (ie self-conscious and organised), a struggle within the class is also needed, if for no other reason than to make struggle itself possible.

In *The Communist Manifesto*, Karl Marx gave a broad theoretical answer to this paradox by defining the role of communists. Communists must never separate themselves from the dominated class. They must always defend the general interests of the movement. At the same time, they must be the most resolute section of the "working class parties" and have the "theoretical" advantage over "the great mass of the working class...of clearly understanding the lines of march, the conditions, and the ultimate general results of the proletarian movement".

The united front revisited

The united front strategy was the practical response to this paradox by the parties of the Third International in the 1920s. The Third International was born out of splits in the parties of the Second International in 1919. But the capacity of the reformist parties in the developed countries to preserve the support of important sections of the working class (if only passively) had led to the failure of the first wave of revolution, notably in Italy and in Germany.

The united front was designed to win over the majority of workers by drawing them into action alongside revolutionaries. Revolutionaries would thereby show in action that they were "the most resolute section of the working class parties" and demonstrate that "theoretically" they had a clear "understanding [of] the lines of march, the conditions, and the ultimate general results of the proletarian movement".

This strategy was elaborated under particular historical circumstances whose characteristics can be succinctly summarised thus: a workers' movement existed that was organised and powerful (despite the war), there was a dominant Marxist culture at the heart of the left, and strong reformist and revolutionary parties contended for leadership of the workers' movement. Under these circumstances unity in action by the class was guaranteed via unity of its organisations (in the first place, of its parties). Detaching workers from reformism was in essence to succeed in detaching them from the reformist party.[4]

The prolonged crisis of hegemony that we have described means that the strategy of the united front is now posed in radically altered historical conditions: we have a new workers' movement that has by and large become unstructured and traditional leaderships with only weak links to the working class, and this in a society in which class ideas have only just rediscovered an audience.

The united front broadened

Sabado fails to approach the NPA within the framework of a united front because his conceptual basis is the "classical" model. This leads him to think of the NPA in terms of a political fight, with the NPA playing the role of a revolutionary party engaged in struggle against a reformist party.

The notion of "united front of a special kind", to which Callinicos refers, is an attempt to supersede the historical model because the situation demands it. This, however, remains an inadequate response for it is conceived as no more than a variation on the model. This leads Callinicos

4: Consideration should be given to the change Stalinism was already making to the application of this united front strategy once neither of the two parties fighting for leadership of the workers' movement was revolutionary. We can say, however, that unity of action among workers was still being formulated in the context of a largely organised workers' movement. See Godard, 2008.

to consider the NPA in the final analysis as failing to correspond to this variation.

While imprisoned by the fascist regime, Gramsci tried to understand the failure of the revolutionary wave of the 1920s. This led him to re-examine the notion of the united front and to extend its scope, based on an analysis of the more complex structure of advanced capitalist countries. From this he drew a broader vision of the united front. As Daniel Bensaïd explains, he attaches to it "as objective the conquest of political and cultural hegemony". He deduces from this, in a very Leninist manner, that at stake in a revolutionary situation "is the resolution in a generalised crisis of the reciprocal relationships between all components in society", which cannot be reduced to a "clash between two antagonistic classes".[5]

The "classical" model, within this broader notion of the united front, is the form that suited particular historical conditions, those in which the reality of the workers' movement and its influence made the struggle for leadership the key question for "resolving this generalised crisis". The fundamental objective of the united front is not, however, unity of action between parties. Its objective is to set the vast mass of society in motion in a multi-levelled confrontation with the ruling class, to organise the working class as the motor force of this movement and to win the movement to revolutionary leadership.[6]

Strategic conception of the NPA

It is in the light of this that we must clarify our conception of the NPA. The issue now for class struggle in France is to rebuild the workers' movement and enable it to pull behind it "all the oppressed sectors"—to build what some call a "counter-hegemony". At a time when the developing process of struggle has already begun to see potential leaderships emerge on many battlefronts against the system, the NPA must aim to regroup, coordinate and provide them with a strategy for confronting the ruling class. If it does so, and relies on the dynamic of the struggle to take things forward, it will not only help these new leaderships to overcome the paralysis due to the current domination by the traditional leaderships and their politics, but will also be key to rebuilding the workers' movement.

This is the basis for establishing the foundations of the NPA as an

5: Bensaïd, 2007.

6: Chris Harman, 2007, sums this up as an attempt to find what gives "an economic force" the potential "to translate itself into a political force with the mass capacity to draw all sections of the oppressed in a bid to overthrow an old political system".

anti-capitalist and class party. It is worth saying from the outset that none of this is guaranteed in advance or can be won by the proclamation of founding principles. The stress on the NPA having precise restrictions during its formation benefited the most battle-hardened propagandisers at the expense of the activists. And the most stridently "revolutionary" elements of these propagandisers, inside and outside the former Ligue Communiste Révolutionnaire, found an echo in "healthy" leftist tendencies from those social sectors recently radicalised by the movement.[7]

The consequences of having the founding process dominated by propagandising are clear. The NPA may have begun to implant itself in the working class and sectors of society. Nevertheless it remains comparatively weak when it comes to organised sections of the movement, particularly in the unions but also in the neighbourhood associations. And, paradoxically, what makes it easier to convince people, at least superficially, about the need for revolutionary programmatic delimitations, makes it more difficult to build on a class basis.

Clearly, involvement in a party requires greater reflection and is a slower business for militants who work in a milieu, let alone those who have responsibilities. But winning such militants to the NPA should be an objective, which the dominant propagandising profile makes more difficult.

Which strategy?

Focusing the debate solely on programmatic delimitations is insufficient and could merely reinforce the obstacles to working out a strategy for the NPA.

It is the growing capitalist crisis and the questions raised in struggle that create the audience for such a strategy. When alongside struggle there is the growth of distrust towards the institutions and leaderships of the workers' movement, we must develop a concrete alternative perspective to stop combativity sinking back into passivity. Fetishising the call for a general strike can prove a double-edged weapon. The demand makes sense if pressure forces trade union leaderships to call for a national day of strikes and demonstrations. But it can create profound pessimism when these same leaderships paralyse action and there is no alternative leadership able to take its place on a more militant basis. That can only reinforce electoralist illusions (and therefore reformism), which then appear the only way to raise the question of power.

7: No matter how spontaneous this leftism may appear, it is nonetheless influenced by autonomist theories. Panos Garganos, 2009, is quite right to stress the need to wage a political and theoretical struggle against these currents. Moreover, the influence of these currents will be all the stronger on significant, if minority, sections of the movement the longer we fail to work out a coherent strategy for the NPA.

Clearly the NPA should articulate a politics that can be defended on every front it is involved in, with the aim of building and developing the movement on a broader and more militant basis. But this should be combined with the equivalent of what the Trotskyist tradition has termed a transitional strategy[8] by putting forward anti-capitalist structuralist reforms. The NPA should be known as the organisation that proposes, argues for, sometimes initiates (in concrete circumstances) forms of what classically used to be called workers' control. It should be arguing for forms of workers' organisation in workplaces that aim to develop greater or lesser forms of control, ones that unite workers and users of public services in the locality, etc.

As Donny Gluckstein's study of workers' councils shows, experiences like these demand and allow for cooperation between two groups. One consists of a layer of "local rank and file militants" in the workplaces who have gained legitimacy among workers. They are often well known for their opposition to trade union leaderships but often limited by constantly having to deal with immediate demands. The other consists of political activists who possess a more global vision but who frequently lack legitimacy and roots in the working class.[9]

The role of revolutionaries

Not only is there no contradiction between an anti-capitalist strategy and a revolutionary strategy but the first must be grasped as an element of the second. Disagreements over the perspective of revolution, above all over the need to overthrow the state or over the role of violence, are not hindrances to sharing an anti-capitalist strategy (this was, after all, the basis for working out transitional demands).

But revolutionaries must demonstrate that clarity about the perspective of revolution helps develop a consistent anti-capitalist strategy.

Moreover, the development, however short lived, of alternative forms of power will raise, this time concretely, the question of how broad

8: The tradition to which I, like Callinicos, belong has long criticised the so-called orthodox Trotskyist tradition for its formal and ahistorical conception of the transitional programme elaborated by Trotsky. A sign of what is new about the period is that this approach must be taken up again and made concrete. The arguments of the International Socialist Tendency, which I believe were valid in the past, should not become an obstacle in the period that is opening up. Conversely, the current that came out of the Fourth International should not go on to consign the transitional approach to the status of an "outdated strategic lesson" or abandon Trotskyism as a tradition of the past.

9: Gluckstein, 1985.

the confrontation with the existing institutions of power must be, and of what methods are needed.

Here we return, as far as revolutionaries in the NPA are concerned, to the role Marx attributed to communists: they are the most resolute when it comes to elaborating and developing an anti-capitalist strategy for the NPA and the most class conscious when it comes to understanding the lines of march, the conditions, and the ultimate general results of this strategy.

That then excludes creating a revolutionary faction within the NPA, the basis of which would be autonomy of action, since the possibility and development of an anti-capitalist strategy are currently conditional upon the development of the NPA. That also excludes its opposite—making do with argument at the purely theoretical level.

The aim of Marxists revolutionaries must be to work out a strategy among themselves and debate and try to get their strategy accepted within the NPA. They must test it not only against other positions but also in relation to the experience accumulated within the framework of the NPA.

References

Bensaïd, Daniel, 2007, "Front Unique et Hégémonie", www.europe-solidaire.org/spip.php?article7177

Callinicos, Alex, 2008, "Where is the Radical Left Going", *International Socialism* 120 (autumn 2008), www.isj.org.uk/?id=484

Callinicos, Alex, 2009, "Revolutionary Paths: A Reply to Panos Garganas and François Sabado", *International Socialism* 122 (spring 2009), www.isj.org.uk/?id=538

Garganas, Panos, 2009, "The Radical Left: A Richer Mix", *International Socialism* 121 (winter 2009), www.isj.org.uk/?id=513

Gluckstein, Donny, 1985, *The Western Soviets* (Bookmarks).

Godard, Denis, 2008, "Redéfinir le Front Unique pour en Faire une Boussole", *Que Faire?*, number 9, http://quefaire.lautre.net/articles/09frontunique.html

Harman, Chris, 2007, "Gramsci, the *Prison Notebooks* and Philosophy", *International Socialism 114* (spring 2007), www.isj.org.uk/?id=308

Kouvélakis, Stathis, 2009, "France, une Crise d'Hégémonie Prolongée", *ContreTemps*, new series, number 1.

Nachtwey, Olivier, 2009, "La Crise de la Représentation de Classe en Allemagne et Die Linke", *ContreTemps*, new series, number 2.

Sabado, François, 2009, "Building the New Anticapitalist Party", *International Socialism* 121 (winter 2009), www.isj.org.uk/?id=512

Confronting the wolf

Chris Harman

Neil Faulkner accused me in our previous issue of not seeing the "wolf" of economic crisis now that it is upon us.[1] It is an accusation that, I must admit, mystified me, since only a year ago Jim Kincaid was accusing me of grossly overestimating the crisis-prone nature of the world system.[2] The accusation is even more mystifying since it relies on an analysis nearly all of which came from my own writings, reinforced by statistics from the same source (as anyone who looks at his footnotes can tell). If plagiarism is the highest form of flattery, I should be flattered indeed.

The core of my analysis has been that we are faced with a crisis in which neither governments nor big corporations can simply rely on the "creative destruction" of the market resolving as some firms cannibalise others.[3] This is leading to intense political and ideological as well as economic crisis as panicking governments turn, with the support of wide sections of capital, to "Keynesian" interventionist policies, including partial nationalisation. The result is that a level of government economic spending, already much higher than in the 1930s, has shot up even further so that the US government deficit this year is set to be 10 percent of GNP—a higher figure than total government spending under Roosevelt in 1936. But, as I wrote, "the major

1: Faulkner, 2009.

2: Kincaid, 2008.

3: Harman, 2009a. All the quotes from me are from this source unless otherwise indicated.

financial and industrial corporations operate on a much greater scale than in the inter-war years and therefore the strain on governments of bailing them out is disproportionately larger." The bail-outs "are bigger than ever in the past but the pool of debt they have to dispose of is also much deeper".

This introduces enormous unknowns into the situation, which exacerbate the sense of social, political and ideological crisis while making the forecasting of exact outcomes difficult. "The panicking politicians and terrified capitalists doing the bailing out can hardly avoid clashing with each other as they try to cope with problems they never thought they would face."

I did suggest it might just be possible "for a state with an economy as big as that of the US" to "prevent recession turning into cumulative collapse" but that this was unlikely to do more than repeat "the Japanese experience" of the 1990s of "a decade and half of paralysis of the economy". Such a paralysis would have "a devastating impact elsewhere" as "US-based capital" tried "to offload the costs of the crisis on to weaker parts of the system". And, I added, many of the world's smaller states do not have the sort of resources even to achieve the paralysis outcome, so that "we could well see multiple examples of the sort of devastating crisis that hit Argentina, causing political turmoil". "Britain", I noted, "is especially exposed to the impact of the global crisis".[4] Finally, central to my argument was that even if the bail-outs are partially successful in preventing complete collapse, the cost of recouping what the banks have lost will lead to attacks on the wages of employed workers and welfare expenditure.

So what is Neil's gripe against me? Insofar as I can follow it, my mistake has been that I am not willing to join with him in proclaiming "the beginning of a new epoch of global slump". Note the word "epoch", which is not one to apply to something that lasts a decade, like the American slump of the 1930s, or a decade and half, like Japan in the early 1990s. It cannot be of "limited duration", according to Neil—which presumably means it will be of unlimited duration, ie will last forever. "We are witness", he tells us, "to perhaps the greatest crisis in the history of the system." By refusing to use such catastrophist language I am doing "nothing to challenge the sense of powerlessness and paralysis that afflicts many workers, including many activists, in relation to the recession".

Yet Neil, while criticising me, is not himself prepared to put all his money on the catastrophist position. His phrasing, note, is that this is "perhaps" the greatest crisis—which implies that perhaps it is not. Similarly, he insists at one point that the money poured into the banking system by the

4: Harman, 2009b.

British government has had "no apparent economic effect" and that the "$2 trillion" put into the US banks by Treasury secretary Timothy Geithner was "ineffective". Yet this completely contradicts his own assertion a few paragraphs earlier that "capitalism's leading finance ministers and central bankers have, since September-October 2008, prevented a global meltdown". He can't have it both ways. I prefer to try to be consistent and to examine the evidence in a critical way, even if it means admitting that, like Marx, Engels, Lenin, Trotsky[5] and Rosa Luxemburg in their time, I cannot foresee in detail how a crisis as serious as this is going to develop.

Marxist analysis is about more than rhetoric. It is about scientifically carrying through "the concrete analysis of concrete situations", as Lenin put it. That is not possible without some care for facts. Unfortunately, Neil does not show such care. He exaggerates in order to justify complete catastrophism. He argues, for instance, that "the global asset bubble" of "$290 trillion…completely dwarfs the $1.9 trillion of state bail-outs since the crisis began". The implication is that the $1.9 trillion has somehow to cover the cost of the 290 trillion—an obvious impossibility. But this assumes all the assets are of negligible value. They are not. Many of us, for instance, are still paying mortgage payments on homes in a way that justifies the valuation of at least some bank assets. What matters is the assets whose price is not justified in this way. The figure for these is big, may get bigger as the recession deepens, and may quite likely mean governments will have to return once more to trying to prop up the banks. The latest estimate is just over $4 trillion dollars; even if, as seems likely, this too turns out to be too low, the real figure will not be Neil's hundreds of trillions.

He similarly gets carried away when he writes of "the Chinese economy" being "now in freefall". I am sorry but, although some 20 million Chinese workers have reportedly lost their jobs and growth is considerably down on last year, the economy is far from being in "freefall" at the time of writing and, in fact, is expected to grow by 6 percent on the basis of a huge government stimulus. I have argued that Chinese capitalism cannot sustain its levels of accumulation and growth indefinitely in the face of falling profit rates and a dependence on exports to sell goods which Chinese workers and peasants cannot afford to buy.[6] Still less can it be a locomotive for the rest of the world system. But its growth continues for the present.

5: For Trotsky's hesitancy in forecasting the detailed short-term trajectory of an economy in crisis because "it is an equation with many unknown elements" and his refusal to say there could not be a limited "upturn", see Trotsky, 1969, where he also recognised he had failed to foresee the depth of the crisis that hit the US in the early 1930s.

6: Harman, 2008.

Does all this matter, if we all agree the crisis is causing immense pain to the world's workers and peasants and has thrown capitalism into turmoil? It does, because there is a long tradition of Marxists making catastrophist analyses and drawing ultra-left practical conclusions—as, for instance, happened with a section of the Comintern leadership in 1920-1,[7] and again with the Stalinised Comintern of 1929-34. The results have been disastrous, both for the revolutionary left and for the wider working class.

There are hints in Neil's piece that point in the same direction, and he has written elsewhere[8] that the behaviour of the British Communist Party after 1929 provides a model for us now, not noticing with his disregard for facts that its membership fell from 4,500 in 1929 to 2,555 in 1931.[9] He sees my practical conclusions as conservative. I actually argued, "Propaganda alone is clearly not enough. Socialists have to try to be present at the myriad points where the pain caused by the recession can lead to resistance—whether it is factory closures, wholesale sackings in call centres, waves of repossessions or the draconian measures imposed on benefit claimants".[10] On top of that I stressed the resistance to the cuts to be expected in the public sector after the next general election.

Neil's own perspective for resistance is much narrower than this. Almost all of his practical suggestions focus on activity by unemployed workers. Agitation among the unemployed will be important as large numbers of young people are thrown on the dole. That is why I included it in my list of activity. But the long history of revolutionaries agitating among the unemployed shows that continuing organisation—as opposed to spasmodic riots and demonstrations—only involves a small minority of their numbers and cannot have the same impact on the system as, for instance, mass strikes. This was certainly true of the Right to Work marches in the late 1970s and early 1980s. The first march involved 80 people at a time when more than a million were on the dole.[11] It was true of the rather larger

---

7: When the view that capitalism could not enjoy any respite, however temporary, from crisis led to the disastrous "March Action" in Germany. For a post-mortem on the damage caused by revolutionaries assuming that crisis automatically opened up a prospect of offensive action, see Trotsky, 1921.

8: In a privately circulated document.

9: Frank, 1979, p634.

10: Harman, 2009b.

11: The highly successful rally that marked the end of the march was in the Albert Hall, London, which only holds about 5,000 people. That was an achievement at the time but not a mass movement against unemployment. It was, in effect, a mobile propaganda column aimed at encouraging struggles from employed workers. See the reports in *Socialist Worker* from 28 February to 27 March 1976.

mobilisations of unemployed by the Communist Party in the 1930s, however effective particular actions were. And it was also true of the most effective unemployed organisations in recent memory, the *piqueteros* in Argentina in 2001-2.[12] What is more, although on occasions the actions of unemployed workers can help precipitate a crisis of the bourgeois state, they do not have the power that comes from being at the point of production to resolve it in a revolutionary direction. That, above all, was the lesson of Argentina.

Things are rather different with struggles of employed workers. The biggest struggle against unemployment in the 1980s was the year long miners' strike of 1984-5, and the really big struggles in the US in 1930s were those which took place with a degree of very limited economic recovery from early 1933 onwards.

There is a certain logic to Neil's catastrophist approach that leads him to prioritise agitation among the unemployed over those with jobs. This makes sense if your perspective is that the system is not merely in deep crisis but collapsing. However, if you grasp the multidimensional character of the crisis, with states pouring in huge sums to prevent complete collapse only to face the problem of how to make workers pay for those huge sums, then you will understand that struggles by employed workers remain crucial. Even if the stimuli do eventually lead to a limited degree of economic recovery, past experiences suggest that a partial and shortlived economic recovery in the middle of a painful recession can encourage resistance from workers.[13] The perspective then is one of a long period of recurrent and intense class struggles, in which employed workers and their organisations will play a central role. That is why it would be disastrous for revolutionaries, out of impatience, to abandon that terrain.

While I have no doubt about the threat of the wolf to us, Neil writes as if the wolf has already eaten us and all we can do is cause it indigestion.

12: The *piqueteros* organisations numbered at the high point perhaps 60,000 at a time when there were four or five million unemployed—that is they involved less than 2 percent of the unemployed.

13: Again see Trotsky, 1921 and 1969.

References

Faulkner, Neil, 2009 "From Bubble to Black Hole: The Neoliberal Implosion", *International Socialism 122* (spring 2009), www.isj.org.uk/?id=536

Frank, Pierre, 1979, *Histoire do l'International Communiste*, volume two (Editions de Breche).

Harman, Chris, 2006 , "China's Economy and Europe's Crisis, *International Socialism 109* (winter 2006), www.isj.org.uk/?id=160

Harman, Chris, 2008, "Misreadings and Misconception", *International Socialism 119* (summer 2008), www.isj.org.uk/?id=462

Harman, Chris, 2009a, "The Slump of the 1930s and the Crisis Today", *International Socialism 121* (winter 2009), www.isj.org.uk/?id=506

Harman, Chris, 2009b, "Brown's Left Bounce?", *International Socialism 121* (winter 2009), www.isj.org.uk/?id=504

Kincaid, Jim, 2008 "The World Economy—a Critical Comment", *International Socialism 119* (summer 2008), www.isj.org.uk/?id=461

Trotsky, Leon, 1921, "Flood Tide", www.marxists.org/archive/trotsky/1924/ffyci-2/06.htm

Trotsky, Leon, 1969 [1938], "Discussion in Mexico City", 20 July 1938, in *Leon Trotsky on the Labor Party in the US* (Merit), www.marxists.org/archive/trotsky/1938/04/lp.htm

Book reviews

Karl Marx in Beijing

Jeong Seong-jin
Translation by Owen Miller

Giovanni Arrighi, ***Adam Smith in Beijing*** *(Verso, 2007), £14.99*

The following review was written by Jeong Seong-jin, professor of economics at Gyeongsang National University, South Korea. Professor Jeong is the author of a number of books in Korean, including Marx and the Korean Economy *and* Marx and Trotsky. *He is also co-editor of the English-language volume* Marxist Perspectives on South Korea in the Global Economy *(Ashgate, 2007), editor of the bilingual journal* Marxism21 *and translator (into Korean) of* An Anticapitalist Manifesto *and* The Revolutionary Ideas of Karl Marx *by Alex Callinicos.*

In South Korea the writings of Giovanni Arrighi have become popular among a section of the intellectual left who have wholeheartedly adopted his reworking of Marxism and welcomed his positive appraisal of a possible China-centred future. Jeong's polemical attack on Arrighi's concept of a "non-capitalist market society" should therefore also be understood in the context of South Korean left politics.

With Beijing the centre of world attention during last year's Olympics, Giovanni Arrighi's recent book *Adam Smith in Beijing* received a lot of attention from progressive scholars around the world.* In South Korea too Arrighi is well known as one of the main theorists of world systems theory along with Immanuel Wallerstein and the late Andre Gunder Frank. Many intellectuals from the Korean PD tendency† have accepted the thesis of "historical capitalism", which constitutes the core of so-called "generalised Marxism", from Arrighi's best known book, *The Long Twentieth Century* (1994).

Many scholars, both in Korea and around the world, were keenly anticipating Arrighi's first new book in 13 years. But this book is like the rumoured banquet where there is nothing to eat. Everything about it, from the eye-catching title (which, as Arrighi himself reveals, is an imitation of Mario Tronti's 1971 book *Marx in Detroit*) onward, is problematic.

* I am deeply thankful to comrade Owen Miller for his excellent translation of my piece, which first appeared in the August 2008 issue of *Candlelight Resistance*.

† PD stands for People's Democracy—one of the two main tendencies dominating South Korea's Stalinist left that originated in the workers' and students' struggles of the 1980s. While the PD tendency believed that Korean society was characterised by "state-monopoly capital" their rivals in the NL (National Liberation) tendency saw South Korea as a semi-colonial society dominated by US and Japanese capital. While the NL tendency has generally remained true to some form of left nationalist politics, and even in some cases to support for the North Korean regime, during the 1990s and 2000s the PD tendency splintered in many different directions, becoming increasingly influenced by post-Marxist and postmodernist ideas.

In *Adam Smith in Beijing* Arrighi claims that today's Chinese society is a "non-capitalist market economy". Thus, for him, modern China is not the capitalist world of Marx's *Capital* but the market economy world of Adam Smith's *Wealth of Nations*. According to Arrighi, in contrast to capitalism, which is characterised by exploitation, inequality, expansionism and "accumulation by dispossession", the market economy is based on principles of reciprocity, equality and "accumulation by possession". For him, the market economy is a preferable social system to capitalism and the problems of our world are due to capitalism rather than the market economy.

Arrighi insists that in today's world the US is the main capitalist state while China is the main market economy. From this premise he goes on to argue that in the 21st century, particularly after the Iraq war, the global hegemony of US capitalism is facing its "terminal crisis", while the swift rise of the Chinese market economy to the centre of the world economy is historically progressive. He even goes as far as to present China and other "non-capitalist market economies" as really-existing alternatives that progressive forces can look to.

The core hypothesis upon which the whole of *Adam Smith in Beijing* rests is a distinction between market economy and capitalism. This distinction is not something thought up by Arrighi, but an idea that was introduced by the social historian Fernand Braudel in his *Civilisation and Capitalism*. But this sort of distinction cannot be found in Marx's critique of political economy. Of course, Stalin and some Marxists such as Ernest Mandel have asserted that a so-called system of "simple commodity production" that corresponds to Braudel and Arrighi's "non-capitalist market economy" existed prior to the establishment of the capitalist commodity system. But Marx himself nowhere used the concept of "simple commodity production".* Marx put forward capitalism as a historical system of generalised commodity production (a market economy) based on the commodification of labour power. He did not suggest anywhere that it was possible for a market economy to be established as a system distinct from capitalism.

In actual history, when the market economy was generalised and established as an independent social system Marx called this capitalism. There is no historical example of a market economy existing as a separate, independent social system. In fact, globalisation—the central characteristic of 21st century capitalism—is simply the expansion of the market economy to the entire globe, in other words the total realisation of commodification, marketisation and the logic of competition.

When one distinguishes between market economy and capitalism in the way that Braudel and Arrighi do, it also makes it impossible to criticise the capitalist system itself, even though this might be quite contrary to their intentions. Arrighi actually ends up closing his eyes to the exploitative and repressive realities and contradictions of Chinese capitalism today by idealising it as a "non-capitalist market economy".

In my view, the capitalist "laws of motion" that were formalised by Marx in *Capital* have functioned more clearly in the development of the Chinese economy since the 1980s than in any other nation in history. These "laws of motion" have appeared in China in the last three decades in their typical forms: the tendency of the organic composition of capital to rise, the resulting cumulative increase in the "reserve army of

* For philological evidence, refer to Christopher Arthur, "Myth of 'Simple Commodity Production'", *Marx Myths and Legends* (2005), http://marxmyths.org/chris-arthur/article2.htm

labour" (what Marx called the "general law of capitalist accumulation") and the tendency of the rate of profit to fall.* Rather than the "socialism with Chinese characteristics" proclaimed by the Chinese ruling class, David Harvey's phrase "neoliberalism with Chinese characteristics" is a more appropriate description of today's China.

It is unfortunate that so soon after Arrighi suggested that China offers a "non-capitalist market economy" and the possibility of "decoupling" from the troubled US economy as alternatives for humanity in the 21st century, its own economy has made an abrupt hard landing and "recoupled" itself with the deepening global economic crisis. Indeed, it turns out that the Chinese economy, rather than providing an alternative engine of growth for the world economy, has been at the centre of the current global economic crisis by exacerbating overproduction and over-accumulation on a world scale. There is a high likelihood that as the domestic contradictions and global imbalances resulting from China's intensive accumulation deepen, and the global ecological crisis worsens, China may turn out to be the trigger for an even bigger world economic crisis.

If we want to hold China up as a possible alternative in the 21st century that can not be in the sense of a "non-capitalist" system that other countries can model themselves on. Rather it should be as a country akin to Russia at the beginning of the 20th century: the "weakest link" of the global capitalist system where the contradictions of uneven and combined development reach their highest level of intensity and compression—in other words, as the country where a workers' revolution against capitalism is most likely to erupt.

Behind the wholesale revival of commercialism, chauvinism and Confucianism seen during the Beijing Olympics last year we see not the "industrious economy" dreamt of by Adam Smith but a capitalist reality marked by super-exploitation and inequality, competition and accumulation, dispossession and the logic of imperialism. It is a society still haunted by the spectre of Marx. In order to analyse this Chinese capitalist reality and consider alternatives, we still need the framework offered by Marx's *Capital*, not Smith's *Wealth of Nations*.

The intellectuals of the PD might consider Arrighi to be one of the core theorists of the "generalised Marxism" they have adapted but his ideas have nothing in common with our tradition of classical Marxism. As with *The Long Twentieth Century*, Marx's problematics of class struggle and the law of value are completely absent from *Adam Smith in Beijing*.

Arrighi instead devotes the whole of his book to a critique of Robert Brenner's *The Economics of Global Turbulence* (2005), a book which could be seen as the state of the art in the analysis of the large-scale dynamics of modern capitalism. However, despite the large number of points on which he takes issue with Brenner, in terms of level of scholarship, there is no comparison between the two books. *The Economics of Global Turbulence* makes a political analysis of primary sources on the basis of an independently constructed Marxist theory of crisis while *Adam Smith in Beijing* simply cuts and pastes a variety of badly interpreted secondary sources. If Arrighi actually had the ability to see reality as it is, he would have to change the title of his book to "Karl Marx in Beijing".

* See Chris Harman, "Misreadings and Misconceptions", *International Socialism 119*, www.isj.org.uk/?id=462 and Lee Jeong Koo, "A Study on the Development of State Capitalism in China since 1990s", PhD dissertation, Gyeongsang National University, 2009 (in Korean).

Precarious reflections

Charlie Kimber

*Kevin Doogan, **New Capitalism? The Transformation of Work** (Polity, 2009), £16.99*

There is a myth that changes in capitalism have made workers virtually powerless. Many commentators and academics suggest that permanent jobs are a thing of the past and that everyone now faces a world of constant turbulence, transient work and rootless employment. If the great majority of us are permanently insecure at work, the balance of power has swung massively towards the employers.

Kevin Doogan robustly challenges such lazy conclusions and the whole idea of "societal shifts based on a more tenuous connection between employers and workers" (p3). Doogan attacks such analysis because "it privileges discontinuity and it 'overdetermines' the role of technological change. In stressing the significance of global flows of finance, and the integration of capital beyond the national economy, it greatly exaggerates the mobility propensity of non-finance capital and neglects the continuing significance of the role of the state in the workings of the market economy" (p6).

This is not an academic debate. One of the prime tactics in the bosses' locker is to serve up a series of attacks and then say that if there is any resistance the firm will move abroad or bring in agency workers. The belief that companies can flit around at will and that it is always easy to find an alternative workforce means, says Doogan, "The spectre of capital mobility and the economic insecurity it engenders has served to constrain wages and union activity in a period of tight labour markets" (p76).

And it is not just open apologists for capitalism who have spread such ideas. The book is particularly harsh on Michael Hardt and Tony Negri for providing "the presence of left wing harmonies in the neoliberal chorus" (p11). Doogan insists that such dreamers should submit to a statistical cold shower. For example, "The labour force survey data from North America and Europe discussed here shows that job stability has not declined and that long-term employment has increased in many sectors of the advanced economies" (p4).

The figures are powerful. "Over both shorter and longer time frames, the growth of the long-term workforce has been significant in Europe and North America. This is all the more remarkable as it has occurred during a period of substantial employment expansion" (p177). You would expect expanding employment, and lots of new starters, to drive down the length of time people stay in jobs. But this has not happened.

It is true that in some sectors, particularly manufacturing, there are examples of downsizing, outsourcing and corporate relocation. But manufacturing has not generally been a template for retail or health and education—which are the areas of the greatest growth in employment. Furthermore it is simplistic to think that corporations have abandoned all domestic attachments and move around the world at will. Even among the largest of the global multinationals, for many "the domestic economy provides the key market and base of operations" (p72).

Analysing the annual surveys of multinationals conducted by United Nations agencies, Doogan shows that the top 100 non-financial corporations have a transnationality index of approximately 50 percent. This means that their sales, employment and value added in the home economy are as important as their combined operations in overseas markets.

Data gathered by the Bureau of Economic Analysis on US multinationals shows that investment and employment in the domestic economy have kept pace with expansion overseas. Three decades of corporate globalisation have left little impression on the balance between the domestic and foreign activities of US multinational corporations. Doogan adds that "analysis of global foreign direct investment patterns also reveals two interesting and counter-intuitive trends. In the first instance FDI [foreign direct investment] expands during boom periods and contracts during recessions. To blame job losses on capital migration is highly questionable.

"Secondly the lion's share of overseas investment goes to the rich rather than poor countries. Between 1980 and 2006 the developed economies' share of global FDI inward stock has grown from 56 percent to 70 percent, consolidating their position as the prime target for overseas investment. In other words, capital moves abroad to access rich markets rather than exploit cheap labour. This shows that fears of exporting jobs are not related to the actuality of capital relocation but to the threat of jobs going overseas. Research in America, where fears of overseas job loss have a much higher profile than in Europe, shows that companies use the threat of corporate relocation in order to maintain the compliance of trade unions during contract negotiations".*

Doogan is not the first or the only person to have pointed out the deficiencies of much conventional analysis. For example, seven years ago one study concluded, "Many of the commonly held assumptions about today's world of work need to be seriously questioned. A wide gulf exists between the over-familiar rhetoric and hyperbole we hear daily about our flexible and dynamic labour market and the realities of workplace life. The evidence simply does not sustain the view that we are witnessing the emergence of a 'new' kind of employment relations, seen in the 'end of the career' and the 'death of the permanent job for life'".† And in this journal Chris Harman's "The Workers of the World" explodes many of the myths around the issue.‡

Nevertheless Doogan's book is very welcome and there is much useful material for socialists. Above all else he underscores the continuing potential power of workers to resist their bosses and governments.

And he is right that "a left wing mindset that sees only temporariness and contingency in new employment patterns is blind to the basic proposition that capital needs labour. Despite all the rhetoric of foreign competition and threats to relocate and outsource, employers generally prioritise the recruitment and retention of labour. Otherwise it would be difficult to explain the international evidence of job stability and rising long-term employment" (p206).

But there are some areas where the analysis needs to be more rounded. Doogan does not really look in enough detail at examples where the number of workers on non-permanent contracts of employment is genuinely high. This reality was already clear in a European-wide study from 1998 which showed that in countries such as Spain (40 percent non-permanent), France (22 percent non-permanent) and Greece (18 percent non-permanent) the scale of non-permanent employment was at a level which would penetrate deeply into

* Kevin Doogan, "Not All that is Solid", *New Humanist*, volume 124, number 3, http://newhumanist.org.uk/2036

† Robert Taylor, "Britain's World of Work—Myths and Realities", ESRC Future of Work Programme Seminar Series, http://tinyurl.com/futurework

‡ *International Socialism* 96, http://pubs.socialistreviewindex.org.uk/isj96/harman.htm

workers' consciousness. It is true that the term "non-permanent" can cover a wide range of situations: the consultant on 1,000 euros a day is not worried if his contract means only six months work. But that is not the dominant reality and these examples need more careful attention.*

A study last year of the Italian labour market found that "while full-time permanent employees account for almost 51 percent of the Italian labour force and 'standard' workers for 72 percent, the extent of atypical workers varies according to the definition adopted...they represent between 8.1 percent and 20.5 percent of the Italian labour force according to the particular definition. Non-standard employment contracts are more likely among young people aged 15 to 29 years and those living in southern regions of Italy. Women are more likely than men to work on such contracts".†

In such an economy there will be swathes of workers who are truly in a "precarious" situation. Many will be students, and Doogan points out the need for increased analysis of the role students play in the labour market. But they are not all students. Many are young workers who do not have the chance of a permanent job.

And it is also true that the economic crisis intensifies certain trends such as the rise in the number of workers who are part time simply because they cannot get a full-time job. A recent TUC analysis of official statistics found that one in nine (11.2 percent) of people in part-time work are in this position. The number of involuntary part-time workers has increased sharply over the last two years to 829,000.

The lack of full-time work is demonstrated in Jobcentres across the UK, with government statistics showing that over one in four (27 percent) of vacancies are for less than 16 hours a week. The majority of involuntary part-time workers are female (451,000 women compared to 378,000 men), reflecting the fact that around 80 percent of the UK's part-time workforce are women. However, one in five (21.2 percent) men working part time are doing so because they cannot secure full-time unemployment.

Recognition of such factors is important in working out why workers believe they are insecure, even when they are not. Doogan sometimes suggests that this is largely an ideological construct driven by neoliberalism and its lackeys, both right and left wing. And he's partly right. A manufactured sense of powerlessness is an important help to the bosses. But, as Doogan admits, it's not simply about useful lies. He recognises that the exposure of new groups to the threat of job losses in the recession of 1989-91 had a powerful effect.

But, particularly today, it may be that when people express a fear of losing their jobs they are pointing to material facts in wider society, even if not in their particular job. In Britain up to 100 universities at present want to get rid of staff. Coming after years of pressure for "flexibility" and the increased use of temporary contracts, the threat of mass redundancies quite rightly engenders thoughts of insecurity. Of course, as Doogan would point out, this should not lead to the belief that lecturers and other staff have no power. But the pervasive feelings that "they are after my job" are not irrational.

To take another example, the British postal service, Royal Mail, is currently trying to force through a root and branch "reform" of its workforce. It is seeking to use the

* See graph 5 in www.eurofound.europa.eu/pubdocs/1998/15/en/1/ef9815en.pdf

† "Use and Abuse of Non-standard Employment Contracts", www.eurofound.europa.eu/ewco/2008/05/IT0805019I.htm

introduction of new technology to transform the mainly full-time workforce into one dominated by part-timers. It seeks to move towards the "Dutch model" pioneered by TNT. This saw 14,000 of 25,000 full-time mail jobs replaced by 20,000 part-time "mail deliverers", who were 50 percent cheaper to employ. Bosses boasted they had found plenty of workers, particularly women, prepared to work for 10 percent above the minimum wage. Now it may be true that union resistance rebuffs this assault at Royal Mail. But it is hardly surprising that workers will feel insecure, or feel that part-time work is a real threat.

Another example comes from developments in the US labour market as the crisis deepens. In April US unemployment hit 13.7 million, pushing the rate to 8.9 percent. But the total number of Americans who are not working full time but ought to be is actually about 22 million, or 15.8 percent, according to the Bureau of Labour Statistics. The recession has swollen the ranks of people working part time because they cannot find full-time work. While this segment constituted only 3.3 percent of the workforce a year ago, it reached 5.7 percent in April. According to the Labour Department, if "discouraged," "marginally attached" and involuntary part-time workers are included, the jobless rate comes to a shocking 15.8 percent.

Again it is hardly staggering if workers fear that the era of secure jobs is finished, and we might doubt just how many part-time workers are satisfied with working the hours they are contracted for. However, whatever criticism I may have, this is a really valuable book which will remind everyone that our side still has power—if we use it.

Origins of the French working class

Henry Heller

Samuel Guicheteau, ***La Révolution des Ouvriers Nantais: Mutation Economique, Identité Sociale et Dynamique Révolutionnaire (1740-1815)*** *(Presses Universitaires de Rennes, 2008), €19*

A revisionist school, premised on the notion that the French Revolution was not bourgeois and capitalist, has dominated the historiography of the revolution in the English-speaking world since the 1970s. Its dominance over academic history was made possible by the cultural turn, neoliberalism and lacunae in the scholarship of the previous generation of Marxist historians like Georges Lefebvre, Albert Soboul and George Rudé. Yet today revisionism is increasingly challenged as a result of a rising tide of new research coming from American scholars such as Steven Kaplan and Jeff Horn, but especially from French researchers. Samuel Guicheteau's study of the development of the working class in Nantes provides a powerful new set of weapons against the entrenched conservative school of historiography.

Using a sophisticated quantitative methodology Guicheteau has been able systematically to sift the departmental archives of the Loire-Atlantique so as to delineate the outlines of the emerging working class of Nantes before and during the French Revolution.

The development of the working class was itself based on the progress of capitalism. Agricultural capitalism made rapid progress in France in the second half of the 18th century. Accompanying this was a spectacular development of concentrated and mechanised cotton factories designed to serve both the internal and overseas markets. The port of Nantes, which was heavily involved in the slave trade with Africa and the plantation-slave economy of the Caribbean, saw the proliferation of such cotton mills serving the expanding overseas trade.

As a prelude to his account of the working class, Guicheteau provides the reader with an overview of the growing economy of Nantes, paying special attention to the proliferation of these concentrated cotton manufactures and their manner of operation. The complex hierarchy of workers within such large new workplaces ranged from highly skilled and well educated fabric designers recruited from Switzerland to locally recruited illiterate and unskilled male and female peasants. Meanwhile traditional industries like metal working, shipbuilding, tanning, glass manufacture and stocking manufacture underwent a certain degree of centralisation of production.

As Guicheteau points out, even dispersed industries experienced a process of modernisation, adapting themselves to the industrial takeoff and overall capitalist economic expansion. The first decade of the revolution brought a decline of the Atlantic orientated economy and a re-focusing of economic activity towards Paris and the north and east of France. Yet Nantes was able to restructure its industries and to thrive throughout much of the Napoleonic period.

The development of capitalist industry saw increasing efforts by the authorities to control the expanding working class population. Political coercion grew as the older corporate order which had restricted both capital and labour decayed during the 18th century. Master artisans lost much of their autonomy while the ranks of unskilled labour expanded. Industrialisation, with its attempts to control the time of workers and intensify their work, threatened their traditional identity, which was based on their skills and a certain sense of independence. In response to repression, workers resorted to frequent strikes and other forms of resistance while strengthening their clandestine and illegal organisations.

On the eve of the revolution workers were united by their common poverty and dependence on wage work. They tended to live in the same areas of the city and increasingly to intermarry. On the other hand, they remained divided by their occupations and the traditional split between skilled and unskilled labour. A sense of working class consciousness was also diluted by workers being profoundly immersed in the overall culture and life of the "people". Nonetheless, sparked by growing poverty, class conflict and working class violence grew as the revolution approached.

With the onset of the revolution the fundamental characteristics of the French path to industrial capitalism became evident: the ongoing importance of skilled work and of small-scale enterprises and the continuing shock of popular insurgency. In the tumultuous initial phase of the revolution militancy among workers was at its height. Yet despite some lessening of repression the new revolutionary regime of the bourgeoisie refused to recognise the legality of workers' organisations.

Nonetheless, workers used their participation in the revolution to strengthen their autonomous organisations. In doing so they helped to democratise the revolutionary process. As part of the "people" they likewise fully participated in the *sans-culottes* movement* and the military mobilisation against counter-revolution.

---

* Literally "without breeches", the *sans-culottes* were a movement of urban poor in the French Revolution.

Guicheteau demonstrates the development of a working class political culture based on enthusiastic adherence to the revolution as witnessed by the proliferation of given names such as Victoire, Montagne, Jean-Jacques and Verité at the height of the popular movement. The habitual brandishing of tools by workers in popular mobilisations represented a distinctive form of working class self-expression. Furthermore, within the revolution workers voiced autonomous claims to the right to work and the right to their own organisations. In other words, they used the political discourse of the revolution to articulate and justify their own autonomous demands. Although a working class consciousness would not fully emerge until the later revolution of 1848, involvement in the 1789 Revolution helped to politically legitimate the economic and social claims of workers, at least in their own eyes.

As we have noted, the first two years of the revolution brought an upsurge of working class strikes and agitation in Nantes as elsewhere in France. Steve Kaplan and other historians go so far as to argue that the emergence of the *sans-culotte* movement controlled by radical elements of the revolutionary elite became a way of channelling and controlling this emergent working class.

Based on the case of Nantes, Guicheteau is unwilling to endorse this view. However, his research does point to a definite split between members of the working class and the bourgeoisie over the National Guard. While acknowledging along with others that the ranks of the National Guard remained open to some workers, he insists that bourgeois control over the guard and its use in repressing workers caused it to be regarded by many workers as an instrument of repression. Likewise some workers expressed their alienation from the bourgeoise revolutionary elite by remaining loyal to the counter-revolutionary Catholic clergy.

The rights of women

Farah Reza

Jeanne Flavin, ***Our Bodies, Our Crimes*** *(New York University, 2009), £30.95*

"When she said, 'rights terminated', I just felt lost... Those are my kids...you snatch them, that was my world. You just took that. What I'm a fight for? What I'm a fight for? You took my babies. I just continued using drugs. I didn't even think."

These are the words of a former prisoner who was deemed an unsuitable mother by the US state. She is one of many working class women in the US who have had their children taken away without ever being offered adequate support to keep them in the first place. They have returned to civilian life unable to see or write to the children they had missed every day in prison. Flavin puts such cases in a historical context that stretches back to the turn of the last century, and argues that the "paternalisic belief that poor people, especially poor people of colour, are not competent to control their own fertility and that government is empowered to intervene still influences reproductive policies today".

Our Bodies, Our Crimes looks at, but also well beyond, the abortion argument, discussing recent government legislation that has introduced "fetal rights" into US law, the treatment of working class mothers, pregnant women, young women whose future reproductive health is being threatened through "abstinence programmes" that neglect the issue of safe sex, and the general lack of affordable sexual health services. Flavin explores the all round policing of women's bodies in terms of reproductive rights, that has, for example, led to pregnant drug addicts being prosecuted for damage to the "unborn" rather than being given support to deal with their addiction.

These women can find themselves being forced into a Caesarean to "rescue" the child and are then led directly to a cell.

Flavin looks at the lack of pre-natal care for women in prison and the way in which it is often assumed by judges that working class women—especially those who are black—cannot be trusted to have children, take care of their bodies while pregnant, or control their own fertility. Flavin shows how the state authorities, however, abuse the same people, ordering incarcerated women to give birth while shackled and in some cases denying imprisoned women in intense pain the chance to get to hospital for emergency treatment—because the prison managers claim they don't run "a taxi service".

This book is well researched, and turns over every piece of relevant US legislation on reproductive rights, as well as exploring women's activism and political protest. The context she provides for her arguments is impressively thorough, and it is entirely possible to come to this book with no prior knowledge of women's rights in the US and walk away feeling like an expert on what needs to change. Flavin's book is unashamedly polemical, and while her perspective is not socialist, it has a left-leaning feminist slant that exclusively focuses on working class women, and especially on the relationship between race and class in America. This means that her chapters on women in prison are particularly strong, as class and race play a massive part in why these women end up in prison and why they are maltreated.

Flavin's exploration of the legacy of the eugenics movement is also pertinent and impassioned. For example, she shows how activists successfully brought an end to "no-procreation orders" and forced sterilisation programmes that targeted mainly black women right into the 1970s—after the Roe v Wade decision had officially granted women the right to determine what happens to their own bodies and lives. By this time between 60,000 and 100,000 women had been forcibly sterilised nationwide. Flavin argues that racist, anti working class eugenicist arguments still play a part in the minds of lawmakers, who generally define the feminine ideal as upper or middle class, married, white, desirous of having children, and possessing "restraint" (ie not getting pregnant more than two or three times). This becomes the basis for institutionalised discrimination against women who do not fit this model, including working class women who simply want regular and affordable access to contraception or smear tests.

This book serves as an invaluable introduction to all of these issues, and points to what needs to be changed. However, Flavin falls into the liberal trap of framing "rights" within a framework of "property" and "privacy". For example, she appears to be limited to the Roe v Wade approach of seeing the right to an abortion as being essentially about the individual's freedom to privacy and the freedom from state interference—an approach that defines our bodies as private property and our family lives as belonging to a private sphere.

This becomes a problem when Flavin starts to discuss the rights of working class women to keep their children. She seems to see the issue as a woman's right to her private life at home (free from intervention) and a right to the things that biologically belong to her. But this appears to define children as property, and in particular as the private property of their mothers.

This view could be used to support the idea that women should not be helped by the state to keep their children through publicly funded services, because the state should not be poking its nose into the private sphere. Such an approach leads to an excessively individualist attitude to child rearing that can actually allow child abuse and domestic violence in general to thrive—because it sees the family as a sacred "private sphere".

Despite this flaw, Flavin has produced an incredibly useful book for activists. It brings together information that we need to be aware of, at least in part because if women in the US can be treated in this way, so could we. Many right wing tactics used in the US have been used by the anti-choice lobby in the UK. For example, the relatively new tactic of focusing on abortion time limits rather than getting rid of abortion completely, has won the anti-choice lobby a new hearing in the UK.

Flavin is also right to see beyond abortion, to stress that it should not be seen as the only reproductive right. Unless the agenda is broadened, it can lead to the neglect of other issues that are incredibly class based, such as access to good, free sexual health services from the NHS or adequate state support for disabled women who want to keep their children. It is also refreshing to read a book that sees all of these issues as related, not separate, and that sees these problems as ones that can be dealt with through a political movement that asks questions and demands a better deal for all women.

Gold dust

Chris Harman

Barry Eichengreen, ***Globalizing Capital: A History of the International Monetary System*** *(second edition) (Princeton, 2008), £19.95*

Occasionally mainstream economists manage to produce works of genuine use. This is one of them. The eruption of the credit crunch and then the deepest recession since the 1930s has led to many people developing a new interest in economic discussions, only then to be mystified by references to things like the gold standard, the Bretton Woods system, and the Plaza Accord. Eichengreen explains such things in easily understandable terms. In doing so, he makes it clear that insofar as there has been an international monetary system it has always depended on negotiated deals between the major powers according to their economic interests rather than pure market relations.

So, for instance, he shows how the use of gold as a common measure for all national currencies through the gold standard only emerged quite late in the 19th century and its maintenance depended on different national banks being prepared to do a favour to each other by turning a blind eye to infractions of its rules. He ends by pointing to the problems posed today for global economic transactions being based upon one no longer all-powerful national currency, the dollar. A book well worth reading if you want to know some of the background to the world economy today.

Marx misread

Jonathon Collerson

Stephen Shapiro, ***How to Read Marx's Capital*** *(Pluto Press, 2008), £12.99*

The left has good reason to return to *Capital*, given the unrest gripping economic wisdom. Images of Nicolas Sarkozy thumbing the pages of *Le Capital* titillated the *Economist* and, in a *Financial Times* op-ed, Harold James wrote, "Marx's description of 'the fetishism of commodities' seems entirely relevant to the complex process of securitisation, in which values seem to be hidden by obscure transactions." But, he warned, "the implication of Marx's renewed popularity is that capitalism is now universally accepted as being fundamentally broken".

In *How to Read Marx's Capital*, Stephen Shapiro gives a near chapter by chapter reading of the first volume of *Capital*. But the act of paraphrasing imbues the text with a definite interpretation and Shapiro's version of Marx's theory of value undermines his otherwise adequate reading of topics such as the working day, the division of labour and primitive accumulation.

Marx argues that the value of a commodity is the amount of labour time required to produce it with the socially valid technique and skill. Exchange-value is the real quantity of one commodity that exchanges for another, the form in which value appears when commodities enter the market. But Shapiro writes, when Marx "uses the word 'value' he really means exchange-value". This does strange things to Marx's argument. Marx writes, "The progress of the investigation will lead us back to exchange-value as the necessary mode of expression, or form of appearance, of value." For Shapiro this reads, "Exchange-value is the form of appearance of exchange-value."

Shapiro argues that the distinction Marx draws in chapter one of *Capital* is merely between use-value and exchange-value, rather than value and exchange-value. The first pair are what immediately appears to us about a commodity: it is something useful and something paid for. The second pair disclose an essence and its form of appearance. This is important if we want to understand where surplus value and thus profit come from. Marx claims that under capitalism equal values exchange. Labour power is itself a commodity, for which the workers receive an equivalent exchange-value, their wage. It also has a use-value: its ability to both replace this equivalent and create a surplus value beyond it. There is nothing fraudulent (in principle) in the sale and purchase of labour power.

Because Shapiro collapses together value and exchange-value, he cannot explain surplus value. This leads to the claim that "fraud is the origin and sole source of surplus value"—the opposite of what Marx tries to show. This in turn leads Shapiro to attribute the views of early 19th century popular political economy to Marx. The influence of Adam Smith and David Ricardo on these early radical economists led them to the belief that the market was a means to social equality. Marx wrote his critique of political economy to combat this current in the workers' movement.

However, in Shapiro's view, Marx establishes that, "once we have moved beyond the very basic, self-sufficient village groups, commodity production is the human condition". He misquotes Marx as saying commodity production (rather than labour in its most generic sense) is an "eternal natural necessity". A communist society would thus be "a modern society that produces commodities, but without the supplement of commodity fetishism", and "if labourers were paid the true value of their work, there would be no price differentials, no surplus value, no capital and no profits".

These issues create problems in a text aimed at students as a cheap and brief introduction. A further issue is the tight focus on the text of the first volume in isolation from Marx's account of capitalism's overall dynamic developed in volumes two and three of *Capital*. As an introduction to Marx's critique of capitalism *How to Read Marx's Capital* can only be partial. There remains space for an introduction that does cover the whole ground.

Starting at the bottom

David Seddon

*Heidi Armbruster and Anna Laerke (eds), **Taking Sides: Ethics, Politics and Fieldwork in Anthropology** (Berghahn Books, 2008), £45*

I enjoyed reading this collection—in part because it reminded me of when I was at the London School of Economics as a graduate student in social anthropology. This was in 1968, when there was a good deal of discussion about the politics of anthropology—mainly coming across the Atlantic from the US and exemplified most memorably by *Current Anthropology*'s "symposium on social responsibilities". Here Kathleen Gough made a central contribution (referred to in the introduction to this book but strangely nowhere else in the collection) about the impossibility of remaining "neutral" in social investigation and analysis. The main reason I enjoyed it, however, is that there is a sense of purpose to the work contained in *Taking Sides*, and that purpose gives the analysis and discussion provided by the various essays a distinctive clarity and personal character.

The book, which aims to re-establish the relevance of what might be termed "critical anthropology", is dedicated to Nancy Lindisfarne (formerly Nancy Starr Self Tapper) by the editors, who identify themselves as students and friends of Nancy's ("We know Nancy as a demanding and exceptionally inspiring supervisor, a fiercely intelligent discussant and, above all, as a lovely friend"). Nancy herself contributes to the book with a remarkable and stimulating essay on "fieldwork, gender and imperialism now", and one of the hardest hitting and, to my mind, most illuminating chapters in the book (the final chapter), is provided by Nancy's partner, Jonathan Neale—anthropologist, political activist, professional writer and university lecturer in creative writing. I have also to admit to a longstanding relationship, as colleague and friend, with Nancy, from the days when I was teaching at the School of Oriental and African Studies (Soas) and she was Nancy Tapper, through to now. So here, in the review as well as in the book reviewed, the personal is political, and vice versa.

Nancy Lindisfarne has lived and worked as an anthropologist in Afghanistan, Turkey and Syria, has taught at Soas (among other institutions), where she supervised the doctoral work of several of the contributors, and has published extensively on various issues, usually concerned with gender and the Middle East. She has also written short stories,* and exhibited paintings, prints, collages and photography. She is evidently also an able linguist and someone who can adapt to immersion in different cultures (eg US, British, Austrian, Afghan, Turkish, Syrian).

For the editors, "the purpose of this volume is to contribute to a clarification of political and ethnical partiality in the formation of anthropological knowledge" (p11). Interestingly, partiality here is used in the sense of both commitment and taking sides, and also of incompleteness and limitation. For the editors at least (p11), and for Nancy Lindisfarne herself (p23), the starting point is fieldwork—for it is in fieldwork, and particularly in participant observation (living and becoming to a greater or lesser extent embedded in another culture and society), that the anthropologist has the experiences and initially constructs the knowledge and achieves the understanding that provide the basis for analysis.

* One collection is *Dancing in Damascus* (State University of New York, 2000).

"Starting from below", as Nancy Lindisfarne herself puts it, undoubtedly provides a distinctive perspective on anthropology, not only studying society but also seeing it "from below"—a position from which, as she puts it, "power and privilege stand out in sharp relief" (p23). But this is only the case if the anthropologist is predisposed to "see" the structures of inequality that permeate all levels of society, from bottom to top, in the contemporary world. It does not automatically follow, as many of the contributors to this collection seem to believe, that fieldwork, and "paying attention to the lives of ordinary people" (as Lindisfarne puts it) result in critical and committed analysis, let alone activism and advocacy.

As Jonathan Neale's contribution makes abundantly clear, anthropological research is not just conducted "in the field"; anthropological practice and the process of "knowledge construction" take place, usually, within a highly articulated and profoundly hierarchical institutional matrix of universities, research institutes, funding agencies, and so on. These effectively conspire to reduce the capacity of the researcher to deviate from the dominant discourses and paradigms of the discipline or dissent from the predominantly "top-down" conventional wisdoms of the day.

For Neale, "writing as an activist is a very different project from writing as an academic" (p243), and requires a powerful predisposition to critical work. Most academic anthropologists are too constrained by the hierarchies of the profession to venture too far into critical analysis. It is certainly possible, but "it is not easy to be both an academic and an activist" (p217).

It is significant that the boldest assertions of critical autonomy in this collection are those by Nancy Lindisfarne and Jonathan Neale, both established mavericks and seasoned campaigners. The contributions by younger anthropologists, whose positions within the academy are more vulnerable and whose intellectual formation as "critical anthropologists" is more recent, are less able to make the links and connections that enable both of these two to range widely, from specifics to generalities, drawing on a wide range of examples and illustrative material, from considerable personal experience, to make a powerful case for "taking sides".

Nevertheless, Heidi Armbruster provides a focused discussion of "The Ethics of Taking Sides" in her introduction to the collection, and also contributes a fascinating study of "Memory, Ethics, Politics" based on her research among what she describes as "a beleaguered community" of Syrian Christians in south east Turkey and Berlin. Panagiotis Geros discusses the discomfort and difficulty—ethical, political and practical—of "Doing Fieldwork within Fear and Silences" in Syria, while Sabine Strasser examines the very different political strategies of three anti-racist activists of Turkish origin in Vienna in her study of "Multiple Belongings, Political Activism and Anthropology in Austria".

Studies that involved the anthropologist more directly in local political practice include Nayanika Mookherjee's account of her own "Friendships and Encounters on the Political Left in Bangladesh", Tayfun Atay's personal "encounter", as a Turkish anthropologist (and only "nominal Muslim"—p61) with an Islamic Sufi Order in London, and Heike Schaumberg's "Taking Sides in the Oilfields"—describing her political engagement with workers and grassroots activists in Mosconi, an oil town in northern Argentina. All three of these, especially Tayfun Atay, are concerned with the personal implications of the fieldwork experience (and of "taking sides"), and all three, especially Mookherjee and Schaumberg, manage to integrate these concerns effectively with an analysis of the wider political context.

Finally, Anna Laerke presents an extraordinary and revealing account of extreme participant observation in a primary school in an English village—where she spent virtually all of her time in class, in playtime and at dinner time with the children (giving her, as she puts it, "a view from the floor"—p144). Her exquisitely sensitive and restrained "Confessions of a Downbeat Anthropologist" involve an account of her own emotional entanglement (throughout the fieldwork, as a "recollected, sad, small and angry me"—p172), and an analysis of power, discipline and socialisation, and forms of resistance. The function of the school as an institution is considered to have been what Anna Laerke calls "uniformation" (I would prefer "standardisation", with its connotation of maintaining standards as well as of ensuring uniformity), assured through a process she calls "bonsai" (trimming or pruning) of young children.

All in all, a challenging and provocative volume, providing much food for thought and implying that anthropology always has the potential to be edgy and uncomfortable, problematic and political—and that this is no bad thing, for then it reveals more than usual. For those who are predisposed to believe that the issue is not so much how to understand the world as how to change it, the fieldwork experience can promote not just a better understanding of the world and how it works, but also—albeit within very real institutional constraints, particularly as far as academics are concerned—can enable more effective action to be taken.

One key concern and criticism: the authors in the collection all appear to take it for granted that such action will always be progressive and broadly supportive of the exploited and oppressed. The cover picture—of a young woman wearing a CND and a "Free Palestine" badge and looking full face at the reader, a man looking sideways towards but not necessarily at her, and a poster behind them both of what may well be Tony Blair—illustrates the point. But, if "taking sides" is unavoidable, and "refusing to take sides" is also, in effect, a political decision in favour of the status quo, it is also possible for fieldwork to be used to "investigate" (or "spy" on) the poor and subaltern and see how better to manage exploitation and oppression.

Historically, it has been argued, this was the function of anthropology, as the handmaiden of colonialism (or imperialism)—to provide knowledge and understanding that would be "useful" to the powers that be. There is no rule to say that "taking sides" necessarily implies taking one side rather than the other, even if there is a tendency for fieldwork to involve a significant degree of identification with those studied, and thus an inherent bias towards taking "their" side against (usually more powerful) "others"; the outcome is not inevitable—unless the anthropologist is already predisposed towards activism of a particular political orientation.

Life and works of a Spanish rebel

Luke Stobart

*Michael Eaude, **Triumph at Midnight of the Century: A Critical Biography of Arturo Barea** (Sussex Academic Press, 2009), £45*

"A lump of grey mass, the size of a child's fist, was flattened out against the glass pane and kept on twitching... A scrap of human brain... I wanted to cry out... If I was to stay on fighting against my nerves and my mind...I had to do something more... So

I continued to write, and I began to speak on the radio."

The trilogy *The Forging of a Rebel* is one of the most powerful and shocking works on the background to the Spanish Civil War, yet as historian Paul Preston writes,* its author, Arturo Barea (1897-1957), has remained a little known figure. Barcelona-based writer and socialist Michael Eaude redresses this anomaly, producing an essential guide to Barea's literary work and life.

Eaude's book follows the self-taught novelist from his childhood in Madrid's slums to his dreadful experiences as conscript in Spain's colonial war in Morocco in the 1920s and then participation in the struggle to defend the Spanish capital against General Franco. During the latter Barea worked as head press censor and started broadcasting—an activity he would continue later in exile in Britain. However, events would take their toll and he suffered a breakdown. According to Barea he then started writing "to discover how and why I became what I am" and why he was "like so many millions" (a reference to the wider breakdown of Spanish society).

Although Barea's autobiographical novels themselves provide much information about their author, Eaude's book fills in the gaps. Furthermore, Eaude's acute literary eye, Marxist politics and careful study of the links between Barea's works and life, cast useful light on the dialectical relationship between art and society.

Reproduced in the biography is the process Barea went through to write his trilogy: "I wanted to wipe the slate of my mind clean of all reasoning" and "go back to my beginnings, to things which I had smelled, seen, touched and felt". Thus, in *The Forge* he described his childhood using a child's voice and filtered political and other events through a child's perspective.

Barea spent his early childhood living with both his poor single mother and his middle class aunt. The latter was a pious "bigot" who sent him to study at a rigid and hierarchical Catholic school. At the age of 13 he left home and by 18 had worked in a shop, an office and even as an international salesman. He also joined the UGT, the Socialist Party union, and started identifying himself as a "proletarian." An early attempt to become a writer was abandoned after he attended literary functions and witnessed the class elitism of the literary establishment.

Barea's transformation into a "rebel" would properly take place after being conscripted at the age of 20 into the Spanish army and its colonial war. In *The Track*, the second part of his trilogy, Barea explains how he was politicised by this experience—which echoed the wider polarisation caused by the war that would eventually lead to the fall of the monarchy. As Eaude explains, *The Track* describes in shocking Scorsese-like detail how war corrupted, maddened and brutalised officers and common soldiers alike, who performed indiscriminate killings against locals (including women and children) as "vengeance". In addition, Barea's writing often contrasted this reality with the humanity and culture of its Moroccan victims.

Barea was given the job of supervising the building of a long "track" (or *ruta* in Spanish, which also means "route") across the desert. A blind local strayed alongside the road searching for the previous path. When Barea suggested he used the straight new track, he laughed, "I'll always walk on the path... This road is full of blood, all of

* In the preface to this, the English version of Eaude's biography of Barea. The original Spanish version, published by Editora Regional de Extremadura in 2001, was entitled *Arturo Barea: Triunfo en la Medianoche del Siglo*.

it... And it will fill with blood again and yet again." The route, which headed nowhere and which Barea said originated from profiteering capitalist enterprises in Spain, thus becomes a symbol for the occupation. The road would also lead backwards, as Spain's colonial adventure created the monstrous military generals Barea served under (Franco and Millán Astray) who would eventually cross the straits of Gibraltar (accompanied by conscripted Moroccan soldiers) to fight the Republic.

While disposing of bodies after a major defeat for the Spanish army in Annual in 1921 Barea contracted typhus, was hospitalised and discharged (returning to the army only temporarily). Before the Spanish war began, Barea bought a house for himself and his wife and four children in a small rural village, Novés. There he organised a Popular Front meeting with left wing and Republican speakers, which ruling class forces attempted to shut down. Through his portrait of this one small village, Eaude argues, Barea neatly and graphically illustrated the dynamics of the advancing class war.

When Franco and his supporters attempted to take Madrid, Barea was at the centre of the working class's dramatic response: inspired by the "force of spontaneous mass solidarity", he participated in the successful armed assault of the Montaña barracks (where he had previously been stationed as a soldier). He also helped train a new workers' militia.

By dissecting Barea's *The Clash*, which covers the civil war period, Eaude demonstrates how the writer conjures up the dizzying violent and revolutionary upheaval taking place, offering a rapidly changing narrative of events in which its working class subjects were constantly "buffeted" by unexpected events. Eaude maintains that Barea's politics shifted left in this period but remained left reformist (he briefly joined the Socialist PSOE) and were increasingly influenced by the (Stalinist) Communist Party of Spain (PCE).

Barea was made foreign press censor and in this job met Ilsa Kulcsar, an Austrian socialist, who would become his lifelong partner. Partly due to her influence, he attempted to limit censorship of foreign reports to those that distorted the events of the war to the detriment of the Republic (a common occurrence). This approach eventually led to tensions with a superior who was a (secret) PCE member and wished to prohibit any news that contradicted "the party line". These difficulties would see Barea sacked, and the situation added to the stress caused by his continual witnessing of violence to spark his breakdown. He then wrote his first book—a Soviet-influenced propaganda piece called *Valor y Miedo*—and, his nerves in tatters, escaped for exile in south east England.

Based in the relative peace of his new places of residence—the villages of Puckeridge, Fladbury and Faringdon (!)—he worked as a broadcaster for the BBC Latin American Service, producing a total of 800 broadcasts. He also wrote his trilogy, many short stories, political analyses, a novel and some impressive literary criticisms (such as *Lorca, the Poet and his People*.) In all of these he tried to be a voice for the Spanish working masses and continue the fight against fascism. He aimed to be an unflinching eye (or "camera eye") recording the dramatic events he had experienced. Eaude skilfully analyses all of the works of this period and concludes that Barea largely succeeded in his objectives.*

* The exceptions to this were when Barea's own trajectory parted from that of the working class, such as in the latter half of *The Clash*, when his work as censor isolated him from events. Here, Eaude argues, his book stops showing the plight of the "millions" and loses its tension.

Eaude emphasises that Barea's autobiographical works partly gain strength from his role as an insider to events, in contrast to other celebrated books on the civil war by outside observers such as George Orwell and Ernest Hemingway. Barea, in his own critical writings, described the latter as "always a spectator." Nevertheless *Triumph at Midnight of the Century* offers a compelling case that Barea's skill as a chronicler derives from also being an "outsider"—either as a working class kid in a middle class school, or an elite employee in a workers' union, and in Barea's many intermediate roles in society (army sergeant, co-operative manager, writer), the Madrid writer was able to see society with "double vision".

This allowed him to penetrate the essence of both Spain's institutions and the ordinary people who would revolt against them. Except in his very last book, his portrayals of his adversaries avoided crude caricature and he refused to prettify the working class. His accounts are partisan yet (possibly because of this) objective, and even critics in Franco's Spain praised his sincerity and truthfulness.

Barea did not prettify his sentimental relationships either, which for much of his life were empty and exploitative. This situation changed, however, when he fell in love with the broadly cultured Ilsa in the midst of revolutionary upheaval, beginning a long "relationship of equals". Eaude concludes that this represented a "revolution in his private life" that was inseparable from the events surrounding him. Eaude also compares Barea's literary examination of this side to his life with the work of gay poet and playwright Lorca. The latter, Barea wrote, clarified the "sediments" of sexual tradition as "perhaps a step towards clearing them away".

Triumph is a readable yet thought-provoking book, full of impressive literary and historical understanding, and its arguments are almost always commanding. In true Barean style it celebrates the Spanish author's achievements but does not flinch from highlighting the negative sides to his life and work. These include Barea's refusal, while working as censor, to block the publication of smear stories about the revolutionary POUM, which he probably knew to be false (like the POUM, Ilsa herself was also accused of counter-revolutionary "Trotskyism" by the Stalinists), and the crude nationalist stereotypes in some of his writings.

However, in my opinion there are some minor weaknesses in Eaude's biography. First, there needs to be more clarification as to which aspects of Barea's "autobiographical novels" were fictional (apart from the names used, which is acknowledged). It is stated that Barea made no "substantial" invention but the vast majority of the account of Barea's early life is gleaned from these books, and the reader is left with nagging doubts as to the novelist's exact history.

Second, while the book gives lots of information about Barea's political ideas, these are not fully clarified, and it is even suggested, somewhat confusingly, that these varied from "revolutionary" to "counter-revolutionary PCE" positions. It seems probable from the account offered by Eaude that Barea had a fluid and contradictory stance (as did a great many other Socialist supporters and UGT members) and one that cannot be reduced to the influence of the Stalinists. I would venture that greater examination of the evolution of the PSOE and its union federation would help illuminate his trajectory. Certainly many of his ideas dovetailed significantly with Second International conceptions: for example when he describes the Moroccan war as a "rotten adventure" promoted by sectional interests (army generals, the king and profiteering industries), as opposed to being related to the inter-imperialist "scramble for Africa" between rival ruling classes. Of course, under the class polarisation of the civil war, the PSOE drew closer to and became dominated by the rising Communist Party, due to their shared opposition to the revolution, and this rapprochement must have influenced Barea.

Finally, it seems a shame that the biography does not explicitly highlight Barea's interesting treatment of the Islamic world in his trilogy. Barea repeatedly denounces the idea that the war against the Rif tribes was fought, as was officially proclaimed, "for civilisation". He contrasted the decrepit and corrupt Spanish army with the locals he met along the way—one of whom he felt knew a lot more about Spanish history than most Spaniards. Tellingly, while he was convalescing in mainland Cordoba, he contrasted the beauty of its mosque with the "destruction" embedded in it in the form of a Catholic chapel.*

But the above reservations are of secondary importance compared to the many achievements of Eaude's book. And *Triumph* remains an impressive and successful attempt at explaining a writer who has too often been ignored and misunderstood. Barea's "focus was on the millions who live history without a voice" for whom and about whom he wrote. Tragically he became cut off from that audience by events beyond his control. It is hoped that Eaude's critical biography and the cheaper recent paperback version of Barea's trilogy (published by Granta) will bring Barea to a new audience. No doubt they will help forge new rebels... and writers!

* See the 4th and 9th chapters of *The Track* in *The Forging of a Rebel* (Granta, 2001).

Black star rising

Ken Olende

*Jeffrey B Perry, **Hubert Harrison: The Voice of Harlem Radicalism, 1883-1918** (Colombia University, 2008), £27*

Hubert Harrison was a towering figure in US black and socialist politics in the early years of the 20th century. He was known as the "father of Harlem radicalism" but has now almost disappeared from the history books. Jeffrey B Perry has already edited a collection of Harrison's writings entitled *A Hubert Harrison Reader* (Wesleyan University, 2001). He is owed a serious debt of thanks for this, the first part of his exhaustive two-part biography, using Harrison's own journals and a sympathetic understanding of the time. It rescues a fascinating historical figure from obscurity, and allows us to see how far ahead of its time much of his analysis was.

The level of racism in the US in which Harrison became politicised was not simply dreadful—it was getting worse. The American Federation of Labour (AFL) union federation had passed through a radical phase in the 1890s, in which it appealed to black workers, who responded enthusiastically. Indeed, Philip S Foner records, "In the opening decade of the 20th century, Southern black workers, far from being 'opposed to unions', were often among the most militant unionists".† But the brief flowering of radicalism was beaten back. The AFL retreated to support almost exclusively white craft unions. The segregationist Jim Crow laws had begun to appear across the Southern states at the end of the 19th century. New laws were enacted right through the period covered by this book.

† Philip S Foner, *Organized Labor and the Black Worker 1916-1981* (International Publishers, 1982), p89.

The competing strategies of Booker T Washington and WEB Du Bois led the struggle against racism. Washington believed discrimination would end once black people had shown through education and hard work that they were worthy of equality. He set up the Tuskegee institute as a centre for such education. By 1915, however, Du Bois's more radical ideas were dominant. He was an activist who demanded equality and was a leader of the new multi-racial National Association for the Advancement of Coloured People (NAACP). However, he still looked to organising a minority of black people, what he called the "talented tenth", which came to annoy Harrison, who wished to bring the mass of black people into the struggle.

Harrison arrived in New York in 1900 from St Croix in the West Indies. His politics shifted from an initial flirtation with Republicanism—which had been the party of Abraham Lincoln, who freed the slaves—through free thought and socialism. He was also a powerful public speaker and always argued for political organisation. His interests were wide ranging. He was an advocate of women's rights, and, as well as discussing on the origins of racism and how to overthrow capitalism, he wrote on religion, theatre and evolution, and had a deep interest in religion and culture.

Many of Harrison's theoretical insights are striking. At the end of 1911 he produced five articles on "The Negro and Socialism". Perry comments that this was "the first such effort at comprehensive analysis by an African American in US socialist history, and on many points it evidences a profound and still incisive understanding" (p159). Perry summarises Harrison's argument: "The historic roots...were 'found in slavery' and the need to supply that system with labourers... [Though he pointed out that] black people were not the first slaves in North America and that 'under Spanish rule, the Indians of Florida and California had been enslaved, and under English rule white men, women and children from Ireland had been sold into slavery'... Black people were treated as chattels, but, 'to the credit of our common human nature', steps had to be taken 'to reconcile the public mind to the system of slavery'. This reconciliation was accomplished by nurturing the belief 'that the slaves were not fully human' and 'wherever the system was most profitable,' that belief 'was strongest'" (p159).

Harrison went on to argue that racism could not be seen as innate, citing examples from the interest of slave owners in black women to the need for legislation to enact segregation. He argued that capitalists foster racism to divide workers. Neither black nor white gain because, with a divided working class, white workers can be told that "other wage slaves are doing as hard work or harder and doing it for less" (p162).

In *Capital* Karl Marx argued, "Labour cannot emancipate itself in the white skin where in the black it is branded." But Marx did not theorise how racism had developed. It was not until the 1940s that the explanation of how racism developed out of slavery was fully articulated in the writings of Eric Williams and CLR James. I am not aware of anyone else prior to the First World War who approached this level of sophistication. Harrison maintained this view even as he moved to a more overtly race centred politics.

Perry writes, "In 1926 [Harrison] explained, 'The conception now prevailing that white people are superior and darker people inferior arose as the mental reflex of a social fact. The fact was the military and political dominations exercised by European whites over the darker people who as late as the 14th century had been superior to them.' He added that the King James version of the Bible 'does not contain the word "race" in our modern sense of a breed of people… as late as 1611 our modern idea of race had not yet arisen, or had not found expression in the English language'" (p121).

Harrison also opposed the First World War, arguing that capitalist competition inevitably leads to armed conflict, "Hence beaks and claws must be provided beforehand against the day of conflict, and hence the exploitation of white men in Europe and America becomes the reason for the exploitation of black and brown and yellow men in Africa and Asia. And therefore it is hypocritical and absurd to pretend that the capitalist nations can ever intend to abolish wars" (p232).

He wrote much of the above in publications associated with the Socialist Party. This had been formed in 1901. It built significant support in the early years of the 20th century. While it was usually dominated by conservative elements, it contained some serious revolutionary socialists. Its presidential candidate, Eugene Debs, won over 900,000 votes in 1912. The party also boasted two Congressmen and many state legislators and mayors. It was later weakened by rows over its opposition to the First World War and how to respond to the Russian Revolution in 1917.

Within the Socialist Party a paternalistic view of black people as at best deprived of education and at worst degenerate held sway. Harrison challenged this. He came to work as a full-time organiser for the party in New York, after being sacked from his job as a post office clerk for his political activity. Initially he was optimistic about the possibilities of winning black workers to socialism.

He argued for an organised strategy to recruit a layer of black workers. He was asked if this meant separate black branches, something that Du Bois specifically objected to. Harrison stated, "There is no intention to establish separate branches or separate organisations for coloured people." However, since black people had a legitimate suspicion of white-led organisations they must be approached, "in part at least, by men of their own race and the work must be done where Negroes 'most do congregate'" (p170). But Harrison's attempt to organise in this field was undermined by the party, which offered no support.

Harrison demanded that the party stopped allowing racism within its ranks. He asked, "Southernism or socialism—which? Is it to be the white half of the working class against the black half, or all of the working class? Can we hope to triumph over capitalism with one half of the working class against us?" (p183). The Socialist Party's 1912 congress passed motions favouring the exclusion of Asian immigrants. Race was put ahead of class and Harrison's views were marginalised. He was pushed out of the party both because of its line on racism and its drift away from anything that could be defined as revolutionary socialism.

He went on to became active in the Industrial Workers of the World (IWW), building support for a number of major strikes in this period and challenging the AFL's complacency. In 1913 he declared to a rally, "We socialists must go to the workers to hear what we must do. The revolution is not coming from above, remember, but from below, working its way up from the depths" (p210). The freedom to speak like this was a relief after the Socialist Party, even if his words also reflect the IWW's admiration of spontaneity at the expense of any consistent and sustained organisation.

In late 1915 Harrison became more concerned with organising Harlem's black community. He increasingly believed that a "race first" view was necessary. Perry says he regarded this as "a self-defence measure under existing social conditions and that it was a necessary corrective to white supremacy" (p278). By 1920 he would advocate separate black unions.

Harrison's shift was a tragic response to the behaviour of the left in this period. Take, for instance, William Z Foster, a former member of both the Socialist Party and the IWW, who would become a leading Communist. Foster wrote a history of the great steel strike of 1919. A section of this attacks black workers for their "open hostility" to organised labour, complaining that they were prepared to be used as strikebreakers and took a "keen delight in stealing the white men's jobs".

Harrison reviewed the book, saying, "It is conceded on all sides that the white organised labour movement has been and still is pronouncedly anti-Negro. And so long as that remains true, just so long will any self-respecting Negro leaders abstain from urging the labouring masses of their race to join forces with the stupid and short-sighted labour oligarchy which refuses to join forces with them" (p279). Harrison may have been wrong to advocate separate unions but his point stands. Unless the socialist movement actively welcomes the oppressed it has no right to condemn them for not taking part.

In 1917 Harrison launched the Liberty League, a broad organisation which promoted black pride, and demanded social change, equality for black people and specifically an end to lynching. A new paper, *The Voice*, argued for the league's policies and galvanised political discussion in Harlem. At its peak it reached a weekly readership of 55,000 but it struggled both because it faced hostility from the black political establishment and because it refused to take adverts for hair straightening and skin lightening products.

He became involved in a campaign against lynching, demanding that, unless the federal government took action to stop this, black Americans should "rise against the government, just as the Irish against England" (p286). That summer a race riot over the use of black labour in St Louis killed at least 39 people. Shamefully Samuel Gompers, president of the AFL, said the cause was "the excessive and abnormal number of Negroes" in the city.

The Liberty League took a hard line. Harrison advised black people to "supply themselves with rifles and fight if necessary to defend their lives and property". He commented on the hypocrisy of US intervention in the First World War: "While they are talking about fighting for freedom and the Stars and Stripes, here at home the whites apply the torch to the black men's homes, and bullets, clubs and stones to their bodies" (p299).

Some Liberty League supporters were unhappy with Harrison's confrontational radicalism and the anti-imperialism of his statements. His consistent opposition to capitalism worried many black leaders. He had built powerful arguments against capitalism and racism, but not an organisation that agreed wholeheartedly with his ideas.

Nonetheless Harrison felt the potential for radical organisation was growing. Despite his differences with the Socialist Party he was heartened by the increase in its vote in New York in the 1917 elections. He was also excited by the active participation in the election by black voters that meant they could not be treated as a block to be bought. In the summer of 1918 Harrison was central to organising a Liberty Congress in Washington DC, demanding rights for black Americans. The meeting had 115 delegates from 35 states and marks the high water mark of Harrison's influence.

From here on he would be overshadowed by a rival movement, Marcus Garvey's

Universal Negro Improvement Association (UNIA), which had been launched in New York in 1917 in direct competition with Harrison's league. Harrison would soon accept the post of editor of UNIA's paper *Negro World*.

In some ways this first volume follows the most interesting part of Harrison's life for socialists. But the later period, when he worked in a genuine mass movement, trying to steer Garvey's UNIA left, is also fascinating. It is easy to get lost in "what if" speculations but it's hard not to imagine what might have happened had Harrison not been pushed away from the socialist left. He was the leading radical activist in Harlem at the time of Garvey's arrival. Imagine if a Marxist with a significant following had been operating in Harlem, working with the fledgling Communist Party, and he had managed to channel the anger of the black masses.

Mark Naison has written about the struggle that Communists faced in trying to gain a foothold among black radicals in Harlem. He notes, "For most of the 1920s the Communist Party represented a marginal phenomenon in Harlem's political life." Furthermore, "Most Harlem organisations...regarded capitalism as a fact of life, if not a positive good".* Naison explains how the first black leaders were recruited after the party was prodded from Russia. Several had already been in Harrison's orbit, notably Cyril Briggs. But by 1921 Harrison is reported to have refused Communist money to help the Liberty League, saying he didn't want to compromise the independence of his black organisation. It is a sad comment on the treatment meted out to such a vibrant and fascinating revolutionary.

* Mark Naison, *Communists in Harlem During the Depression* (Grove, 1985), p3.

A history lacking in hindsight

John Rose

Gerd-Rainer Horn, ***The Spirit of '68—Rebellion in Western Europe and North America 1956-1976*** *(Oxford University, 2008), £19.99*

When *International Socialism*'s editors asked me to review this book I was in the middle of a speaking tour of the wave of new year student occupations in solidarity with Gaza. Now, there was a just a hint of 1968 about these protests. So what an excellent accompaniment, I thought, to all those annoying train journeys. Alas, it was not to be. While the book certainly lives up to its title, it collapses over the political legacy of 1968.

Nevertheless, as an introduction I strongly recommend it. The author has complete command of the research and adds a wealth of new material, especially from Holland, Belgium, Italy and Spain. In addition, the tracing of all the bewildering variety of sinews that finally exploded in 1968 is superb. I doubt whether anyone else could get away with showing how "Howl", the US beat-poem masterpiece of Allen Ginsberg, led simultaneously to the Beatles' most radical moments and the streets around the Sorbonne in Paris in 1968. And the book is worth reading just for the passage "Marlon Brando turns Communist", a wonderful exposition on the Italian *teppisti*—Italy's teddy boy rebellion that turned red!

The book captures brilliantly the great mass democratic upsurges from below on campus, factory and street. The demand for *autogestion* (self-management), arguably the single most important demand of 1968, is fully grasped. The book bursts with examples of "participatory democracy at the point of production"—in the French May, of course, but also in many other countries, especially during Italy's long hot autumn in the late 1960s and early 1970s:

"Springing up in the midst of a huge national wave of social movement activity paralysing universities and factories alike, the average Italian delegate was rather different...graphic descriptions of the origins of the *delegati* at the giant Fiat works... demonstrate the new phenomenon: 'We jumped on tables in the canteen and organised assemblies and the first strikes...*delegati* elections were immediate and the most combative were chosen...whoever displayed the most amount of rage and whoever was most experienced politically'."

Yet how to go beyond this? The author locates precisely that pivotal moment when, in his words, the new left had to give way to the far left. Spontaneity was not enough; revolutionary political organisation was essential. To go into jargon mode, this was the moment that the game was up for anarcho-libertarianism and autonomism:

"Aiming to avoid a repetition of the French post-May 1968 defeat, the far left's eyes were suddenly opened to the perceived lessons of the Bolshevik Revolution. Here...the organisational antidote to new left passivity and disorganisation was beckoning...[for those] disillusioned with the tyranny of new left structurelessness."

And yet it is here that the book stalls. This is very frustrating, given the encyclopedic promise of the book. This hinges on the extraordinarily limited way the author approaches Maoism and Trotskyism, the two political strands which he acknowledges offered a potential link back to the Bolshevik Revolution from 1968 and forward again.

Now, it is true that in 1968 both of these strands were roughly equally weighted in the eyes of the youthful revolutionaries looking for a way forward. But the author has the benefit of hindsight, which he rightly uses to draw a link between 1968 and the new social movements of the 21st century. With hindsight, we can confidently conclude that Maoism proved to be a catastrophe whereas Trotskyism, *creatively adapted* to late 20th century circumstances, offered then, and offers now, a way forward.

Horn's approach leads to unacceptable omissions. The Italian revolutionary student leader Renato Curcio is celebrated several times in the book. Yet, in passing, we are told Curcio became one of the "guiding spirits of the terrorist Red Brigades". This is the only reference to the urban terrorism that grew directly out of one way to adapt "Maoism" to the post-1968 movement. And it was an unmitigated disaster, in Italy with the Red Brigades, in Germany with Baader-Meinhoff, in America with the Weathermen. It fuelled the intense disillusion with 1968 that led to postmodernism and the ex-Marxist B52 liberals of the Bush/Blair era.

The failure to explore what I am calling Trotskyism creatively adapted is even more serious. Again, using the hindsight test, this is very marked. Which Trotskyist tendencies are alive and well in the 21st century, intervening in the new social movements, as well as in the workers movement? The answer is the Fourth International of Ernest Mandel and the International Socialist (IS) Tendency of Tony Cliff. Mandel and Cliff played vital roles in 1968, both as theoreticians and as active builders of revolutionary organisations. Cliff's intervention ensured that the IS Tendency became dominant in the British revolutionary student movement, Mandel's intervention in France ensured that the Ligue Communiste Révolutionnaire played a central part both in the French May and afterwards. Indeed it is the Ligue that is the backbone of the new Anti Capitalist Party in France launched this year and very obviously the inheritor both of the French May 1968 and France's new social movements.

Yet neither Mandel nor Cliff is mentioned in this book. Nor is there a mention for either Tariq Ali or *International Socialism* editor Chris Harman, who were effectively Mandel and Cliff's respective representatives in the 1968 student movement (though at least Tariq, unlike Chris, makes it to the bibliography!). It may be that Cliff is dismissed because Britain itself is dismissed as a 1968 backwater. But there is no similarly easy explanation for the excision of Mandel. I think the answer lies with a kind of intellectual political loss of nerve by the author.

In the final part of the book the author searches for a theoretical retrospective on 1968. This involves a retreat from the far left, back to the new left. Surprisingly, he thinks he discovers it with a remnant of the British new left that previously he had almost ignored. It is the public row at the end of the 1970s between the historian E P Thompson and *New Left Review* editor Perry Anderson that is given this exalted status.

The row was about the tension within Marxism between "determinism" and "voluntarism", about structure and agency, the limits that social and political structure places on potential agents of social and political change. Now, it may well be that the row reflected, as the author suggests, "the impasse of 1968". And clearly this is a useful framework for reflection. And yet not a single insight is derived from the row. None of the historical practical consequences are discussed: the conservative role of the reformist structures, especially the trade unions and parliament; the persistence at the time of the conservative Stalinist structures, both within the West and in global East/West "Cold War" terms; the structure of capitalism itself and the implications of the return of its crisis symptoms in the 1970s. The row disappeared almost as suddenly as it appeared.*

And this raises the most glaring omission in the book. While Marxism is recognised abstractly as the guide, the classical Marxist tradition is ignored. Marx, Lenin, Trotsky, Luxemburg (heroine of the German revolutionary students) even Gramsci (particularly surprising because Italy, rather than France, is given pride of place as the 1968 showcase) are never mentioned.

Yet the legacy of 1968 cannot be understood without the creative adaptation of the writings of the classical Marxist revolutionaries. They are the essential tool to explore the dynamics of how "agency" could have overcome then, and can overcome now, the conservatism of structures. This is not just about restating the centrality of the working class as the agency of change, more globally rooted than ever before. It is also about the fight for political clarity about what are the socialist or communist (with a small "c") objectives—never achieved properly in 1968 and its immediate aftermath.

To creatively paraphrase one of Marx's most famous aphorisms, workers need to interpret, as accurately—as scientifically—as possible, the world as they struggle to change it. Indeed, it does not at all ring hollow to emphasise as *scientifically* as possible, especially in this, the epoch of rapidly degenerating climate change.

* Though written in obtuse, scholarly language, by far the best response to the Anderson/Thompson argument is to be found in Alex Callinicos's *Making History* (Brill, 2004).

China's place in the world

Charlie Hore

Shaun Breslin, ***China and the Global Political Economy*** *(Macmillan, 2009), £19.99*

Jenny Clegg, ***China's Global Strategy*** *(Pluto, 2009) £19.99*

Nobody knows how long or how deep the world economic recession is likely to be. For China the stakes are especially high. Will the world's fastest economic growth rate turn into the worst decline? Or will the innate dynamism of the Chinese economy allow the country to survive relatively unscathed?

This isn't the first recession to hit China since its turn to the world economy in the late 1970s. From mid-1988 until late 1991 the economy shrank or stagnated, giving rise to the "Tiananmen Square movement" of May and June 1989, the consequences of which further deepened the recession. That recession was particular to China, however, produced by the overheating of a newly marketised economy and the excessive austerity measures of the government's anti-inflation strategy. Since then China has grown almost uninterruptedly through both the East Asian currency crisis of the late 1990s and the bursting of the dot-com bubble in the early years of this decade.

What's different now is that China's economy is much more integrated into the world economy in general, and in particular that exports of consumer goods and business electronics have been the major source of economic growth for most of the past 20 years. The immediate signs are that parts of China have been devastated by the impact of the recession, with some reports speaking of one third of toy factories closing and possibly up to 20 million migrant workers losing their jobs.

One of the subsidiary themes of Shaun Breslin's book is the unreliability of statistics about China. But where most authors simply note this, he explains some of the reasons and tries to provide some more accurate figures, particularly for understanding foreign investment in and trade with China.

His main concern, however, is to understand the disjunction between the external image of China as the world's most dynamic economy and the internal realities of growing protests, deepening inequalities and continuing rural poverty. In doing this, he provides a useful counter to the dominant view of China as the "world's next superpower".

Part of this involves understanding the extent to which the export industries that provided most of China's growth are separate from the rest of the Chinese economy. He shows in particular how dependent those industries are on imported components and raw materials, and how this ties in to a wider division of labour across eastern Asia. He also shows how dependent those industries have been on foreign investment, and how little control the central state has over their development.

This is highlighted by the fact that a significant part of this "foreign" investment is actually capital from China, recycled through Hong Kong or offshore tax havens. Necessarily there are no authoritative figures for this, but Breslin gives a sense both of its extent, and of why it matters.

One crucial part of the post-Mao economic strategy is the deliberate devolution of power from central government to different layers of local government, from provinces to villages. The idea was to allow for greater flexibility in order to stimulate innovation, and in that it has undoubtedly succeeded. But it has also necessarily led to the central state losing much of its control over what local authorities actually do. Breslin argues, "If China is becoming a regulatory state, it is becoming a voluntary regulatory state, with local authorities still able to decide whether to adhere to central regulation or not" (p72).

That lack of control has led to corruption becoming endemic at most levels of government, and a wasteful duplication of investments as each group of officials seeks to develop its own particular patch. Towards the end of the book he quotes one official in north eastern China as saying that their biggest competitor is "the export processing zone down the street" (p188). And in his very useful account of the impact of China's entry into the WTO, he suggests that the central government was keen on joining the WTO in part because it offered a way of disciplining local officials.

Breslin also gives a critical account of the growth and influence of private capital within China. While private capital has undoubtedly flourished over the past ten years, this does not necessarily weaken either the state or the Communist Party. He shows how private capital has become entwined with state enterprises and individual bureaucrats, and how entrepreneurs have been welcomed into the Communist Party. Connections with the various levels of the state bureaucracy remain as important as ever for both small and big businesses. In passing he also knocks down the fashionable theory that the "new middle classes" will force an end to Communist Party rule, pointing out just how many of them are part of, or reliant on, the state bureaucracy.

His final chapter looks at the growth of inequality and the consequent rise in protests that have accompanied China's rapid economic growth. This is one of the most useful books on China's economic development before the world recession that I have read for some time. It is very detailed and at times over-academic, but the detail doesn't get in the way of his central argument.

China's global strategy takes a quite different approach, welcoming the emergence of China as a world power, both because it provides a counter-weight to US imperialism, but also because China offers the prospect of a new post-imperialist world order.

The idea that China is challenging American domination of the world is a very popular one on the left, and of course it is not entirely wrong. More than a decade of rapid economic growth has led to China pulling in imports from across Africa and Latin America, and in the process offering an alternative means of support to governments which are out of favour with the US. Left-leaning governments, in particular Hugo Chavez's in Venezuela, are better placed to stand up to the US because of their trade with China.

As I write this, the Chinese government are suggesting a new world currency to replace the dollar as part of their plans to end the recession. It is unlikely ever to happen but the fact that they have the capital to make it feasible shows the extent to which China has become both a political and economic competitor for American imperialism—arguably the only major power that challenges American hegemony.

China's challenge to the US has gone furthest in Asia, and Clegg documents well the various political and economic structures that link China with other Asian governments, such as the Shanghai Cooperation Organisation (SCO). This alliance of most major central and south Asian governments began as a political and military alliance, and is now also becoming a forum for economic cooperation—all without any US involvement.

Yet the SCO also shows the limits of her argument. In one rare critical sentence she writes, "The weakness of the democratic systems within individual SCO member-states is problematic" (p109). This is an understatement of the highest order—the central Asian states in the SCO include some of the world's worst dictatorships. It is also the case that the SCO was originally built on Asian governments' own "war on terror". She rightly attacks George Bush's concept of the "war on terror" as an excuse for both US military intervention in Asia and greater repression in the US itself but sees no contradiction in then accepting it as a reality for China, Russia and Uzbekistan.

There is nothing necessarily progressive about the governments that China supports—Chinese support is conditional on trading or political links, rather than any "progressive" credentials. This is particularly obvious in Africa, where China is involved in supporting some of the most repressive regimes on the continent. However, there is almost nothing about Africa in this book. Other awkward areas are similarly glossed over—there is just one mention of strikes, for instance, and almost nothing about the mass protests by workers and peasants which have marked the past 15 years. Tibet gets less than one page, with the suggestion that Chinese repression is the fault of the Dalai Lama!

This is primarily a study of Chinese policy, rather than the actual history, and its main value is in giving a clear account of how China presents itself to Third World governments. The author does gloss over the contradictory positions this involves and does not offer any more than the mildest of criticisms. She does, however, acknowledge left critiques of China, quoting in particular from a number of regular contributors to this journal, but she doesn't actually engage with the detail of their arguments.

What is also missing is any real account of the transition from the essentially closed economy under Mao, to the open and dynamic world power that China is today. This is essentially a nationalist defence of China, rather than an attempt to paint the current regime as socialist.

Clegg is absolutely right to point to the long historical account of US aggression against and pressure on China, which helps explain why much of the left wants to line up behind China. But that is only half the story. The other side of the Chinese-American relationship is that both economies are deeply intertwined, and both ruling classes are jostling for position while at the same time propping each other up. For a more rounded sense of the complexities and contradictions of that relationship, Shaun Breslin's book is the better bet.

Pick of the quarter

The most interesting easily accessible article this quarter is "From Çayönü to Çatalhöyük" on the English version of the website Urkommunismus ("Early Communism").* It is an analytical account by Bernhard Brosius of the results of archaeological excavations of one of the world's oldest cities—Çatalhöyük, in central Anatolia, Turkey. The excavations have revealed that in the Neolithic period, 8,000 to 10,000 years ago, 5,000 or more people lived there in houses packed right up against each other, growing grains, herding sheep and hunting wild animals.

It seems to have been an egalitarian society with no evidence of class distinctions. All the dwellings are more of less the same size; they all show signs of being sites of manual work; the "grave goods" buried alongside bodies reveal no distinction between rich and poor. Nor are there any signs of the superior status males usually have in urban societies; there were "no significant differences concerning nutrition, body height and lifestyle between men and women. Men and women performed very similar tasks. Both sexes stayed in and outside the house equally long and were equally active in the kitchen as in tool production." This was, in fact, a society before the development of private property, the state and the patriarchal subordination of women.

Brosius contrasts Çatalhöyük with another, older, Anatolian Neolithic city, Çayönü, which was much more typical of early cities across the globe. Here there was "a destructive, patriarchal and hierarchical society of enormous cruelty". A few houses show signs of wealth, but the others were half the size and contained nothing but "the few tools needed for daily living". The big houses contained all the resources for making tools but only the poor ones showed any signs of labour with such tools. In other words, "There was a small group of people who possessed without working and a large group of people who worked without possessing—in other words, there were classes." Alongside all this there were "gloomy temples" filled with bloody signs of human sacrifice, with skeletons of more than 400 different individuals "neatly stacked up to the ceiling".

But here the excavations reveal class struggle as well as class. "On a certain day 9,200 years ago the manorial houses were burnt down... The temple was torn down and burnt, and converted into a municipal waste dump. The slums in the west disappeared for good... The new Çayönü was erected. There were no more houses or shacks built to an inferior standard... All hints to social differences were erased." In short, there was a revolutionary overthrow of the ruling class.

Brosius argues, "Not only did the revolutionaries of those remote times succeed in overthrowing a regime thousands of years old, bloody and exploitive—moreover, they also succeeded in developing their own alternative society, devising and realising it. The social revolution of the year 7200 BC is the hour of the birth of

* www.urkommunismus.de/catalhueyuek_en.pdf

Neolithic communism." He sees this as having spread across Anatolia to produce societies of the Çatalhöyük type. These then lasted until "around 4000 BC" when an exploiting class began to establish itself, finally getting into power by 3000 BC using "the most effective mechanisms of oppression available to an exploitative ruling class"—"metal weapons, a writing system and a ruling authority".

The author leaves unexplored an important area of inquiry: the processes that led people to permit a class society to arise in the first place. But his account suggests that the initial transition to the agriculture that characterised Neolithic societies was associated in the region with the crystallising out of an exploiting class—only for people then to find that they could continue to use the new methods and enjoy better lives by overthrowing it. Egalitarian societies could then flourish for thousands of years until new techniques associated with the transition from the Neolithic period to the Bronze Age encouraged the formation of new social relations between people and eventually renewed polarisation into classes. There have been theories about revolutionary uprising overthrowing class societies similar to Çayönü, for instance among the Maya people of Central America about a thousand years ago, but if Brosius is right people did not in this case then abandon city dwelling.

The April issue of *Anthropology Today* contains a fascinating article on the US military's attempts to use anthropology in its wars in Afghanistan and Iraq. The author, Roberto Gonzalez, writes that most anthropologists today are wary of using the term "tribe" but that it suits the military to focus on it as a cover for their "divide and rule" approach—financing and arming powerful figures in each locality to control the population for them. "Tribalism" then becomes both an excuse for their presence and a means of maintaining it, even though the effect is to encourage the tearing apart of society.

In our previous issue we recommended Henry Heller's article on the French bourgeoisie before the revolution in *Historical Materialism* (volume 16, number 1). In the same issue is a piece by Marcus Green and Peter Ives providing a rare examination of Antonio Gramsci's ideas on language, class and common sense.

The year's first issue of the *Cambridge Review of International Affairs* will be a treat for many readers of this journal, crammed with articles by some of our contributers. Sam Ashman, Alex Callinicos, Jamie Allinson and Neil Davidson are all there, as well as Gonzalo Pozo-Martin, Alex Anievas, Justin Rosenberg, Adam Morton and others. It is a pity it is one of the many academic journals to which access is only widely available via university libraries, either directly or via the Athens system. Let's hope some of the arguments appear elsewhere in a more accessible form.

Also for those with such access is a piece on the argument among Egyptian revolutionaries on how to relate to the Muslim Brotherhood, "'With the Islamists?—Sometimes. With the State?—Never!' Cooperation between the Left and Islamists in Egypt", in the *British Journal of Middle Eastern Studies*.

One place where ideas are freely available is the Marxist Internet Archive. It has just added pieces by the Peruvian Marxist of the 1920s Mariategui,* as well as Hal Draper's article on Marx's often abused encyclopedia entry on Simón Bolívar.†

JC and *CH*

---

* www.marxists.org/archive/mariateg/works/

† www.marxists.org/archive/draper/1968/winter/bolivar